The Chemistry of the Non-Metals

Chapman and Hall Chemistry Textbook Series

CONSULTING EDITORS

R.P. Bell, M.A., Hon. L.L.D., F.R.S., Professor of Chemistry at the University of Stirling.

N.N. Greenwood, Ph.D., Sc.D., Professor of Inorganic and Structural Chemistry at the University of Leeds.

R.O.C. Norman, M.A., D.Sc., Professor of Chemistry at the University of York.

OTHER TITLES IN THE SERIES

Symmetry in Molecules J.M. Hollas
Introduction to Molecular Photochemistry C.H.J. Wells
N.M.R. and Chemistry J.W. Akitt
Principles and Applications of Electrochemistry D.R. Crow

FORTHCOMING

Pericyclic Reactions G.B. Gill and M.R. Willis
Organometallics in Organic Synthesis J. M. Swan and D.St C. Black

The Chemistry of the Non-Metals

P. Powell

Department of Chemistry
Royal Holloway College
University of London

P.L. Timms

School of Chemistry
University of Bristol

LONDON

CHAPMAN AND HALL

First published in 1974
by Chapman and Hall Ltd
11 New Fetter Lane, London EC4P 4EE

© *1974 P. Powell and P.L. Timms*

Set and printed in Great Britain by
William Clowes & Sons Limited
London, Colchester and Beccles

SBN 412 12200 6

Distributed in the U.S.A.
by Halsted Press, a Division
of John Wiley & Sons, Inc., New York

   Library of Congress Catalog Card Number 73–13383

Contents

Preface

This book is a new attempt to interrelate the chemistry of the non-metals. In the early chapters, simple compounds of the non-metals with the halogens, hydrogen, and oxygen are surveyed, permitting a large area of chemistry to be discussed without the burden of too many facts. The structural relationships in the elemental forms of the non-metals are then used as an introduction to the catenated compounds, including the boron hydrides. In the concluding chapter, selected heteronuclear chain, ring, and cage compounds are considered. In some chapters, we have thought it useful to outline important features of a topic in relation to chemical theory, before giving a more detailed account of the chemistry of individual elements. The book is certainly not comprehensive and the bias in the material selected probably reflects our interest in volatile, covalent non-metal compounds.

Suggestions for further reading are presented in two ways. A selected bibliography lists general textbooks which relate to much of our subject matter. References in the text point to review articles and to a few original papers which we consider to be of special interest.

Although there are few difficult concepts in the text, the treatment may be appreciated most by students with some previous exposure to a Group by Group approach to non-metal chemistry. We have assumed an elementary knowledge of chemical periodicity, bonding theory, thermodynamics, and spectroscopic methods of structure determination. For these reasons, we consider the book to be most suitable for students in their final two years of an Honours degree course.

We should like to thank several of our immediate colleagues and friends who made helpful criticisms and suggestions during the preparation of the manuscript. We greatly valued the comments of Professor N.N. Greenwood, acting as consulting editor for the Series. Albright and Wilson and Imperial

Chemical Industries kindly gave us up-to-date information on some of the important industrial processes which involve the non-metals.

Finally, we are grateful to the Publisher for being patient in spite of all the deadlines we missed in completing the manuscript.

P.P.
P.L.T.

ERRATA

Page 13: The molecular orbital energy level diagram for N_2 should have been represented as shown below.

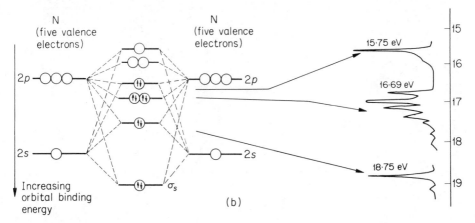

Page 80, line 15: for $(3p–3p)\pi$ read $(2p–3p)\pi$.

Page 123, Figure 3.17: for $H_5IO_6^-$ read $H_3IO_6^{2-}$.

Page 126: The sentence beginning on line 2 is more correctly written:
Reduction potentials for xenon couples are:

$$H_4XeO_6 \xrightarrow{\;2\cdot3\text{ V}\;} XeO_3 \xrightarrow{\;2\cdot10\,\pm\,0\cdot01\text{ V}\;} Xe \quad \text{(acid solution)}$$

$$HXeO_6{}^{3-} \xrightarrow{\;0\cdot9\text{ V}\;} HOXeO_3{}^- \xrightarrow{\;1\cdot24\,\pm\,0\cdot01\text{ V}\;} Xe \quad \text{(basic solution)}$$

perxenate   xenate

Page 157, Figure 4.2: for $\sigma^*(2p_z)$ read $\sigma^*(2p_x)$.

Page 254: The formula on the left in the middle of the page should read:

The Chemistry of the Non-Metals, P. Powell and P. Timms

Principles of structure and bonding

1

1.1 Introduction

This book concerns the non-metallic elements and the compounds which they form one with another. Many of these compounds and some of the elements themselves exist as discrete small molecules both in the vapour and in the condensed states. The bonding in such molecules can generally be described as covalent, involving a sharing of electrons between two or a few atoms only. Even when infinite lattice structures are formed, the same generalization of covalent bonding still applies.

On the other hand, many compounds formed between metals and non-metals are best considered as ionic in the solid state, having lattices bound by electrostatic interactions between metal cations and non-metal anions. On the whole, we shall not deal with such compounds here. Another contrasting form of bonding occurs in the metals themselves, the electrical conductivity and optical properties of which indicate appreciable electron delocalization over the complete array of atoms in the structure. Indeed, one traditional distinction between metals and non-metals is based on whether or not the element is an electrical conductor.

As the type of bonding found in compounds formed between the non-metals is fairly uniform, their chemistry might be expected to present a coherent, logical picture. We shall see that many useful generalizations can certainly be made. In Chapter 2 we consider the binary hydrides and halides, which have particularly simple structures. Next the binary oxides are discussed (Chapter 3), pointing out the delicate balance between simple and macro-molecular species which sometimes exists. The elemental forms of the non-metals (Chapter 4) serve as models both for the catenated compounds, which are based on skeletons composed of one type of atom only (Chapter 5), and

1

in part, for the molecules with heteronuclear frameworks treated in Chapter 6. As is common in inorganic chemistry, however, periodic trends are sometimes obscured where changes in several factors can occur at once. It is therefore not surprising if some facts do appear rather isolated and do not fit neatly into any general pattern.

1.2   Some properties of atoms

The ground state electronic structures of the atoms of the non-metals and of some neighbouring elements are listed in Table 1.1. Also shown are three parameters, the ionization energy, the electron affinity, and the electronegativity, which relate to the ease with which the atoms lose or gain electrons. The ionization energy is the enthalpy change for the process:

$$A(gas) \rightarrow A^+(gas) + e^-$$

while the electron affinity can be defined as the enthalpy change when the A^- ion loses an electron:

$$A^-(gas) \rightarrow A(gas) + e^-$$

On the whole there is an increase in both of these quantities across a row as the p electron shell is being filled, although the noble gases with closed p shells have low electron affinities. Irregularities occur when loss or gain of electrons changes the electronic structures between ns^2 and ns^2np^1, owing to the lower binding energy of electrons in an np than in an ns shell, or between np^3 and np^4, on account of electron pairing in the np^4 configuration.

The electronegativity is a measure of the relative attractive power for electrons of the atoms forming a chemical bond. Numerous attempts have been made to define it quantitatively. A theoretically satisfying approach was due to Mulliken who suggested that the electronegativity of an atom should be proportional to the arithmetic mean of its ionization energy and electron affinity. The difference between the electronegativities of two atoms A and B in a compound A—B is thus proportional to the enthalpy change in the reaction:

$$A^-(gas) + B^+(gas) \rightarrow A^+(gas) + B^-(gas)$$

A more widely applicable scale, however, was devised by Pauling, and the values quoted in Table 1.1 have been derived by his method. Any bond formed between two atoms of differing electronegativities has some polar character. On account of this, the strength of the bond A—B is found to be greater by an amount Δ kJ than the mean of the bond energies of the homopolar bonds A—A and B—B. Pauling found empirically that Δ could be

TABLE 1.1
Electronic properties of non-metal atoms

	II	III	IV	V	VI	VII		
H							He	
$1s^1$							$1s^2$	
1311							2372	
72							—	
2·20							—	
	Be	B	C	N	O	F	Ne	
	$2s^2$	$2s^2 2p^1$	$2s^2 2p^2$	$2s^2 2p^3$	$2s^2 2p^4$	$2s^2 2p^5$	$2s^2 2p^6$	
	899	801	1086	1403	1312	1681	2080	First ionization energy kJ
	~−20	~30	113	~−30	142	333		Electron affinity kJ
	1·57	2·04	2·55	3·04	3·44	3·91	—	Pauling electronegativity
	Mg	Al	Si	P	S	Cl	Ar	
	$3s^2$	$3s^2 3p^1$	$3s^2 3p^2$	$3s^2 3p^3$	$3s^2 3p^4$	$3s^2 3p^5$	$3s^2 3p^6$	
	736	577	786	1012	999	1255	1521	
	~−50	~26	~135	~60	~200	348	—	
	1·31	1·61	1·90	2·19	2·58	3·16	—	
METALS	Ga	Ge	As	Se	Br	Kr		NON-METALS
	$3d^{10} 4s^2 4p^1$	$4s^2 4p^2$	$4s^2 4p^3$	$4s^2 4p^4$	$4s^2 4p^5$	$4s^2 4p^6$		
	579	760	947	941	1142	1351		
	—	~130	~60	~200	324	—		
	1·81	2·01	2·18	2·55	2·96	~2·9		
	In	Sn	Sb	Te	I	Xe		
	$4d^{10} 5s^2 5p^1$	$5s^2 5p^2$	$5s^2 5p^3$	$5s^2 5p^4$	$5s^2 5p^5$	$5s^2 5p^6$		
	558	708	854	869	1008	1169		
	—	~140	60	~200	295	—		
	1·78	1·96	2·05	2·30	2·66	~2·6		
	Tl	Pb	Bi	Po	At	Rn		
	$4f^{14} 5d^{10} 6s^2 6p^1$	$6s^2 6p^2$	$6s^2 6p^3$	$6s^2 6p^4$	$6s^2 6p^5$	$6s^2 6p^6$		
	589	715	703	813	—	1037		
	—	—	—	—	—	—		
	2·04	2·33	2·02	2·0	~2·2	—		

expressed in terms of the electronegativities of A and B, χ_A and χ_B, by the equation:

$$\Delta = 96 \cdot 4(\chi_A - \chi_B)^2$$

The electronegativity of hydrogen was given the value 2·20. It will be seen from the table that electronegativities increase across each row, reaching a maximum with the halogens. Values for Kr and Xe are quoted, but these are not well established, as so few compounds of these elements are known.

The size of an atom should be considered both in bonding and non-bonding situations. Half the length of a single bond A—A is equal to the bonding or covalent radius of the atom A. Half the distance of closest approach of one atom to another in the solid element, where no chemical bond exists between these atoms, i.e. the non-bonding distance A—A···A—A, is equal to the non-bonding or van der Waals radius of A. The non-bonding radius is often roughly equal to the radius of the anion A^-, and is always greater than the bonding radius. As shown in Table 1.2, there is an overall increase in radius down each Group. The covalent radii in Groups IV and V, however, change little between

TABLE 1.2
Atomic radii of the non-metals (pm)

	III	IV	V	VI	VII	0
H						He
37						–
130						180
	B	C	N	O	F	Ne
Covalent radii	90	77	75	73	71	–
van der Waals radii	~180	170	160	150	150	160
		Si	P	S	Cl	Ar
		118	110	102	99	–
		210	190	180	190	190
		Ge	As	Se	Br	Kr
		122	120	117	114	110
		210	200	190	190	200
		Sn	Sb	Te	I	Xe
		140	~140	135	133	130
		220	220	210	210	220

the second- and third-row elements. The contraction in atomic size which occurs across the first transition series, when the inner $3d$ electron shell is being filled, cancels almost exactly the expected expansion in radius on descending these Groups.

The experimentally determined bond length in a compound often does not correspond exactly with the sum of the covalent radii of the atoms forming that bond. This indicates that the size of an atom can vary from one situation to another. We saw above that polar character can strengthen a bond; it can also shorten one. Thus, in a compound AB the bond length A—B will be the sum of the radii derived from A—A and B—B bond lengths only if the electronegativities of A and B are the same. An empirical correction to the bond length in polar bonds, devised by Schomaker and Stevenson, takes the form:

$$\text{Bond length A—B} = r_A + r_B - 9(\chi_A - \chi_B)$$

Multiple-bond radii can be assigned to a few atoms such as C, N, and O, in the same way as single-bond radii. Multiple bonding leads to shortening of bonds as in the series: C—C 154 pm; C=C 133 pm; C≡C 120 pm. Sometimes the extent of multiple bonding is much more difficult to assess than in carbon compounds such as ethylene or acetylene. In BF_3, for example, the B—F bond distance is found to be 130 pm, whereas the sum of the covalent radii gives a value of 161 pm, or 144 pm after correction by the Schomaker–Stevenson equation. One explanation is that further bond contraction arises from π bonding by donation of electrons from lone pair orbitals on fluorine into the empty p orbital of the boron atom.

1.3   Structures and properties of molecules

Two models are often useful in discussing bonding in covalent molecules. A molecule, AX_n, for example, can be thought of as being composed of n individual A—X bonds, localized between the central atom A and each of the n X atoms. Alternatively, the molecule can be treated as one complete unit, by considering the valence orbitals of all the atoms together, and combining them to form molecular orbitals delocalized over the whole.

Both of these descriptions have a useful place in the study of non-metal compounds, and we shall use each of them when appropriate in the following

5

discussion. For example, properties such as molecular shape, molecular dimensions, and thermochemical data are most conveniently considered in terms of localized bonds. On the other hand, the delocalized orbital description gives a picture of bonding which in favourable cases can be related directly to spectroscopic results.

1.3.1 *The shape of molecules*

A simple semi-empirical approach for predicting the shapes of molecules was put forward by Sidgwick and Powell in 1940 and subsequently developed by Gillespie and Nyholm [1]. The model considers repulsion between pairs of valence electrons which, according to the Pauli exclusion principle, cannot occupy the same position in space. The shape of a molecule AX_n is then dictated by that arrangement of the electron pairs which leads to the least mutual repulsion. The most favoured arrangements for two to six equivalent electron pairs around a central atom are shown in Fig. 1.1(a). Where lone pairs of electrons are present on A, in addition to the n bonding pairs, significant deviations from these symmetrical arrangements are normally observed. It has been found that the correct shape of such a molecule can usually be predicted by assuming that the lone electron pairs occupy more space over the surface of the central atom than the bonding electron pairs, which are extended away from it into the bonds. The repulsive forces therefore fall in the order: (lone pair–lone pair) > (lone pair–bonding pair) > (bonding pair–bonding pair). All the interactions show a strong angular dependence. Thus, interactions at 120° or greater are negligible compared with those at 90°.

These ideas are illustrated by the chlorine trifluoride molecule ClF_3. In ClF_3 there are ten electrons in the valence shell of the central chlorine atom (seven from Cl and one from each of the three F atoms). These five electron pairs distribute themselves approximately towards the corners of a trigonal bipyramid. The three possible arrangements of three bonding and two lone electron pairs about the central chlorine atom are shown in Fig. 1.1(b). Of these, structure (iii), in which there are only two lone pair–bonding pair and two bonding pair–bonding pair interactions at 90°, seems favoured over (i) and (ii), in which the mutual electron pair repulsions are greater. Structure (iii) is close to that determined experimentally by microwave spectroscopy

[1] Gillespie, R. J. (1970), *J. Chem. Educ.*, **47**, 18.

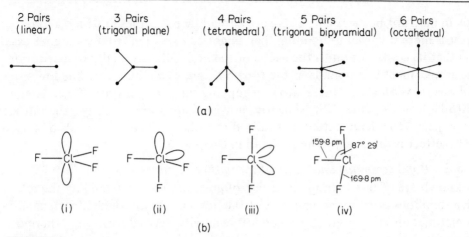

| 2 Pairs (linear) | 3 Pairs (trigonal plane) | 4 Pairs (tetrahedral) | 5 Pairs (trigonal bipyramidal) | 6 Pairs (octahedral) |

(a)

(i)   (ii)   (iii)   (iv)

(b)

FIGURE 1.1
(a) Arrangements of electron pairs minimizing repulsions
(b) The possible structures of chlorine trifluoride

(iv). Note that the axial Cl—F bonds are tilted away slightly from the two lone pairs, and also that they are longer than the equatorial Cl—F bond. Such small deviations from the regular structure can readily be understood if electron pair repulsions, especially those involving lone pairs, must be minimized. Structures of other halides which are correctly predicted by the Gillespie–Nyholm theory are shown in Fig. 2.2.

To apply the theory to compounds which contain multiple bonds such as A=O or A≡N, only the σ electron pairs are considered to contribute to the gross molecular shape. Thus, CO_2 and HCN are both linear. The basic shape of each of the isoelectronic molecules $F—SiF_3$ (SiF_4), $O=PF_3$, and $N≡SF_3$ is tetrahedral, as the central atom in each case is surrounded by four σ electron pairs. Electrons in multiple bonds, however, are presumed to occupy more space over the surface of the central atom than a single bonding pair. In fact, the effect of the grouping A=O is very similar to that of a lone pair (p. 76). In agreement with these ideas, the FAF bond angles decrease from 109° in SiF_4, through 102° (OPF_3), to 94° in NSF_3.

The theory in this simple form succeeds in predicting correctly the approximate structures of many covalently bonded molecules or ions. Where the total number of electron pairs is greater than six, as in XeF_6 (p. 22). several structures of similar energy may be possible, so that the decision between them may not be clear-cut. There are also a few molecules in which a lone pair is more involved in bonding than might be expected from analogous cases, so that its contribution to the shape of the molecule is actually reduced. For example, most compounds of the type NX_3 are pyramidal, with the lone pair of electrons on the nitrogen atom occupying the apex position. Trisilylamine $N(SiH_3)_3$ has a planar NSi_3 skeleton, however, apparently because the nitrogen lone pair is to a large extent delocalized into the unfilled $3d$ orbitals of silicon. This effect is discussed in more detail in Chapter 6.

1.3.2 Bond strengths and heats of formation of molecules

A knowledge of bond strengths proves of great use in understanding the relative stabilities of many compounds of the non-metals, although kinetic factors sometimes distort a picture of chemical reactivity derived from such thermodynamic data.

The different ways of considering bond strengths need careful definition. The dissociation energy $D(A-B)$ of the bond in a diatomic molecule AB is defined as the enthalpy change at 298 K for the process:

$$AB(gas) \rightarrow A(gas) + B(gas)$$

In a polyatomic molecule AB_n, the mean bond dissociation energy $\bar{D}(A-B)$ is given by $1/n$ of the enthalpy change for the process:

$$AB_n(gas) \rightarrow A(gas) + n\,B(gas)$$

Except for diatomic molecules, $\bar{D}$ differs from the enthalpy changes in stepwise atomization of a molecule. Thus, in boron trifluoride, the mean bond dissociation energy is 645 kJ mol^{-1}, whereas the dissociation energies of successive bonds are $D(BF_2-F)$ 605, $D(BF-F)$ 565, and $D(B-F)$ 756 kJ mol^{-1}.

Where a molecule contains two or more different types of bonds, another parameter to define the various bond energies must be introduced. The energy of atomization of ethane:

$$C_2H_6(gas) \rightarrow 2\,C(gas) + 6\,H(gas)$$

may be represented as the sum of bond energy terms $E(C-H)$ and $E(C-C)$ such that:

$$6\,E(C-H) + E(C-C) = 2\,\Delta H_f^\circ[C(gas)] + 6\,\Delta H_f^\circ[H(gas)]$$
$$- \Delta H_f^\circ[C_2H_6(gas)]$$

Similarly, 8 $E(C-H)$ and 2 $E(C-C)$ could be obtained from the heat of formation of propane. Since it is found that bond energies in molecules of related chemical type often have similar values, the data for ethane and propane combined permit the terms $E(C-H)$ and $E(C-C)$ to be evaluated. In this way, reasonably self-consistent sets of terms covering a wide range of bonds have been compiled, but they cannot be transferred successfully from one compound to another in which the relevant bonds are in very different chemical environments.

Table 1.3 shows bond energy terms for some single bonds between non-metals. Two major factors seem to influence these values. First, the greater the

TABLE 1.3
Selected energy terms for some bonds between non-metals; values in kJ mol^{-1}

	C—C	356			N—N	167		O—O	146	F—F	158
	Si—Si	226			P—P	209		S—S	226	Cl—Cl	242
	Ge—Ge	188			As—As	180		Se—Se	172	Br—Br	193
	Sn—Sn	151			Sb—Sb	142		Te—Te	149	I—I	151
C—H	416	C—Cl	327	N—H	391	N—F	272			
Si—H	323	Si—Cl	391	P—H	322	P—F	490			
Ge—H	289	Ge—Cl	342							
Sn—H	250	Sn—Cl	320							
C≡C	602	C=O	735	N≡N	944					
Si=Si	314	Si=O	640	P≡P	485					

electronegativity difference between the atoms the stronger the bonds. This follows from the way in which Pauling derived his scale of electronegativity. It reflects the contribution to bonding from the electrostatic attraction $A^+ X^-$ in a bond $A-X$ ($\chi_X > \chi_A$) which is superimposed on the attraction due to electron sharing between A and X. Second, the overlap between orbitals of higher principal quantum number generally produces weaker bonds than overlap of orbitals of lower principal quantum number. This trend can be distorted by major changes in the electronegativity difference between atoms, e.g. $E(C-Cl) < E(Si-Cl) > E(Ge-Cl)$ but $E(C-C) > E(Si-Si) > E(Ge-Ge)$. A more subtle reversal of the trend is observed in the bond energy sequences $E(N-N) < E(P-P)$, $E(O-O) < E(S-S)$, and $E(F-F) < E(Cl-Cl)$. One explanation of this order of bond energies is that repulsion between lone pairs on N, O, or F lengthens and weakens the bonds between these atoms, whereas such repulsion would be of less consequence for P—P, S—S, and Cl—Cl because these bonds are longer. In another explanation, P—P, S—S, and Cl—Cl bonds are thought to be strengthened by donation of electrons from a filled $3p$ orbital on one atom to empty $3d$ orbitals on the other atom. This $(p-d)\pi$ bonding is not possible for the first-row elements as there is no $2d$ electron shell. Irrespective of the cause, the lower bond energies in the first row influence the chemistry of these elements. In particular, the reactivity of fluorine F_2 is enhanced relative to the other halogens, as the molecule is so easily dissociated into atoms (p. 183).

Multiple bonds, i.e. those which involve both σ and π orbital overlap (p. 13). have the highest bond energies of all. It is important to note that, relative to the single bonds, multiple bonds between first-row elements are much stronger than those which involve an element from the second or subsequent rows; π overlap between $2p$ orbitals is much more effective than such overlap using p orbitals of higher principal quantum number. Consequently, multiply bonded compounds are commonly formed between first-row elements (e.g. CO_2), whereas the corresponding compounds of second-row elements, if they exist at all, normally adopt structures in which formal single bonds are present. Examples of this effect are discussed on p. 74.

The relationship between bond energies and the heat of formation of a compound from its elements is shown by an energy cycle:

$$
\begin{array}{ccccc}
A & + & nX & \xrightarrow{\Delta H_f^\circ(AX_n)} & AX_n \\
\uparrow{\scriptstyle -\Delta H_a(A)} & & \uparrow{\scriptstyle -n\Delta H_a(X)} & & \downarrow{\scriptstyle \Delta H_v(AX_n)} \\
A(gas) & & X(gas) & & AX_n(gas) \\
& & \xrightarrow{n\bar{D}(A-X)} & &
\end{array}
$$

$$\Delta H_f^{\circ}(AX_n) = \Delta H_a(A) + n\Delta H_a(X) - n\bar{D}(A-X) - \Delta H_v(AX_n)$$

A, X, and AX_n are in their 'standard states', commonly the most stable forms of the elements or of the compound at 298 K and 1 atm pressure. For most inter-non-metal compounds which exist as discrete molecules in the condensed phase, the heat of vaporization term $\Delta H_v(AX_n)$ will be small. In these cases, the heat of formation is effectively decided by a balance of two sets of energy terms, $n\bar{D}(A-X)$ and the heats of atomization $\Delta H_a(A)$ and $\Delta H_a(X)$. For some elements it is a good approximation to equate the heat of atomization with half the single bond energy $E(A-A)$ or $E(X-X)$, so that:

$$\Delta H_f^\circ(AX_n) = \tfrac{1}{2}E(A-A) + \tfrac{1}{2}nE(X-X) - n\bar{D}(A-X)$$

$$= -96\cdot4n(\chi_A - \chi_X)^2$$

The last relationship follows from Pauling's derivation of electronegativity. Heats of formation calculated from electronegativities are inaccurate for compounds containing nitrogen or oxygen because the dissociation energies of N_2 and O_2 are greater than $3E(N-N)$ and $2E(O-O)$ respectively, but correction terms can be included.

1.4   Bonding

When considering bonding in compounds of the non-metals, we shall use the molecular orbital (MO) approach. The theoretical background to MO theory is beyond the scope of this book (see Bibliography), but in this section we illustrate the application of the theory to a few molecules, and we use these concepts where appropriate in later chapters.

Molecular orbitals are formed by combination of atomic orbitals provided that (a) the atomic orbitals have comparable energies, and (b) the atomic orbitals have the same symmetry properties with respect to some of the symmetry elements of the molecule which is formed. The number of molecular orbitals formed will be equal to the number of atomic orbitals which combine. Some combinations of atomic orbitals which form molecular orbitals are shown in Fig. 1.2.

The relative energies of the molecular orbitals in a compound can be calculated, and in some cases they can also be determined experimentally by spectroscopic methods, particularly by photoelectron spectroscopy [2]. In this last technique, molecules are ionized by irradiation in the vacuum ultra-violet region of the spectrum. The energies of the electrons produced are, in favourable cases, a direct measure of the ionization energies from the various

[2] Turner, D. W., Baker, A. D., Baker, C. and Brundle, C. R. (1970), *Molecular Photoelectron Spectroscopy*, Wiley, London; Baker, A. D., Brundle, C. R. and Thompson, M. (1972), *Chem. Soc. Revs.*, **1**, 355.

occupied molecular orbitals. This interpretation of the spectrum accepts in principle Koopmans' theorem, that the same order of MOs serves both for the neutral molecule and for the positive ion.

Fine structure appears in a photoelectron spectrum when molecular parameters (bond length, bond angle) differ in the ground vibrational states of the neutral molecule and of the positive ion which is formed. Fine structure arises because ionization from the neutral molecule, which essentially is entirely in its ground vibrational level, may, according to the Franck–Condon principle, produce the molecular ion in different vibrational states. This has the effect of reducing the energy of the ejected electron by an amount corresponding to one or more vibrational quanta of the ion.

The form of each band in a photoelectron spectrum can distinguish the character of the molecular orbital from which ionization has occurred. Thus, ejection of a bonding electron leads to an increase in bond length and decrease in vibrational quanta in the ion relative to the neutral molecule. The 'fine structure' then has a spacing less than that of a vibrational quantum for the molecule. If the electron is ejected from an antibonding orbital, the converse applies. Electrons which come from non-bonding orbitals are not coupled with molecular vibrations and have essentially a single energy.

Bonding descriptions of N_2, H_2O, and CH_4 are given in Figs. 1.2–1.4, together with the photoelectron spectra. The relative energies of the atomic orbitals shown in these diagrams have either been calculated or have been determined spectroscopically from atomic ionization or promotion energies. The valence s and p orbitals of the non-metals are all sufficiently similar in energy for molecular orbitals to be formed if symmetry allows, although in some cases the interaction may be weak, e.g. that between H ($1s$) and O ($2s$) in H_2O (Fig. 1.3). Energies of atomic orbitals change much more as the nuclear charge increases across a row than as the principal quantum number varies down a Group.

For the N_2 molecule (Fig. 1.2) both calculation and a variety of spectroscopic evidence show that there is sufficient mixing of s and p orbitals to lower the energy of the π bonding MOs below that of the highest σ bonding MO. In the O_2 molecule, however, the larger separation between $2s$ and $2p$ atomic levels reduces mixing, so that the σ orbital is now lower in energy than the π orbitals.

The molecular symmetry of H_2O permits mixing of s and p orbitals, but

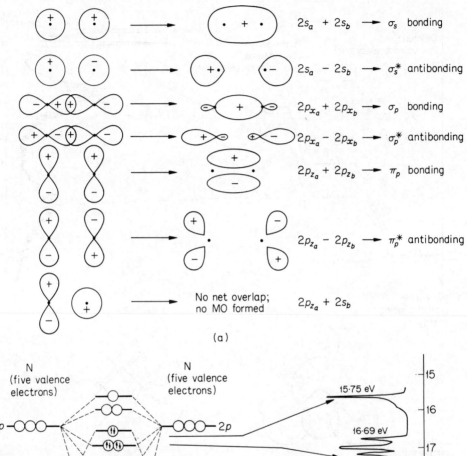

$2s_a + 2s_b \longrightarrow \sigma_s$ bonding

$2s_a - 2s_b \longrightarrow \sigma_s^*$ antibonding

$2p_{x_a} + 2p_{x_b} \longrightarrow \sigma_p$ bonding

$2p_{x_a} - 2p_{x_b} \longrightarrow \sigma_p^*$ antibonding

$2p_{z_a} + 2p_{z_b} \longrightarrow \pi_p$ bonding

$2p_{z_a} - 2p_{z_b} \longrightarrow \pi_p^*$ antibonding

No net overlap;
no MO formed $\quad 2p_{z_a} + 2s_b$

(a)

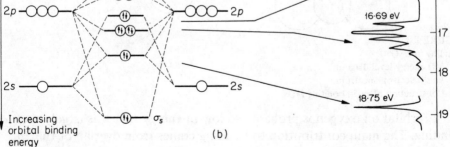

N
(five valence
electrons)

N
(five valence
electrons)

$2p$

$2p$

15·75 eV

16·69 eV

$2s$

$2s$

18·75 eV

σ_s

Increasing
orbital binding
energy

(b)

FIGURE 1.2
Bonding in N_2
(a) The formation of molecular orbitals from atomic orbitals
(b) Molecular orbital energy levels and the photoelectron spectrum

13

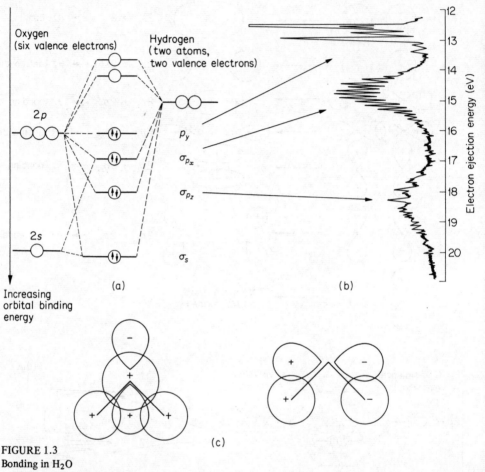

FIGURE 1.3
Bonding in H_2O
(a) MO energy level diagram
(b) Photoelectron spectrum
(c) Construction of main bonding MOs

the $2s$ orbital on oxygen is probably so low in energy that it is largely non-bonding. The main contribution to bonding comes from overlap of the $2p_x$ and $2p_z$ orbitals on oxygen with the hydrogen $1s$ orbitals. The $2p_y$ orbital on oxygen is non-bonding on symmetry grounds.

A delocalized molecular orbital energy level diagram for methane is shown in Fig. 1.4. Each of the hydrogen atoms in methane is bound in the same way

14

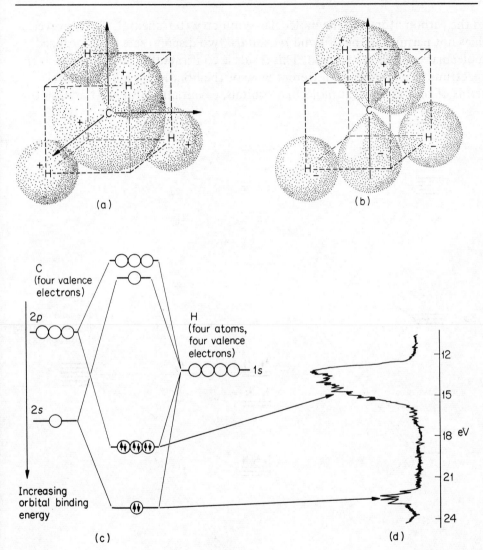

FIGURE 1.4

A representation of bonding in methane

(a) Overlap of carbon $2s$ and hydrogen $1s$ orbitals

(b) Overlap of carbon p_z and hydrogen $1s$ orbitals

(c) MO energy level diagram

(d) Photoelectron spectrum

15

to the carbon atom. As the molecular symmetry (tetrahedral, T_d), however, does not permit mixing of s and p orbitals, two discrete sets of delocalized molecular orbitals are formed. This result is confirmed by the photoelectron spectrum. A qualitatively different view of the bonding in methane is in terms of four equivalent molecular orbitals, essentially localized between the

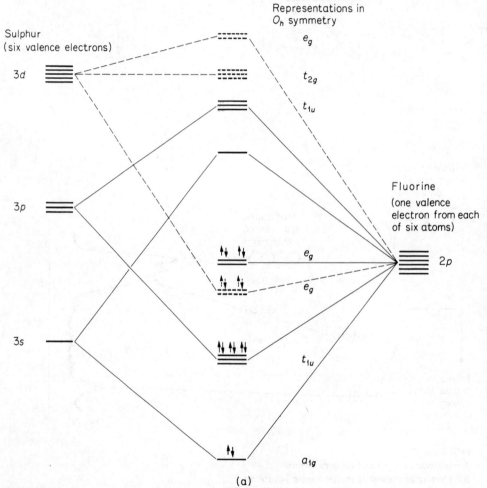

(a)

FIGURE 1.5
(a) Qualitative molecular orbital energy diagram for σ bonding in SF_6 showing the possibility of bonding with or without the involvement of sulphur $3d$ orbitals

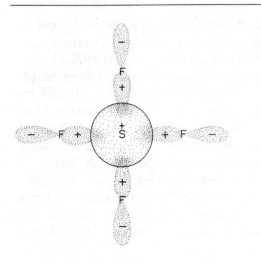

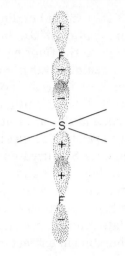

Part of the atomic orbital overlap forming the a_{1g} molecular orbital; the two remaining fluorine atoms supply p orbitals which overlap with the sulphur $3s$ orbital perpendicular to the plane of the paper

Part of the atomic orbital overlap forming the t_{1u} molecular orbital; the sulphur p_x and p_y orbitals bond in a similar way to fluorine p orbitals

(b)

FIGURE 1.5

(b) Bonding molecular orbitals of SF_6

central carbon atom and each hydrogen atom. It can be shown [3] that these two descriptions are equivalent in calculating the overall energy of the molecule. The concept of hybridization of orbitals (e.g. sp^3 hybrids for carbon in methane), which is very useful especially in organic chemistry, represents a close approximation to the localized molecular orbital model. It often has serious limitations in understanding bonding in compounds of the non-metals, as the following example shows.

The non-metallic elements of the second and later rows of the Periodic Table form a number of compounds, especially with fluorine and other electronegative atoms or groups, in which the central atom apparently must accommodate more than four electron pairs in its valence orbitals. Common examples are PF_5, SF_6, and IF_7. One approach to this problem is to assume

[3] Bernett, W. A. (1969), *J. Chem. Educ.*, **46**, 746.

that d orbitals are used in bonding; in the case of SF_6 it is the $3d$ orbitals of sulphur. A combination of $3s$, $3p$, $3d_{x^2-y^2}$, and $3d_{z^2}$ orbitals can create six equivalent bonds to the fluorine atoms in octahedral symmetry (d^2sp^3 hybridization of sulphur valence orbitals). The energy required to promote electrons from $3s$ or $3p$ to $3d$, however, is probably large compared with the energies of the S—F bonds, although relative to the free sulphur atom it may well be lowered, and the $3d$ orbitals contracted in the presence of strongly electronegative ligands. The qualitative MO diagram in Fig. 1.5 shows that a bonding scheme for SF_6 need not necessarily involve $3d$ orbitals. Some mixing of d orbitals with s and p orbitals, however, is allowed by the molecular symmetry, and could lead to a reduction in the energy of the molecule. Note that the high electronegativity of fluorine enables the six fluorine atoms to accommodate four valence electrons in orbitals which are non-bonding or only weakly bonding in character.

1.4.1 *Isoelectronic compounds*

The concept of isoelectronic species often proves useful in non-metal chemistry in predicting new compounds and in suggesting likely structures for them. It is based on the observation that compounds in which the constituent atoms have the same types of valence orbitals occupied by the same total number of electrons often have similar molecular structures, and related physical and chemical properties. Thus, there are striking similarities, especially in physical properties, between the isoelectronic compounds N_2 and CO, N_2O and CO_2, and borazine $B_3H_3N_3H_3$ and benzene C_6H_6. Several other sets, including both neutral molecules and ions, are shown in Table 1.4.

The bonding theories discussed above indicate why these groups of molecules are so alike. First, their shapes, which are dictated by the number of electron pairs and their mutual repulsion, might be expected to be essentially the same. Secondly, the sets of molecular orbitals which describe the bonding in each member of an isoelectronic series will be similar in number and shape, and will be occupied by the same total number of electrons. This has been verified experimentally in several cases; the photoelectron spectra of N_2O and CO_2, for example, are almost identical.

Although structural similarities exist between neutral molecules and the ions which are isoelectronic with them, the chemical properties of charged and uncharged species are, of course, not readily compared. Chemical differences arise within series such as N_2, CO, and BF since the electronegativities of the atoms in the molecules diverge. While N_2 and CO show many common features, BF is chemically very dissimilar. Fluorine is so much more electronegative than boron that the fluorine atomic orbitals are nearly non-bonding, leaving the boron atom relatively electron deficient. This renders the compound very liable to polymerization or nucleophilic attack (p. 47).

TABLE 1.4
Some isoelectronic species

Structural type	Species
Isoelectronic groupings	BH_3 CH_2 NH O
'Triply bonded' species	$^-C{\equiv}C^-$ N_2 CO NO^+ CN^- BF HNC HCN
Linear triatomics	N_3^- NCO^- NNO NO_2^+ CO_2 FBO FCN NNF^+
Bent triatomics	NO_2^- FNO
Trigonal planar	BF_3 BO_3^{3-} CO_3^{2-} NO_3^- F_2CO FNO_2
Polymeric	$(BN)_n$ and C_n (both diamond and graphite structures)
Cyclic	C_6H_6 $H_3B_3N_3H_3$ $H_3B_3O_3$ $(HCN)_3$
Oligomeric and polymeric compounds	$(X_2SiO)_n$ $(X_2PN)_n$ $(X_2SiNH)_n$ $(PO_3^-)_n$ $(X_2SiCH_2)_n$ $(FS(O)N)_n$

Despite these limitations, new compounds of the non-metals can often be predicted, and their structures and properties forecast by comparison with known isoelectronic species. For example, the anions OCF_3^- and $O_2CF_2^{2-}$, which are isoelectronic with BF_4^-, have been discovered recently. The reaction of carbonyl fluoride with caesium fluoride leads to the caesium salt of the trifluoromethoxide ion [4] OCF_3^-:

$$CsF + OCF_2 \rightarrow Cs^+ OCF_3^-$$

The difluorodioxocarbonate ion [5] $O_2CF_2^{2-}$ is obtained from caesium fluoride and carbon dioxide under pressure:

$$2 CsF + OCO \rightarrow Cs_2^+ O_2CF_2^{2-}$$

As OCF_3^- is also isoelectronic with ONF_3 (p. 134), one would expect the two species to have similar structures. Moreover, by analogy with $O_2CF_2^{2-}$, the existence of the ion $O_2NF_2^-$ might be predicted.

Several other examples of isoelectronic species are mentioned in the text.

[4] Redwood, M. E. and Willis, C. J. (1965), *Canad. J. Chem.*, **43**, 1893.
[5] Martineau, E. and Milne, J. B. (1971), *Chem. Comm.*, 1327.

Simple hydrides and halides 2

Hydrides and halides of general formula AX_n are considered in this chapter. The first part of the chapter surveys the main features of the structure and properties of the compounds, and the second part considers special properties within each Group. More complex hydrides and halides containing chains or clusters of non-metal atoms are discussed in Chapter 5.

2.1 The experimentally observed range of compounds

The range of hydrides which can be isolated and manipulated at room temperature is quite straightforward. Each of the elements from carbon to iodine forms a simple hydride AH_n, in which n is the number of electrons required to fill the s and p valence electron shells for each element, i.e. 4, 3, 2, and 1 for Group IV, V, VI, and VII elements respectively. These hydrides obey what is commonly called the octet rule.

In addition to the stable compounds, hydrides are known which contain less than eight electrons around the non-metal. Some of the best characterized are BH_3, CH_2, CH_3, SiH_2, NH, and NH_2, but they are all short-lived gases at room temperature, unstable with respect to a polymerization or disproportionation process.

The range of stable halides is much greater than for the hydrides. In addition to compounds in which the non-metal has a formal eight-electron configuration, elements of the second and subsequent rows show a strong tendency to undergo octet expansion, especially with the most electronegative halogens fluorine and chlorine. The highest possible valency corresponds to the Group number, which implies use of all the outer s and p electrons in bonding.

As with the hydrides, a number of simple halides are known which are too

TABLE 2.1
Simple halides of the non-metals

	Group III	Group IV	Group V	Group VI	Group VII	Group 0
F	BF[a], BF_3	CF_2[a], CF_3[a], CF_4, SiF_2[a], SiF_4, GeF_2, GeF_4, SnF_2, SnF_4	NF[a], NF_2[a], PF_2[a], NF_3, PF_3, AsF_3, SbF_3, PF_5, AsF_5, SbF_5	SF_2[a], SF_4, SF_5[a], SF_6, SeF_4, SeF_6, TeF_4, TeF_6	F_2, ClF, ClF_3, ClF_5, BrF, BrF_3, BrF_5, IF, IF_3, IF_5, IF_7	KrF_2[a], XeF_2[a], XeF_4, XeF_6
Cl	BCl[a], BCl_3	CCl_2[a], CCl_3[a], CCl_4, $SiCl_2$[a], $SiCl_4$, $GeCl_2$, $GeCl_4$, $SnCl_2$, $SnCl_4$	NCl[a], PCl[a], NCl_3, PCl_3, $AsCl_3$, $SbCl_3$, PCl_5, $SbCl_5$	OCl[a], OCl_2[a], SCl_2, SCl_4, $SeCl_2$, $SeCl_4$, $TeCl_2$, $TeCl_4$	Cl_2, $BrCl$, ICl, ICl_3	$XeCl_2$[a]
Br	BBr_3	CBr_2[a], CBr_4, $SiBr_2$[a], $SiBr_4$, $GeBr_2$, $GeBr_4$, $SnBr_2$, $SnBr_4$	(NBr_3), PBr_3, $AsBr_3$, $SbBr_3$, PBr_5	OBr_2, $SeBr_4$, $TeBr_2$, $TeBr_4$	Br_2, IBr	
I	BI_3	CI_2[a], CI_4, SiI_2[a], SiI_4, GeI_2, GeI_4, SnI_2, SnI_4	(NI_3), PI_3, AsI_3, SbI_3	SeI_2, TeI_4	I_2	

[a] Not stable at room temperature.

unstable to be isolated at room temperature. These are mostly compounds containing the non-metals in low valency states which are unstable with respect to polymerization or disproportionation. The complete range of halides, including the most fully characterized of these unstable species, is shown in Table 2.1.

2.2   Structures in the gas phase

The structures of the gaseous halides and hydrides are generally very well predicted by application of the Gillespie–Nyholm rules on electron repulsion discussed in Chapter 1. With the exception of XeF_6, each of the observed structures of the compounds shown in Table 2.2 represents a minimum for electron repulsion effects, with repulsions from the non-bonding electron pairs being dominant. It should be noted that there are diagonal relationships in the table. Starting with structures with no non-bonding valence electrons on the non-metal, and moving upwards and to the right, structures are found with progressive replacement of bonding electron pairs by non-bonding pairs. Thus, successive replacement of equatorial bonding electrons by non-bonding electrons in the trigonal bipyramidal PF_5 structure gives the structures observed for SF_4, ClF_3, and XeF_2.

Several methods have been used to determine the structures. The molecular symmetry has often been found by infrared and Raman spectroscopy, but accurate bond lengths and bond angles have been obtained from microwave spectroscopy or electron diffraction studies.

The simple model of electron repulsion does not give an adequate picture for XeF_6. The diagonal relationship with IF_7 of D_{5h} symmetry suggests replacement of an axial or equatorial bonding pair by a non-bonding pair to give structures with either C_{5v} symmetry or equatorially distorted octahedral symmetry. However, despite intensive efforts using electron diffraction and Raman and infrared spectroscopic methods, the gas phase structure still defies exact analysis. In the ground vibrational state of the molecule the lone pair may occupy a position effectively in the centre of one face of an octahedron causing distortion from O_h to C_{3v} symmetry. At temperatures at which the molecule has an appreciable vapour pressure it is vibrationally excited and its observed symmetry is no longer exactly O_h or C_{3v}.

Methylene CH_2 has two unpaired electrons occupying separate orbitals in its triplet, lowest energy state. The wide bond angle of 150° (Fig. 2.1) can be attributed to the lesser bonding pair to non-bonded electron interaction from orbitals occupied by only one electron compared with orbitals occupied by two electrons, e.g. water.

The strength of bonding pair–non-bonded pair repulsion must decrease rapidly as the enclosed angle exceeds 90°. Thus, small deviations from co-linearity away from the non-bonded pair are observed for the axial bonds in SF_4 (or ClF_3), and in BrF_5 the bromine atom lies slightly below the plane of the four fluorine atoms.

2 orbitals
2 electrons

2 orbitals
4 electrons

FIGURE 2.1
Bond angles in CH_2 and H_2O

Bond lengths among the simple halides and hydrides can be predicted roughly from the sum of covalent radii as discussed in Chapter 1. Poor agreement between the predicted and experimental bond lengths for some halides may be due to $(p–d)\pi$ bonding, e.g. $d(Si—F)$ in SiF_4, predicted 167 pm, experiment 156 pm.

It seems to be a general effect, in halides containing five or six electron pairs, that bonds which are subject to the strongest interaction with adjacent lone or bonding electron pairs are longer than other bonds, e.g. bond lengths in ClF_3, SF_4, and BrF_5.

2.3   Structures in the condensed phase (Table 2.3)

Differences in structures between molecules in the gas phase and molecules in the condensed phase generally arise from the formation of new intermolecular bonds in the condensed phase. These bonds are stronger than van der Waals and other polarization forces which are essentially electrostatic and do not involve the formation of new molecular orbitals.

23

TABLE 2.2
Structures of the gaseous halides and hydrides

Type of molecule	Number of lone pairs of electrons			
	0	1	2	3
AX₂		C_{2v} CH₂ {~150° triplet, 102° singlet} BH₂ 130° CF₂ 105° SiF₂ 102° GeF₂ 97°	C_{2v} H₂O 104° H₂S 92° H₂Te 89° OF₂ 103° OCl₂ 110°	$D_{\infty h}$ XeF₂ KrF₂ XeCl₂
AX₃	D_{3h} BH₃ BX₃ CH₃	C_{3v} NH₃ 106° PH₃ 94° AsH₃ 92° NF₃ 102° PF₃ 98° AsF₃ 96° PCl₃ 100° AsCl₃ 98°	C_{2v} ClF₃ 87° $d_1 > d_2$ BrF₃	
AX₄	T_d All Group IVA tetrahalides and hydrides	C_{2v} SF₄ SeF₄ TeCl₄ $\alpha = 101°$ $\beta = 87°$ $d_1 > d_2$	D_{4h} XeF₄	

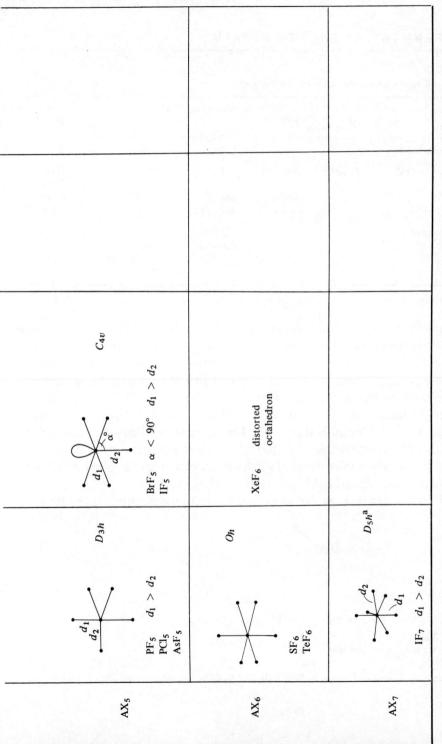

AX$_5$	D_{3h}	C_{4v}
PF$_5$ PCl$_5$ AsF$_5$ $\quad d_1 > d_2$		BrF$_5$ $\quad \alpha < 90°$ $\quad d_1 > d_2$ IF$_5$
AX$_6$	O_h	
SF$_6$ TeF$_6$		XeF$_6$ $\quad$ distorted octahedron
AX$_7$	$D_{5h}{}^a$	
IF$_7$ $\quad d_1 > d_2$		

^{a} Other symmetries for AX$_7$ structures are possible, e.g. TaF$_7{}^{2-}$ is a capped trigonal prism with C_{2v} symmetry, but they have not been observed in the non-metals. There is some distortion in IF$_7$ from exact D_{5h} symmetry, which is to be expected as the energy differences between the possible forms are very small.

TABLE 2.3
Hydrides and halides associated in the condensed phase

	III	IV	V	VI	VII
				Group	
Hydrogen-bonded			NH_3	H_2O	HF
Halogen-bridged	BF_3(w)	SiF_4(w)	SbF_5	SF_4(w)	ClF_3
					BrF_3
		GeF_2	$SbCl_5$?	SeF_4?	(IF_3)
		SnF_4	AsI_3, SbI_3	TeF_4	ICl_3
Auto-ionized			PCl_5	$SCl_4,$	
			PBr_5	$SeCl_4$?	
				$TeCl_4, TeBr_4$	
				TeI_4	

(w) = Weak association

The two main types of new bonds are hydrogen bonds [1] and halide bridge bonds. The former give rise to unexpectedly high boiling points for ammonia, water, and hydrogen fluoride, and are most apparent with electronegative first-row elements joined to hydrogen. The strongest hydrogen bonds are observed with hydrogen fluoride. The F—H—F bond is sufficiently strong for a mixture of linear and cyclic polymers $(HF)_n$ (n = 1 to 6) to appear in the gas phase when the liquid is vaporized. The structure of the solid is shown in Fig. 2.2(a). The hydrogen atom appears to be mid-way between the two fluorine atoms. The exact position of the hydrogen atom has been more clearly established in the related FHF⁻ ion [Fig. 2.2(b)].

The bonding can be regarded as due to the extreme polarity of the H—F

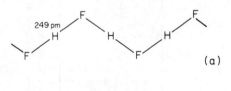

(a)

$(F \underset{113\ pm}{\underline{\hspace{2em}}} H \underset{113\ pm}{\underline{\hspace{2em}}} F)^{-}$ (b)

FIGURE 2.2
Hydrogen bonding in HF and HF_2

[1] Pimentel, G. C. and McClellan, A. L. (1960). *The Hydrogen Bond*, Freeman, San Francisco.

bond, and can be described as a donation of a lone pair of electrons from one fluorine atom to a proton as in Fig. 2.3(a). However, a simple molecular orbital picture of the bonding has been proposed as shown in Fig. 2.3(b).

Less strong hydrogen bonds are observed in water although their effect dominates its physical properties. No polymers of H_2O are observed when water vaporizes. The structure of ice shows unsymmetrical hydrogen bonding of type $O-H \cdots O$. Each oxygen atom is involved in two short and two longer $O-H$ bonds (see p. 58).

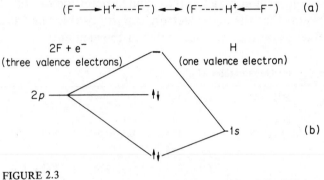

$$(F^- \longrightarrow H^+ ----- F^-) \longleftrightarrow (F^- ----- H^+ \longleftarrow F^-) \qquad (a)$$

FIGURE 2.3
Bonding in HF_2^-

The extent of halide bridge bonding increases down a Group as the acceptor power of the elements increases. The interaction in solid SiF_4 is extremely weak and does little to decrease the volatility of the compound, while SnF_4 is held together by strong fluorine bridges which make it a relatively high-melting, involatile solid. Similarly, PF_5 is not associated in the solid, while SbF_5 shows fluorine bridges. Although bridge bonding is most common among the fluorides, owing to the strongly polar character of A—F bonds, other halides of the heavier elements also show some bridging, e.g. $SbCl_5$, ICl_3, AsI_3.

A third way in which solid structures differ from those in the gas phase is through auto-ionization. This is not a common effect but X-ray studies have shown that stable solid forms of PCl_5 and PBr_5 must be represented as $PCl_4^+PCl_6^-$ and $PBr_4^+Br^-$ respectively. The tellurium tetrahalides have structures which tend towards a $TeX_3^+X^-$ form, although some degree of covalent halogen bridging is preserved especially in the fluoride.

2.4   Aspects of thermodynamic stability

The heats of formation and bond energies of most of the halides and hydrides can be understood qualitatively in terms of the electronegativity and orbital overlap considerations discussed in Chapter 1. Thus, a larger number of stable fluorides than of other halides is observed (Table 2.1). There is little difference between the mean bond energies in fluorides which obey the octet rule and in those which have expanded octets, e.g. PF_3 and PF_5 (Table 2.4). In contrast, a much sharper drop in the mean bond energy occurs between octet and expanded octet chlorides and bromides, and no expanded octet iodides or hydrides are known. It seems that the high electronegativity of fluorine has a particular stabilizing influence on high valency states of the elements.

TABLE 2.4
Mean bond dissociation energies (kJ mol^{-1}) in fluorides AF_n

8 Electrons	SiF_4	598	PF_3	497	SF_2	(355)	ClF	251		
10 Electrons			PF_5	464	SF_4	343	ClF_3	171		
			AsF_5	384	SeF_4	318	BrF_3	201	KrF_2	50
12 Electrons					SF_6	328				
					TeF_6	339	IF_5	263	XeF_4	130

With reference to the qualitative molecular orbital bonding schemes for SF_6 (Fig. 1.5) and XeF_4 (Fig. 2.11), this effect can be explained in two ways. Using only s and p orbitals of sulphur or xenon, both MO schemes require localization of electrons on the fluorine atoms, which would be less possible with elements of lower electronegativity. There is evidence from transition metal chemistry and from calculations on the non-metals that, when an atom has a positive charge, the energy of d orbitals decreases relative to s or p orbitals. Under the electron withdrawing influence of fluorine atoms, vacant d orbitals around a non-metal atom may become more available for overlap with filled p orbitals on the fluorine, as is allowed by symmetry in SF_6 and XeF_4.

The noble gas fluorides have bond energies which are close to values obtained by extrapolation from the bond energies of fluorides in neighbouring Groups. On this basis, the bond energy of ArF_2 can be predicted to be very low, explaining why this compound has not yet been isolated.

The experimentally observed instability of low valency halides or hydrides

28

such as BF, CH_2, or NH, relative to BF_3, CH_4, or NH_3 respectively, is not due to weak bonds. For example, the bond in BF has a higher dissociation energy than the mean dissociation energy in BF_3 (756 compared with 643 kJ mol^{-1}), but chemically BF is very unstable and polymerizes to compounds in which boron is formally trivalent, or disproportionates to boron and BF_3. The enthalpy changes in the disproportionation can be evaluated from a cycle:

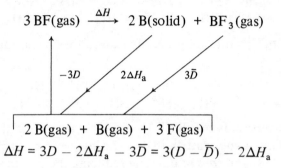

$$\Delta H = 3D - 2\Delta H_a - 3\overline{D} = 3(D - \overline{D}) - 2\Delta H_a$$

Each boron atom is held by at least three bonds in the solid, so ΔH_a is a large term (546 kJ mol^{-1}). Although $D(BF)$ is appreciably greater than $\overline{D}$(B—F in BF_3), ΔH is negative and the disproportionation highly favoured.

Similar thermodynamic instability can be demonstrated for all the low-valent compounds of B, C, and Si, and most of the low-valent species of N and P.

2.5 Physical properties

2.5.1 *Volatility and melting point*

Most non-metal hydrides and halides form condensed phases in which there are discrete molecules held together by van der Waals forces. The strength of binding will depend on the polarizability and dipole moments of the molecules. The compounds listed in Table 2.3 have stronger bonding interactions in the condensed phase, often decreasing their volatility relative to compounds which form purely molecular condensed phases.

The non-metal hydrides and halides are generally quite volatile, with boiling points among compounds forming molecular condensed phases ranging from $-161°$ for methane to $348°$ for stannic iodide SnI_4. Very sharp increases in boiling points are observed for some compounds on the borderline between

29

metals and non-metals, reflecting the difference in bonding between 'ionic' and 'molecular' solids, e.g. BF_3 $-101°$, AlF_3 $+1300°$; GeF_4 $-30°$, SnF_4 $+705°$. Two main trends can be observed in volatility:

(1) Boiling points will increase for a class of compounds going down a Group as the molecular weight and polarizability increase, e.g.

$$NF_3 \ -129° \quad PF_3 \ -101° \quad AsF_3 \quad \ 63° \quad SbF_3 \ \ 376°$$
$$CH_4 \ -161° \quad SiH_4 \ -112° \quad GeH_4 \ -88° \quad SnH_4 \ -52°$$

Exceptions to this rule are generally caused by association in the condensed phase, e.g.

$$HF \quad \ \ 19° \quad HCl \ -90° \quad HBr \ \ -67° \quad HI \quad \ \ -35°$$
$$NH_3 \ -33° \quad PH_3 \ -88° \quad AsH_3 \ -58° \quad SbH_3 \ -17°$$

A curious inversion is that $SiCl_4$ (b.p. $57°$) is more volatile than CCl_4 (b.p. $77°$). This has been attributed to the involvement of chlorine lone pair electrons of $SiCl_4$ in $(p–d)\pi$ bonding reducing the polarizability of the molecule compared with CCl_4.

(2) For a class of compounds AX_n, the boiling points will increase in the order $H \leqslant F < Cl < Br < I$ owing to the increasing polarizability of the heavier halogen atoms. Hydrides and fluorides often have comparable boiling points. Fluorine binds its electrons tightly, making fluorides surprisingly volatile for their molecular weights. As fluorides are more commonly involved in bridge bonding than the other halides, the above sequence can be distorted.

There are few smooth trends in boiling points across rows since, even in the absence of specific bonding interactions, changes in dipole moment and changes in polarizability may compete with each other. For example, the dipole moment in the second-row hydrides increases uniformly from zero with SiH_4 to a maximum with HCl yet the boiling point sequence is $SiH_4 < PH_3 < H_2S > HCl$. The polarizability of diatomic HCl, lower than that of triatomic H_2S, must outweigh the dipole effect. A boiling point sequence such as SiF_4 $-95°$, PF_5 $-85°$, and SF_6 $-64°$ in molecules with zero dipole moment reflects a decrease in volatility with increasing polarizability and molecular weight.

Melting points depend on the packing of molecules in the solid, and are

30

more strongly affected by symmetry and weak intermolecular interactions than boiling points. Among fluorides, it is generally those of highest symmetry which have melting points close to their boiling points, e.g. SiF_4 and GeF_4 of T_d symmetry, SF_6, SeF_6, and TeF_6 of O_h symmetry, and IF_7 of D_{5h} symmetry all sublime, while BF_3, PF_5, and AsF_5 of D_{3h} symmetry have liquid ranges of less than 30°. Liquid ranges of 50–100° are common for fluorides of C_{3v} or C_{2v} symmetry. Carbon tetrafluoride is exceptional with a liquid range of about 40° despite T_d symmetry. Most hydrides, chlorides, and bromides have longer liquid ranges, but there is still a rough correlation with symmetry.

2.6 Chemical properties

2.6.1 *Acid-base properties:* [A] *Proton donor and acceptor properties of the hydrides* [2]

The strengths of the hydrides as protonic acids can only be meaningfully compared with one another relative to a particular proton acceptor such as water. The strength of the acid determines the position in the equilibrium:

$$HA + H_2O \rightleftharpoons H_3O^+ + A^-$$

The acid strength is conveniently quoted as $-\log [H_3O^+][A^-]/[HA]$, the pK_a value. A scale of acid strengths based on pK_a values is only partly determined by direct measurement of the above equilibrium; comparisons with other proton acceptors, whose strength relative to water is known, are also used.

Acid strength in the hydrides is influenced by three main factors:

(1) The energy of dissociation of the A—H bond; weak bonds favour proton release.
(2) The electron affinity of the atom A; high electron affinities favour polarization in the sense H^+A^-.
(3) The energy of solvation of the anion; small anions have high solvation energies, so that A^- derived from HA is likely to be more strongly solvated than $(HA')^-$ derived from H_2A', other things being equal.

[2] Bell, R. P. (1969), *Acids and Bases; Their Quantitative Behaviour*, 2nd Edn., Chapman and Hall, London.

The balance of these energy terms is such that trends in acid strength follow the decrease in dissociation energies of A—H bonds fairly closely. It can be seen from Table 2.5 that pK_a values increase down the Groups and across the rows just as bond energies decrease down the Groups and across the rows. For example, it is certainly the very high bond strength of the H—F bond which outweighs the high solvation energy of F^- and the high electron affinity of fluorine, to make hydrofluoric acid substantially weaker, with water as solvent, than hydrochloric acid. Hydrides with pK_a values greater than that of

TABLE 2.5
pK_a values for the hydrides

CH_4	NH_3	H_2O	HF
~58	39	16	3
SiH_4	PH_3	H_2S	HCl
~35	27	7	−7
GeH_4	AsH_3	H_2Se	HBr
25	~19	4	−9
SnH_4	SbH_3	H_2Te	HI
~20	~15	3	−10

water must be considered extremely poor proton donors. Nevertheless, in practical terms it is possible to deprotonate hydrides with pK_a values up to about 30 using solid potassium hydroxide and up to about 45 using alkali metal hydrides as the proton acceptors, e.g.

$$2\,KOH + GeH_4 \xrightarrow{\text{dimethyl sulphoxide}} KGeH_3 + KOH\cdot H_2O$$

$$NaH + NH_3 \xrightarrow{\text{liq. } NH_3} Na^+ + NH_2^- + H_2$$

Most of the hydrides are rather weak proton acceptors. Proton acceptor power depends on the availability of electrons on the non-metal to overlap with the vacant $1s$ orbital of a proton. If the electrons are in orbitals which are either too diffuse, as with most hydrides of the heavier non-metals, or too tightly bound, as with electronegative elements, acceptor power will be low. In practice, only NH_3, H_2O, and PH_3 form well characterized cations by addi-

32

tion of a proton. The acceptor strength and the observed range of salts with the cations falls sharply from NH_3 to H_2O to PH_3.

Ammonium salts, containing tetrahedral NH_4^+, are well known. Hydroxonium salts containing the cation H_3O^+ include many compounds once classified as 'acid hydrates', e.g. $HClO_4,H_2O$ is $H_3O^+ ClO_4^-$, with crystals isomorphic with $NH_4^+ ClO_4^-$. The H_3O^+ ion is isoelectronic with NH_3 and has a pyramidal structure with HOH angle about $115°$. Aqueous solutions of acids contain H_3O^+ but there is a rapid exchange of protons with H_2O giving an average lifetime of about 10^{-13} s for individual H_3O^+ ions. Phosphine forms salts only with the strongest acids, particularly the hydrogen halides (p. 55).

Both water and ammonia are auto-ionized:

$$2\,H_2O \rightleftharpoons H_3O^+ + OH^- \quad K = [H_3O^+][OH^-] \approx 10^{-14} \text{ at } 25°$$
$$2\,NH_3 \rightleftharpoons NH_4^+ + NH_2^- \quad K = [NH_4^+][NH_2^-] \approx 10^{-30} \text{ at } -50°$$

The chemistry of liquid ammonia solutions is closely comparable to that of water solutions. Thus, solutions of ammonium halides in liquid ammonia are acidic, giving NH_4^+ just as acids in water give H_3O^+:

$$NH_4Cl \xrightarrow{NH_3} NH_4^+ + Cl^-$$
$$\text{(acidic ion)}$$
$$H_3O^+Cl^- \xrightarrow{H_2O} H_3O^+ + Cl^-$$

Similarly, alkali metal amides behave as bases in liquid ammonia like metal hydroxides in water since they generate a proton acceptor ion NH_2^-:

$$NaNH_2 \xrightarrow{NH_3} NH_2^- + Na^+$$
$$\text{(basic ion)}$$
$$\text{cf.} \quad NaOH \xrightarrow{H_2O} OH^- + Na^+$$

Some other properties of liquid ammonia are considered on p. 55.

No salts of the CH_5^+ ion have yet been isolated, but the gaseous species is well known in mass spectrometry from the ion–molecule reaction:

$$CH_4^+ + CH_4 \rightarrow CH_5^+ + CH_3$$

2.6.2   *Acid-base properties:* [B] *Lewis acid-base behaviour* [3]

Proton donor or acceptor power is only one aspect of the broader field of acid–base interactions. We shall now consider other electron pair donor or electron pair acceptor reactions, the so-called Lewis acid-base behaviour. The halides and hydrides which have well defined properties as Lewis acids and bases are listed in Table 2.6. Three main types of interactions will be considered:

(1) The reaction of uncharged acid A with an uncharged base B: to give A:B.
(2) The formation of stable anionic and cationic complexes involving halide ion (X^-) acceptance and donation.
(3) Acid–base interactions which lead to subsequent chemical reactions, especially hydrolysis reactions, i.e.

$$X_nA + OH_2 \rightarrow (X_nA \leftarrow OH_2) \rightarrow X_{n-1}A(OH) + HX$$

TABLE 2.6
Electron pair donors and acceptors

Donors				
	NH_3		H_2O	
	PH_3, PX_3		H_2S, SF_4	
	AsH_3, AsX_3			
Acceptors				
$(BH_3), BX_3$				
	SiX_4	$PX_3 < PX_5$	SF_4	ClF, ClF_3
	GeX_4	$AsX_3 < AsX_5$	SeX_2, SeX_4	BrF, BrF_3, BrF_5
	SnX_4	$SbX_3 < SbX_5$	TeX_2, TeX_4, TeX_6	IF, IF_3, IF_5

(i)   *Formation of neutral complexes* A:B.   One measure of the strength of an acid–base interaction is the enthalpy of the reaction:

$$A(g) + B(g) \rightarrow A:B(g)$$

The complex AB will be isolable at $25°$ if the enthalpy is more negative than about -40 kJ mol^{-1}, although enthalpies for donor–acceptor reactions may be as negative as -150 kJ mol^{-1}.

[3] Satchell, D. P. N. and Satchell, R. S. (1971), *Quart. Rev.* **25,** 171. Lewis acidity; quantitative aspects.

The factors influencing the stability of A:B can be conveniently discussed by reference to the sequence of experimentally determined stabilities shown below:

	Base	Acid strength
1.	NMe_3	$BF_3 < BCl_3 < BBr_3 < BI_3$
2.	NMe_3	$BF_3 > SiF_4 < PF_5$
3.	NMe_3	$PF_5 < AsF_5 < SbF_5$
4.	NMe_3	$BF_3 > (BH_3)$
5.	PMe_3, PF_3, or CO	$BF_3 < (BH_3)$

	Acid	Base strength
6.	BBr_3	$NH_3 > PH_3 > AsH_3 \gg SbH_3?$
7.	SiF_4	$NH_3 > PH_3$

The acid strength of the boron halides (sequence 1) is in the opposite order to that expected in terms of the electronegativity difference between boron and the halogen atoms. It seems that $(p-p)\pi$ bonding, which decreases in the sequence $F > Cl > Br > I$, causes sufficient filling of the 'vacant' boron p_z orbital to reduce its ability to accept electrons from a base. Although SiF_4 is a somewhat weaker acid than BF_3 (sequence 2), the Group V pentafluorides are all stronger acids than BF_3, and their acid strength increases markedly down the Group. This trend to stronger acid properties down a Group is observed in Groups IV, V, and VI and is the result both of the increasing electronegativity difference between fluorine and the non-metals, and the increasing size of the non-metal allowing easier access of an incoming base.

Sequences 4 and 5 raise an important point of classification of acids and bases. The experimental observations can be summarized thus:

(a) BH_3 (from B_2H_6) forms complexes with nearly all neutral electron pair donors. This includes compounds such as CO and PF_3 which appear to have no basic strength towards many Lewis acids. The H_3B—base bond is essentially covalent.

(b) BF_3 tends to form its strongest complexes with bases which bond through nitrogen or oxygen. It will form complexes with bases which bond through other elements, e.g. BF_3PMe_3 and BF_3SMe_2, but these may not be as stable as the BH_3 complexes of these bases. It does not complex with CO or PF_3.

35

The p_z orbital in BH_3 is vacant and thus BH_3 bonds readily with almost any lone pair of electrons from another atom in an orbital of the right symmetry. The p_z orbital in the boron halides is partly filled, and strong complexes are formed only when the donor can compete with the $(p-p)\pi$ bonding from the halogen atoms. This is most likely to occur with nitrogen and oxygen bases, donating $2s$ and $2p$ orbitals. The resulting complexes will be stabilized by a polar contribution to bonding, e.g. $F_3B^{-+}NMe_3$.

Phosphorus trifluoride (like CO) forms stable complexes with some transition metals in low-valence or zero-valency states, e.g. $Ni(PF_3)_4$ [4]. The dominant effect here is not the strength of the transition metals as σ acceptors, but their ability to donate electrons from filled d orbitals to vacant orbitals of suitable symmetry on the base. In the case of PF_3 it may be the vacant $3d$ orbitals which accept electrons from the transition metal, but with CO it is the vacant antibonding π orbitals (see p. 93).

The above classification of acids and bases is related to a more comprehensive scheme developed by Pearson [5]. In his terminology acids and bases are classified as soft or hard. For a base, 'soft' and 'hard' describe graphically the looseness or tightness respectively with which the valence electrons are held. Soft and hard acids are those which form the most stable complexes with soft and hard bases respectively. Thus, CO and PF_3 are soft bases and BH_3 a soft acid, while NH_3 and H_2O are hard bases and BF_3 and SiF_4 are hard acids.

Steric hindrance can distort sequences of acid or base strength. The effect can be illustrated by the pyridine and 2-substituted pyridine complexes with boron acids shown below:

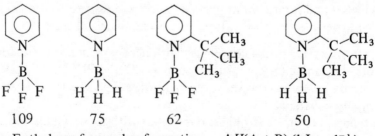

109	75	62	50

Enthalpy of complex formation, $-\Delta H(A + B)\,(kJ\,mol^{-1})$

[4] Nixon, J. F. (1973), *Endeavour*, **32**, 19.

[5] Pearson, R. G. (1969), *Survey of Progress in Chemistry*, **5**, 1. A detailed account of soft and hard acids and bases.

It is seen that the effect of a bulky substituent is to reduce the stability of the complexes with both BF_3 and BH_3 but the effect is larger for BF_3. Measurements on the strength of pyridine and the 2-substituted pyridine as a proton acceptor show that the latter is slightly stronger, confirming that the effect on the boron acids must be steric and not due to a reduction in 'intrinsic' base strength of the pyridine.

(ii)   *Anionic and cationic species.*   The ability of the non-metal halides to form complex anions by addition of halide ions is generally similar to their ability to form neutral complexes with Lewis bases. The anionic complexes are ions of large radius. They are most stable when paired in crystalline compounds with relatively bulky cations. The stability of a complex $M^+(AX_{n+1})^-$ will depend on the constant for the equilibrium:

$$MAX_{n+1} \rightleftharpoons MX + AX_n$$

With large cations, e.g. Cs^+ or NMe_4^+, the lattice energy of MX and of MAX_{n+1} will be more nearly equal than with small cations. The latter give a high lattice energy to MX and shift the equilibrium to the right. Lattice stabilization is similarly important for cationic halide complexes.

A greater range of fluoride complexes is known than for the other halides. This is in part caused by the stronger σ-donor power of the fluoride ion (cf. bases bonding through oxygen and nitrogen), but, in addition, the resulting anions are not as bulky as those with the larger halogen atoms and can be more easily stabilized by readily available cations, e.g. K^+. (Stable crystal lattices usually require that anions and cations, regarded as charged spheres, just touch. For most salts of complex anions a cation/anion radius ratio of at least 0·4 is required if the crystals are to be easily isolable.)

Cationic halide complexes are generally formed only when a very strong halide ion acceptor, particularly Group V pentahalides, abstracts a halide ion from the non-metal halide. Some examples of the resulting complexes are shown in Table 2.7.

The structures of the complex anions and cations are well predicted by the Gillespie–Nyholm rules as shown in Fig. 2.4. The species such as $TeCl_6^{2-}$, with fourteen electrons in the valence shell around the non-metal, provide the same structural problem as already discussed for XeF_6. X-Ray structure determinations on $(pyH^+)_2(TeCl_6^{2-})$ and K_2TeBr_6 indicate octahedral symmetry,

37

TABLE 2.7
Some cationic species formed by reaction of halides with strong Lewis acids

	$PCl_4^+ PCl_6^-$	$SF_3^+ SbF_6^-$	$ClF_2^+ AsF_6^-$	
	$PBr_4^+ Br^-$		$Cl_2F^+ AsF_6^-$	
			$Cl_3^+ AsF_6^-$	
$AsF_2^+ SbF_6^-$	$AsCl_4^+ AsF_6^-$	$SeF_3^+ Nb_2F_{11}^-$	$BrF_2^+ SbF_6^-$	$KrF^+ Sb_2F_{11}^-$
			$Br_3^+ AsF_6^-$	
SbF_2^+	$SbCl_4^+ SbF_6^-$	TeF_3^+	$ICl_2^+ SbCl_6^-$	$XeF^+ AsF_6^-$
			I_3^+	$Xe_2F_3^+ AsF_6^-$
			IF_4^+	$XeF_3^+ Sb_2F_{11}^-$
			$IF_6^+ AsF_6^-$	

suggesting that the lone pair is in a spherically symmetrical orbit which does not distort the structure. However, the vibrational spectra of some of these fourteen-electron species in solution suggest that they may then be distorted from O_h symmetry.

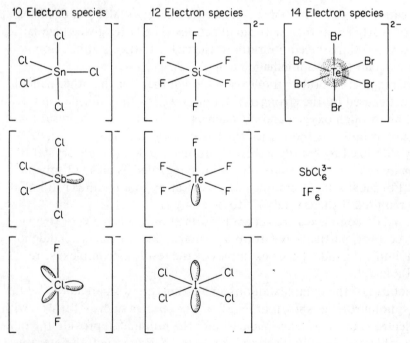

FIGURE 2.4
Structures of some complex anions

With many of the cationic species which are stabilized only with complex halide anions, halide bridging may reduce the extent to which the cations can be regarded as discrete entities. This is illustrated by the XeF^+ and $Xe_2F_3^+$ ions which show fluorine bridges externally to an $Sb_2F_{11}^-$ ion or internally between xenon atoms (Fig. 2.5). The larger anions like $Sb_2F_{11}^-$ are more effective in stabilizing cations containing elements in high valence states than are the simple anions like SbF_6^-. This is due to better delocalization of the negative charge over the larger anion, reducing the tendency for the cation to oxidize the anion and liberate F_2.

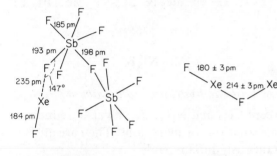

XeF₂.2SbF₅
(bond lengths ± 4 pm)

$Xe_2F_3^+$ in $Xe_2F_3^+$ AsF_6^-

FIGURE 2.5
The structures of $XeF_2.2SbF_5$ and of $Xe_2F_3^+$ in $Xe_2F_3^+.AsF_6^-$

2.6.3 *Hydrolysis of the halides*

The halides with the largest kinetic barriers to hydrolysis are those with low or zero Lewis acidity, since these will not complex with water. They include the carbon tetrahalides, NF_3, NCl_3, PF_3, SF_6, and SeF_6. The non-metal fluorides often hydrolyse less completely and rapidly than the other halides. This is because A—F bonds may be much stronger than A—O bonds, and the hydrolysis equilibrium:

$$A—F + H_2O \rightleftharpoons A—OH + HF$$

is shifted to the right only in the presence of an excess of water. With the other halides the equilibria lie farther to the right. The thermodynamics of hydrolysis become less favourable down the Groups and across the rows as the resulting oxides or hydroxides become less stable relative to the strong O—H bonds in water.

The halogen atoms in halides which are readily hydrolysed can often be replaced by other groups such as NH_2, NR_2, OR, or SR (R = alkyl or aryl) by the action of the corresponding Lewis bases, i.e. NH_3, NHR_2, ROH, or RSH. Replacement of halogen atoms occurs stepwise, e.g.

$$BCl_3 + HNMe_2 \xrightarrow{\text{low temperature}}$$

$$\underset{\underset{Me_2N-BCl_3}{|}}{\overset{H}{|}} \xrightarrow{HNMe_2} Me_2N-BCl_2 + Me_2\overset{+}{N}H_2\ Cl^-$$

$$\downarrow 2HNMe_2$$

$$(Me_2N)_3B$$

2.6.4 *Oxidizing and reducing power of the hydrides and halides*

Group III, IV, and V hydrides, except CH_4 and NH_3, are powerful reducing agents towards halogens or aqueous solutions of metal ions. They are all oxidized by air, and SiH_4 is spontaneously inflammable.

Low-valency halides of Group III and IV elements are reducing agents but only the tin compounds, e.g. $SnCl_2$, find much practical use. Phosphorus trifluoride and trichloride can be readily oxidized to the oxo-halides and may function as reducing agents.

The ability of the halides to act as oxidizing agents depends to a large extent on the strength of the A—X bonds. Thus, all the interhalogens and noble gas halides are powerful oxidizing agents, e.g.

$$Ag + Sb + 2\,BrF_3 \rightarrow AgSbF_6 + Br_2$$

$$2\,CF_3CF=CF_2 + XeF_4 \rightarrow 2\,CF_3CF_2CF_3 + Xe \text{ (see p. 67).}$$

but most other halides show oxidizing power only towards strong reducing agents. Some exceptions are PCl_5 and $SbCl_5$ which readily lose chlorine and return to the trivalent state, SCl_4 which loses chlorine above $-20°$, and NCl_3, NF_3, and OF_2. Both NF_3 and OF_2 are potentially almost as powerful oxidizing agents as molecular fluorine although they often react slowly at room temperature; e.g. OF_2 can be mixed with hydrogen at $25°$ without exploding unless a spark is applied.

2.6.5 *Replacement of halogen atoms by alkyl groups*

The halides of Groups III, IV, and V (except C and N) are common starting materials for the formation of organo-derivatives of these elements. They react with various organometallic compounds in which the metal is strongly electropositive with a high affinity for halogens, e.g.

$$SnCl_4 \ + \ 2\,C_8H_{17}MgCl \ \xrightarrow{\text{ether}} \ (C_8H_{17})_2\,SnCl_2$$
$$\text{(used in stabilizing PVC)}$$

$$BF_3 \ + \ Al(C_2H_5)_3 \ \longrightarrow \ B(C_2H_5)_3 \ + \ AlF_3$$

$$PCl_3 \ + \ LiC_4H_9 \ \longrightarrow \ C_4H_9PCl_2 \ \xrightarrow{LiC_4H_9} \ P(C_4H_9)_3 \ + \ LiCl$$

2.7 Synthesis

The possible ways of synthesizing a compound depend on thermodynamic and kinetic factors. These can be considered in general terms. However, the best way of making any particular compound will depend on the availability of starting materials and practical difficulties in the preparation, factors about which it is quite difficult to generalize.

2.7.1 *Hydrides*

The exothermic hydrides can, in principle, all be formed by direct combination of the elements. In practice, the method is used industrially on a large scale for NH_3 and HCl, and on a very limited scale for HBr and HI. There is essentially no reaction between hydrogen and nitrogen at room temperature, and iron and other catalysts are used to aid the reaction at 400–500° under pressures of several hundred atmospheres (Haber process). The pressure favours the forward reaction:

$$N_2 \ + \ 3\,H_2 \ \rightleftharpoons \ 2\,NH_3$$

Carbon and hydrogen react only at very high temperatures ($>1500°$) to give CH_4, but some acetylene is also formed.

41

The most important approaches to making endothermic hydrides [6] are as follows:

(1) Reaction of a compound between a non-metal and an electronegative element with an anionic hydride, e.g.

$$LiAlH_4 + SiCl_4 \xrightarrow{\text{ether}} AlCl_3 + LiCl + SiH_4$$

$$BH_4^- + HOGeO_2^- \xrightarrow{\text{KOH solution}} HOBO_2^{2-} + GeH_4$$

(2) Reaction of a compound between the non-metal and an electropositive metal with a protonic acid. For example, reactions of magnesium silicide or calcium phosphide:

$$Mg_2Si + 4H_3O^+ \xrightarrow{\text{20\% } H_3PO_4} 2Mg^{2+} + 4H_2O + SiH_4$$

$$Ca_3P_2 + 3H_2O \longrightarrow 3Ca(OH)_2 + 2PH_3$$

This is analogous to the well known preparation of the hydrogen halides by the action of a strong, non-volatile acid like H_2SO_4 on metal halides. These reactions of metal borides, silicides, etc. with acids commonly give some catenated hydrides in addition to the simple compounds (Chapter 5).

2.7.2 *Halides*

The great majority of non-metal halides are exothermic compounds and can be formed by direct combination of the elements, but with polyvalent elements it is sometimes difficult to stop the reaction at a desired intermediate stage. In addition, elemental fluorine is a hazardous reagent. Thus, many halides are more conveniently made by exchange or displacement reactions from other compounds by processes such as the following.

(1) Chlorine for fluorine exchange [7]; common reagents for fluorine exchange in non-metal chemistry are AgF, NaF, HF, ZnF_2, and SbF_3. Their effectiveness depends in part on the difference $\delta G°$ in free energy of formation

[6] Jolly, W. L. (1968), *Preparative Inorganic Reactions*, 4, 1. A good account of the preparation of Group IV and V hydrides.

[7] Muetterties, E. L. and Tullock, C. W. (1965), *Preparative Inorganic Reactions*, 2, 1 (Ed. Jolly, W. L.); a chapter on binary fluorides.

42

between their fluoride and chloride forms, e.g.

$$-\delta G^\circ(\mathrm{HF}) = \Delta G^\circ(\mathrm{HF}) - \Delta G^\circ(\mathrm{HCl})$$

The smaller the difference, the greater their fluorinating power. The above reagents have δG° values per halogen atom ranging from 75 kJ mol^{-1} for AgF to 180 kJ mol^{-1} for HF. This makes them all capable, in principle, of converting PCl$_3$ into PF$_3$ (δG° = 209 kJ), PCl$_5$ into PF$_5$ (δG° = 246 kJ), or SiCl$_4$ into SiF$_4$ (δG° = 250 kJ). Hydrogen fluoride is the preferred halogen exchange reagent in industry, but is less commonly used in the laboratory because of its corrosiveness and toxicity. Some typical fluorine–chlorine exchange reactions are

$$\mathrm{SbCl_5} + 5\,\mathrm{HF} \xrightarrow{20^\circ} \mathrm{SbF_5} + 5\,\mathrm{HCl}$$

$$2\,\mathrm{SCl_2} + 4\,\mathrm{NaF} \xrightarrow{\mathrm{CH_3CN}} 4\,\mathrm{NaCl} + 2\,[\mathrm{SF_2}] \xrightarrow{\mathrm{SCl_2}} \mathrm{SF_4} + \mathrm{S_2Cl_2}$$

$$\mathrm{PCl_3} + \mathrm{SbF_3} \xrightarrow{\text{trace } \mathrm{SbCl_5}} (\mathrm{PCl_2F} + \mathrm{PClF_2} + \mathrm{PF_3}) + \mathrm{SbCl_3}$$

(2) Fluorine exchanged by other halogens; the most general reagent for converting a non-metal fluoride into another halide is the appropriate aluminium trihalide. The main driving force in a reaction such as:

$$\mathrm{BF_3} + \mathrm{AlI_3} \rightarrow \mathrm{BI_3} + \mathrm{AlF_3}$$

is the stability of the ionic solid AlF$_3$.

(3) Formation from hydrides; direct halogenation of methane is an important route to carbon halides; nitrogen halides can also be formed by halogenation of ammonia but in few other cases are the hydrides sufficiently accessible to make this a worthwhile preparative method.

(4) Formation from oxides; with the first- and second-row elements, oxides are generally more stable than corresponding chlorides, bromides, or iodides. Thus, with these elements direct replacement of the oxygen is common only using elemental fluorine or certain fluorides, particularly BrF$_3$, SF$_4$, and HF, e.g.

$$4\,\mathrm{BrF_3} + 3\,\mathrm{SeO_2} \xrightarrow{100^\circ} 3\,\mathrm{SeF_4} + 3\,\mathrm{O_2} + 2\,\mathrm{Br_2}$$

$$(\mathrm{C_6H_5})_3\mathrm{PO} + \mathrm{SF_4} \xrightarrow{150^\circ} (\mathrm{C_6H_5})_3\mathrm{PF_2} + \mathrm{SOF_2}$$

$$\mathrm{SiO_2} + 2\,\mathrm{CaF_2} + 2\,\mathrm{H_2SO_4} \xrightarrow{100^\circ} \mathrm{SiF_4} + 2\,\mathrm{CaSO_4} + 2\,\mathrm{H_2O}$$

43

With elements in later rows, chlorides can sometimes be formed conveniently from oxides, e.g.

$$GeO_2 + HCl(conc.) \xrightarrow{\text{KCl, HCl gas}} K_2GeCl_6$$

A good method of displacing oxygen by halogens is in the presence of carbon at high temperatures. The driving force is the large entropy increase when CO is liberated, e.g.

$$B_2O_3(l) + Br_2(g) + 3C(s) \xrightarrow{700°} 2BBr_3(g) + 3CO(g) \quad \text{(cf. p. 86)}$$

2.8 Mixed hydride-halides

Compounds containing both hydrogen and halogen atoms joined to a non-metal are well known for Group IV elements and for boron, nitrogen, phosphorus, and oxygen. The compounds are commonly formed by controlled halogenation of the hydrides or by partial reduction of the halides, e.g.

$$CH_4 + Cl_2 \xrightarrow{300°} CH_3Cl, CH_2Cl_2, CHCl_3, CCl_4$$

$$PF_2I + HI + 2Hg \longrightarrow PF_2H + Hg_2I_2$$

Some of the mixed compounds, especially those rich in hydrogen, readily decompose to a mixture of hydride and halide or hydride–halide, e.g.

$$6HBCl_2 \xrightarrow{0°} B_2H_6 + 4BCl_3$$

$$GeH_3Cl \xrightarrow{20°} GeH_4 + GeH_2Cl_2 \longrightarrow GeH_4 + GeHCl_3$$

Such reactions may involve halogen bridged dimeric intermediates, and, as expected on this theory, the tendency to decompose in this way is small for carbon, nitrogen, and oxygen compounds, but it increases sharply down a Group.

Few hydride–halides of elements in higher valency states are stable. Thus, HPF_4 and H_2PF_3 are known (trigonal pyramidal molecules with axial F atoms) but not HSF_5 or $HClF_2$ which would have a great tendency to eliminate HF.

Generally, the physical and chemical properties of the mixed compounds are intermediate between those of the hydrides and halides. Difluoramine HNF_2 is one exception as it is dangerously explosive, unlike NF_3 or NH_3, presumably because HF can be eliminated with liberation of heat.

2.9   Mixed halides

The possibility of making compounds containing mixtures of different halogens joined to a non-metal depends on their stability with respect to the dissociation reaction:

$$(n + m) \, AX_nX'_m \rightarrow n \, AX_{n+m} + m \, AX'_{n+m}$$

This reaction is influenced by the pathways available for intermolecular halogen exchange and by the electronegativity difference between X and X'.

The most facile halogen exchange occurs with the boron halides. The mechanism is not certain but a dimeric intermediate seems likely, e.g.,

$$BCl_3 + BF_3 \; \rightleftharpoons \; \underset{\substack{Cl \quad \quad F}}{\overset{\substack{Cl \quad Cl \quad F}}{B \diagup\diagdown B}} \; \rightleftharpoons \; Cl_2BF + ClBF_2$$

Figure 2.6 shows a series of ^{19}F n.m.r. spectra obtained from simple mixtures of BF_3 with BCl_3 and BBr_3 at room temperature. The spectra give good evidence for the triply mixed halide BFClBr. The scrambling is so rapid with these boron halides that the mixed compounds have not been obtained pure by distillation even at low temperatures. When BF_3 and BI_3 are mixed there is no evidence for any fluoroiodoborane. It is typical of mixed halides that fluoro-iodo-compounds are the least stable to dissociation. Electron withdrawal by fluorine may tend to weaken the non-metal–iodine bonds, so that the unmixed compounds are thermodynamically more stable than fluoro-iodo-compounds. In Groups IV and V the formation of mixed halides by direct scrambling requires more vigorous conditions than for Group III compounds. Extreme conditions are required to cause scrambling in carbon halides. Conversely, many of the compounds are relatively stable to dissociation at room temperature and can be separated from mixtures by distillation. Mixed chlorofluoromethanes are important commercially as inert gases and liquids in refrigeration, and CF_3Br is used as a fire extinguisher.

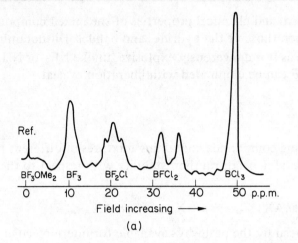

(a)

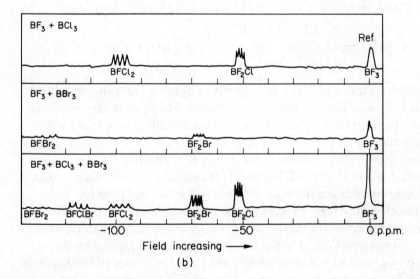

(b)

FIGURE 2.6
N.m.r. evidence for the formation of mixed boron trihalides
(a) ^{11}B spectrum of BF_3 + BCl_3 [Lappert, M. F., Litzow, M. R., Pedley, J. B. and Tweedale, A. (1971), *J. Chem. Soc.* (A), 2426]
(b) ^{19}F spectra of three mixtures [Coyle, T. D. and Stone, F. G. A. (1960), *J. Chem. Phys.*, **32**, 1892]

The compounds are commonly made by partial halogenation with halogen exchange reagents (p. 43), although selective methods giving a single product are preferred, e.g.

$$SiF_2(g) + I_2(g) \rightarrow SiF_2I_2$$

$$PF_3 + HNMe_2 \rightarrow PF_2NMe_2 \xrightarrow{HCl} PF_2Cl$$

Only a limited number of mixed higher-valency halides is known. Thus, all the chlorofluorophosphorus(v) and some of the bromofluorophosphorus(v) compounds have been isolated, but only SF_5Cl and SF_5Br are known with sulphur(VI) (p. 61).

2.10 Special features of hydrides and halides considered in Groups

2.10.1 *Group III: Boron*

(i) *Monovalent compounds.* The boron monohalides are stable with respect to boron and BX_3 only at very high temperatures; e.g. the equilibrium:

$$2\ B(s) + BF_3(g) \rightleftharpoons 3\ BF(g)$$

is appreciably shifted to the right above 1600° at 1 mm pressure. Under all other conditions they are short-lived gases, but when condensed with other compounds at very low temperatures they are chemically very reactive. Thus, BF and BCl both react with acetylenes giving 1,4-diboracyclohexadienes:

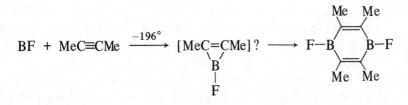

(ii) *Trivalent compounds.* The chemistry of trivalent boron is dominated by the effect of the vacant p_z orbital which becomes involved either in intra-molecular $(p-p)\pi$ bonding or multicentre bonding (p. 219), or in intermolecular reactions with lone pairs of electrons on other molecules.

47

The boron trihalides are monomeric in the gas and liquid phase, although there is some evidence for association of BF_3 at very low temperatures presumably through B—F—B bridges. By contrast, monomeric borane BH_3 is a very short-lived gas which has been characterized only recently from the pyrolysis of BH_3CO. Low-temperature infrared studies indicate that it is a planar molecule like the boron trihalides. It very readily undergoes an exothermic dimerization, liberating about 150 kJ per mole of B_2H_6 formed. The bonding in B_2H_6, which is discussed on p. 219, allows a more effective distribution of electrons among available orbitals than is possible with BH_3. The boron trialkyls are monomeric, and models suggest that this is due to steric hindrance in associated forms involving B—(alkyl)—B bridges.

Boron trifluoride complexes with water at low temperatures to give isolable solids BF_3H_2O and $BF_3(H_2O)_2$. The mode of attachment of the second water molecule in the latter is not known. These are partly ionized in the liquid state, presumably forming $(H_3O—BF_3)^+$ and BF_3OH^- ions. Hydrolysis of the other boron trihalides is immediately complete and very exothermic; it is almost explosive in the case of BBr_3. The equilibrium is shifted markedly in favou of the B—O bonds in the resulting boric acid or oxide, but the B—F bond is of comparable stability to the B—O bond, hence there is partial and reversible hydrolysis in that case. Diborane is immediately hydrolysed by water forming hydrogen and boric acid as the final products.

Under suitable conditions, reactions of the kind:

$$BX_3 + X^- \rightarrow BX_4^-$$

occur with all the boron halides and with BH_3 (as diborane). The most stable of the complex ions are the tetrafluoroborates. Boron trifluoride will react with solid fluorides like CsF to give $CsBF_4$. As in general in tetrahedral 4-coordinate boron compounds, the B—F bond length of 143 pm in BF_4^- is considerably longer than in BF_3 (130 pm). It is a relatively bulky anion and its salts have solubilities comparable to those of the perchlorates (Chapter 3).

The other tetrahaloborates are much less stable than the tetrafluoroborates although compounds such as $KBCl_4$, NR_4BBr_4, and NR_4BI_4 (R = alkyl group) are known. These compounds, unlike the tetrafluoroborates, are immediately hydrolysed by water forming boric acid and the halide ion.

48

The borohydride ion BH_4^- can be formed by reaction of lithium hydride with diborane, i.e.

$$2\,LiH + B_2H_6 \xrightarrow{\text{ether}} 2\,LiBH_4$$

This is formally addition of H^- to BH_3. In practice, $NaBH_4$ is made from trimethyl borate and sodium hydride, i.e.

$$4\,H^- + B(OMe)_3 \xrightarrow{250^\circ} BH_4^- + 3\,OMe^-$$

Treatment of $NaBH_4$ with conc. H_2SO_4 and other non-aqueous acids liberates diborane. Neutral or alkaline solutions of $NaBH_4$ in water are stable for short periods, but have very strong reducing properties, e.g. the reduction of GeO_3^{2-} to GeH_4.

Complexes of BH_3 with ethers react almost quantitatively with unsaturated organic compounds, a process known as 'hydroboration' which is of considerable synthetic use [8], e.g.

$$Bu^nCH{=}CH_2 + BH_3OR_2 \longrightarrow Bu^nCH_2{-}CH_2BH_2 \xrightarrow{Bu^nCH=CH_2}$$
$$(Bu^nCH_2CH_2)_3B \ (94\% \text{ yield})$$

An important result of the acid properties of the boron trihalides is their use as 'catalysts' in organic syntheses. Broadly, their function seems to be to promote formation of cationic organic species by complexing, e.g.

$$RCOOCH_3 + BF_3 \rightarrow RCO^+ + CH_3OBF_3^-$$

RCO^+ can then attack benzene, e.g. to give C_6H_5COR. Boron trifluoride is most commonly used. The other boron trihalides have a tendency to halogenate unsaturated organic compounds because the difference in bond energy between $C{-}X$ and $B{-}X$ is less for these than for the fluorides.

The idea of the chemical similarity between isoelectronic molecules, discussed in Chapter 1, is well illustrated with borane carbonyl which is isoelectronic with CO_2. Treatment of borane carbonyl with potassium hydroxide gives a borano-carbonate [9]:

$$BH_3CO + 2\,KOH \xrightarrow{\text{alcohol}} K_2BH_3CO_2 \quad (\text{cf. } K_2OCO_2)$$

[8] Brown, H. C. (1972), *Angew. Chem. Internat. Edn.*, **11**, 692.
[9] Malone, L. J. and Parry, R. W. (1967), *Inorg. Chem.*, **6**, 817.

Acidification of the salt with 85% phosphoric acid re-liberates BH_3CO almost quantitatively, just as CO_2 is liberated from a metal carbonate. However, in dilute aqueous solution, acidification with HCl first gives the $H(BH_3CO_2)^-$ ion, but then H_2 and CO are liberated and boric acid is formed, marking a limitation to the analogy with carbon dioxide. The ion $H_2P(BH_3)_2^-$, isoelectronic with the hypophosphite ion $H_2PO_2^-$, has also been reported.

2.10.2 *Group IV*

(i)   Divalent and trivalent compounds.   The divalent hydrides and halides of carbon and silicon are short-lived species either in the gas phase or in solution; nevertheless their chemistry has been extensively studied [10]. In contrast, the germanium and tin dihalides are solids with structures on the borderline between ionic and covalent compounds. They are much less reactive than the carbon or silicon compounds.

The carbon compounds are usually generated *in situ*, i.e. in the presence of a compound with which they will react, by chemical reactions or photolysis, e.g.

$$CHCl_3 + OH^- \longrightarrow {:}CCl_2 + H_2O + Cl^-$$

$$CH_2N_2 \xrightarrow{h\nu} {:}CH_2 + N_2$$

The silicon dihalides are best formed by reduction of the tetrahalides with silicon at high temperatures and low pressure, e.g.

$$Si(s) + SiCl_4(g) \xrightarrow[1\ mm]{1200^\circ} 2\ SiCl_2(g)$$

The short-lived gaseous dihalides are caused to react with other compounds by co-condensation on a surface cooled by liquid nitrogen. The dihalides react very rapidly even at -196°, and products of the reactions are isolated on warming to room temperature.

The short lifetime of the carbon compounds is due to dimerization to olefins, but the silicon compounds form catenated polymers or disproportionate to $Si + SiX_4$. Both CF_2 and SiF_2 are longer-lived ($t_{1/2} = 1\ s$ and $150\ s$ respectively at 0.2 torr pressure) than the other divalent compounds.

[10] Kirmse, W. (Ed.) (1970), *Carbene Chemistry*, 2nd Edn., Academic Press, New York.

Methylene CH_2 is thermodynamically most stable as a diradical (triplet) with two unpaired electrons (p. 23) although the expected paired electron (singlet) form is only slightly less stable.

The two most important reactions of the divalent compounds are:

(1) Insertion into suitable A—H or A—X bonds, e.g.

$$SiCl_2(g) + PCl_3(g) \xrightarrow[\text{warm to room temperature}]{\text{condense together at } -196°} SiCl_3PCl_2$$

(2) Addition to carbon–carbon multiple bonds, e.g.

$$CF_2 + F_2C{=}CF_2 \longrightarrow \begin{array}{c} F_2C{-}CF_2 \\ \diagdown\;C\;\diagup \\ F_2 \end{array}$$

Silicon difluoride often gives products containing at least two silicon atoms. A diradical dimer has been suggested as an intermediate, e.g.

$$2\,SiF_2(g) \xrightarrow{-196°} [F_2\dot{S}i\dot{S}iF_2] \xrightarrow{BF_3} F_3SiSiF_2BF_2$$

The crystal structure of GeF_2 shows Ge—F$\cdots$Ge bridges. When the compound is heated under vacuum to 200°, fluorine-bridged species Ge_2F_4 and Ge_3F_6 are formed in the vapour in addition to monomeric GeF_2. Both germanium and tin dihalides are powerful reducing agents and form complex anions with halide ions, e.g. GeF_3^- and $SnCl_3^-$. Surprisingly, the compounds show some carbene-like reactions, e.g. GeI_2 reacts with diphenylacetylene at 200° to give a 1,4-digermacyclohexadiene derivative.

Carbon is the only element in Group IV which readily forms trivalent radicals. The methyl and trihalomethyl radicals are very short-lived species of high chemical reactivity. The methyl radical is planar. Its structure was determined by an infrared spectroscopic study in a noble-gas matrix below 30 K. Trifluoromethyl radicals can be formed by the action of an electrical discharge on C_2F_6, and then used directly to make derivatives; e.g. SnI_4 and CF_3 give $Sn(CF_3)_4$ and I_2. Dissociation of a catenated silicon compound Si_2X_6 tends to give SiX_2 + SiX_4 and not SiX_3 radicals.

(ii)   Tetravalent compounds.   Methane and the carbon tetrahalides are much less chemically reactive than the other Group IV tetrahydrides or tetrahalides. This fact can be attributed to the availability of vacant *d* orbitals on

51

silicon, germanium, and tin which permit an increase in coordination number of these atoms from 4 to 5 or 6.

The thermal stability of the gaseous hydrides AH_4 decreases uniformly from methane (rapid decomposition above 1200°) to stannane SnH_4 (rapid decomposition to tin and hydrogen above 50°). However, silane is the most easily oxidized of the hydrides; it is spontaneously inflammable in air and oxidized by water in alkaline solution:

$$SiH_4 + 2\,H_2O \xrightarrow{\text{OH}^-} SiO_2 + 4\,H_2$$

Small amounts of oxygen actually stabilize SnH_4. Its decomposition is auto-catalysed by the tin formed, but oxygen coats the surface of the metal with an oxide layer that reduces its catalytic action.

Direct chlorination of methane occurs only at temperatures above 300°, but silane inflames in chlorine or bromine at room temperature; controlled halogenation is possible, e.g.

$$GeH_4 + Br_2 \xrightarrow{-50°} GeH_3Br + HBr$$

There is no reaction between methane and the hydrogen halides; HCl and HBr can be added to SiH_4, GeH_4, or SnH_4, although a catalyst is required with SiH_4:

$$SiH_4 + HCl \xrightarrow[100°]{\text{AlCl}_3} H_2 + SiH_3Cl \xrightarrow{\text{AlCl}_3,\ \text{HCl}} SiH_2Cl_2 + H_2$$

Silyl, germyl, or stannyl metal 'salts' can be made by deprotonation reactions (p. 32). Silane reacts with potassium to give $KSiH_3$ and hydrogen; this and the corresponding $KGeH_3$ are useful in the synthesis of silyl or germyl derivatives, e.g.

$$KGeH_3 + CO_2 \rightarrow H_3GeCO_2K$$

potassium germaacetate

The photoelectron spectrum of CH_3Cl differs markedly from that of SiH_3Cl or GeH_3Cl as shown in Fig. 2.7. The bands are thought to arise in each case by ionization of a $3p$ electron from a lone pair on a chlorine atom. The band structures indicate that the $3p$ electron is non-bonding in CH_3Cl but bonding in SiH_3Cl and GeH_3Cl, suggesting that the lone pairs may be involved

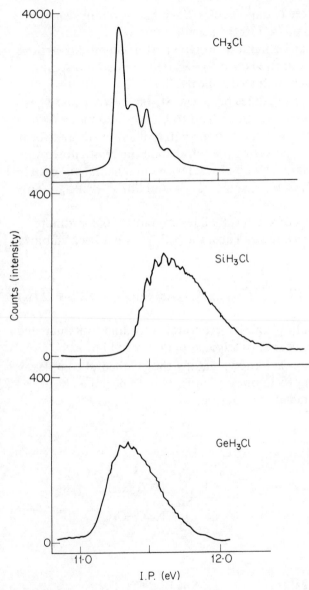

FIGURE 2.7
The photoelectron spectra of methyl chloride, silyl chloride, and germyl chloride [Cradock, S. and Ebsworth, E. A. V. (1971), *Chem. Comm.*, 57]

53

in $(p-d)\pi$ bonding in the latter two molecules. Such back-bonding is not possible in CH_3Cl as there is no $2d$ electron shell.

The carbon tetrahalides can be induced to take part in chemical reactions only under fairly energetic conditions, e.g. at elevated temperatures, on exposure to light, or by attack with free radicals.

The remaining Group IV tetrahalides behave as strong Lewis acids. They are hydrolysed by water but the reactions tend to be slow and incomplete except with $SiCl_4$, $SiBr_4$, and SiI_4 which immediately liberate HX and form silica. The halide ion acceptor power of the tetrahalides increases down the Group as indicated by the range of well characterized octahedral anions which has been isolated, i.e. SiF_6^{2-}, GeF_6^{2-}, and $GeCl_6^{2-}$, and SnF_6^{2-}, $SnCl_6^{2-}$, $SnBr_6^{2-}$, and SnI_6^{2-}.

Although stable complexes of the tetrahalides are mostly 6-coordinate, some 5-coordinate species are known. Thus, the SiF_5^- ion has been stabilized by bulky cations, e.g.

$$(C_6H_5)_4AsCl + SiO_2 + 5\,HF \xrightarrow{\text{MeOH}} (C_6H_5)_4As^+SiF_5^- + HCl + 2\,H_2O$$

The ion is isoelectronic with PF_5, and its structure, according to Raman and infrared spectroscopic evidence, is also trigonal pyramidal [11].

Both *cis* and *trans* structures are known among the octahedral complexes; SiF_4, $SiCl_4$, $SnCl_4$, and $SnBr_4$ form *trans* complexes with pyridine, but $SnCl_4.2\,CH_3CN$ has a *cis*-octahedral structure.

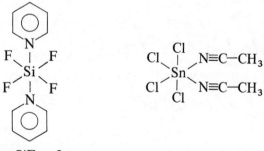

trans-SiF$_4$. 2 py   *cis*-SnCl$_4$. 2 CH$_3$CN

[11] Clark, H. C., Dixon, K. R. and Nicholson, J. G. (1969), *Inorg. Chem.*, 8, 450.

2.10.3 *Group V*

The most common valency states in Group V are 3 and 5, but lower-valency compounds are known. Imine NH is the best characterized of the monovalent compounds as it is readily formed by photolysis of hydrazoic acid:

$$HN_3 \xrightarrow{h\nu} :NH + N_2$$

The N—H bond in imine is longer and weaker than the N—H bonds in ammonia (103·8 *vs.* 101·5 pm; 352 *vs.* 389 kJ).

The NF_2 radical is the most important divalent species. It is formed in a reversible reaction from F_2N-NF_2. The equilibrium is shifted markedly in favour of NF_2 above about 200°. This is similar to the equilibrium between NO_2 and N_2O_4 (p. 131). The electronic spectrum of NF_2 indicates that the odd electron occupies a π molecular orbital. Although PF_2 is formed by thermal dissociation of F_2P-PF_2 there is no evidence that this is a truly reversible reaction.

(i)   *The hydrides.*   The hydrides AH_3 show a regular progression of properties down the Group. Stability decreases, base strength decreases, and acid strength increases. Ammonia is just exothermic, arsine and stibine are strongly endothermic. Only the strongest bases will deprotonate ammonia, e.g. the alkali metals forming amides $M^+NH_2^-$, but phosphine can be deprotonated by KOH (p. 32). Phosphine forms salts with hydrogen halides equivalent to ammonium salts. The difference in stability between these phosphonium halides and the ammonium halides is illustrated by the temperature at which dissociation into the gaseous trihydride and the hydrogen halide gives a pressure of 1 atmosphere:

$$NH_4Cl \ \ 337° \quad NH_4I \ \ 405°$$
$$PH_4Cl \ -27° \quad PH_4I \ \ \ 62°$$

The Lewis base strength of ammonia is much greater than that of phosphine. The latter does form complexes with transition metals in low valency states; e.g. $Ni(PH_3)(PF_3)_3$ is quite stable but $Ni(PH_3)_4$ is said to decompose at $-30°$.

As has been discussed already (p. 33), ammonia is an excellent solvent for ionic compounds [12]. It also dissolves the alkali metals to form blue solutions

[12] Fowles, G. W. A. and Nicholls, D. (1971), *Reactions in Liquid Ammonia*, Elsevier, Amsterdam.

which contain solvated electrons. When the concentration of metal is less than about 0·03M, there is essentially no pairing between the electrons and the metal ions each surrounded by ammonia molecules. The electron paramagnetic resonance spectrum of these solutions shows a very narrow signal (0·1 gauss) with a g-factor of 2·0012, close to the value of 2·0023 for entirely free electrons. Solutions of electrons in liquid ammonia have also been formed by electron pulse techniques; the light absorption maximum (1500 nm) and e.p.r. spectrum of these solutions are identical to those containing electrons produced by 'chemical' means.

It must be stressed that on a practical level ammonia is a very important chemical. It is produced on a scale of millions of tons a year by the Haber process (p. 41) for use in fertilizers and as a basic raw material in chemical synthesis.

(ii)   *The trihalides.*   The phosphorus trihalides are thermodynamically much more stable than the nitrogen compounds but also chemically more reactive; cf. CX_4 and SiX_4. Hydrolysis of NCl_3 and PCl_3 takes different paths:

$$NCl_3 + 2\,H_2O \xrightarrow{\text{slow}} NH_3 + 3\,HOCl$$

$$PCl_3 + 3\,H_2O \longrightarrow HPO(OH)_2 + 3\,HCl$$

This may be due both to a difference in mechanism, i.e. no octet expansion with nitrogen, and to the sequence of bond energy terms:

$$E(N-H) > E(N-O) \quad \text{but} \quad E(P-O) > E(P-H)$$

Lewis acidity among the trihalides increases from phosphorus to antimony. While PCl_3 and PBr_3 form weak 1:1 adducts with trimethylamine, and are weak halide ion acceptors, $SbCl_3$ is a powerful halide ion acceptor. Both molten SbF_3 and $SbCl_3$ are electrical conductors probably owing to auto-ionization, i.e. $SbF_2^+\ SbF_4^-$. The halide ion acceptor power of the SbF_3 must enhance its effectiveness as a fluorinating agent for non-metal chlorides (p. 43).

Phosphorus, arsenic, and antimony trihalides are used in the synthesis of organic derivatives of these elements. Nitrogen trifluoride has a limited use in the preparation of N_2F_4 (p. 213), but the other nitrogen trihalides are avoided because of their explosiveness. The well known sensitive explosive 'nitrogen triiodide' obtained from ammonia and iodine is $NI_3.NH_3$. An X-ray structure

56

determination [13] has shown it to contain NI_4 tetrahedra connected at the corners to build a zig-zag chain. The ammonia molecule is coordinated to one iodine atom in each tetrahedron.

(iii)   The pentahalides.   Although no covalent pentahalides of nitrogen are known, there is some evidence [14] that NF_3 can be made to react with fluorine at low temperatures using gamma-ray excitation, to form a very unstable salt $NF_4^+ F^-$. Salts of NF_4^+ with large anions, e.g. BF_4^- and SbF_6^-, can be made under milder conditions from NF_3, F_2, and the corresponding Lewis acid.

It is surprising that $AsCl_5$ has not yet been synthesized, since PCl_5 and $SbCl_5$ are easily made. There is no reaction between $AsCl_3$ and chlorine under ordinary conditions, but $AsCl_5$ may eventually be formed by a reaction of chlorine atoms and $AsCl_3$ at low temperatures (cf. 'NF_5' above, and $XeCl_2$, p. 66).

The pentafluorides PF_5, AsF_5, and SbF_5 are powerful Lewis acids. The fluoride ion affinity of AsF_5 and SbF_5 is evident from the range of complexes containing AsF_6^- or SbF_6^- shown in Table 2.7. There is strong association in liquid SbF_5; ^{19}F n.m.r. studies indicate an octahedral arrangement of fluorine atoms around each antimony atom with two *cis* fluorine atoms shared with two adjacent octahedra.

The ^{19}F n.m.r. spectrum of PF_5 shows only one resonance. This is not consistent with the known trigonal pyramidal structure of the molecule in which the axial and equatorial fluorine atoms should be distinguishable. The explanation appears to be fast intramolecular exchange of axial and equatorial fluorine atoms, possibly via a square pyramidal intermediate as shown in Fig. 2.8, although other intermediate structures have been proposed [15].

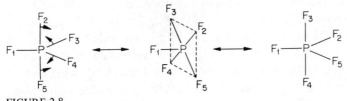

FIGURE 2.8
A mechanism for rearrangement in PF_5

[13] Hartl, H., Barnighausen, H. and Jander, J. (1968), *Z. Anorg. Chem.*, **357**, 225.
[14] Wilson, J. N. *et al.* (1972), *Inorg. Chem.*, **11**, 1696.
[15] Ugi, I., Marquarding, D., Klusack, H. and Gillespie, P. (1971), *Accounts Chem. Research*, **4**, 288.

The ^{19}F n.m.r. spectra of PF_3Cl_2 and PF_3Br_2 at very low temperatures show two fluorine signals corresponding to two fluorine atoms in axial positions and one in an equatorial position. As the temperature is raised the lines broaden and finally coalesce owing to rapid exchange. The rates of exchange can be determined from the temperature dependence of the n.m.r. signals. These pentahalides are representatives of the large class of 'fluxional molecules' which can undergo intramolecular rearrangements [16].

2.10.4 *Group VI*

(i) Hydrides.   The OH radical is a transitory but well established intermediate in the combustion of hydrogen and from decomposition of HOOH (p. 217).

Hydrogen bonding in water gives it physical properties which are quite out of line with the properties of the other dihydrides in the Group, as can be seen from Table 2.8.

TABLE 2.8
Some properties of the Group VI dihydrides

	H_2O	H_2S	H_2Se	H_2Te
Melting point	0·0°	−85·6°	−60·4°	−51°
Boiling point	100·0°	−60·7°	−41·5°	−1·8°
H_{vap} (kJ mol^{-1})	46·0	18·7	19·9	23·8
Density of liquid near m.p. (g ml^{-1})	1·00	1·96	2·12	2·60

Below 0° at 1 atm pressure, ice has a structure in which the oxygen atoms at the centre of OH_4 'tetrahedra' are arranged in puckered hexagonal nets similar to the tridymite structure of silica (p. 83). Two of the O—H distances in the OH_4 units are at 101 pm and two are at 174 pm. Ice exhibits a residual entropy at 0 K of 3·4 ± 0·2 J K^{-1} mol^{-1}, in excellent agreement with residual entropy calculated on the assumption of two short and two long O—H distances. Under pressure, ice can be transformed into at least six other forms differing in the arrangements of the OH_4 units.

When ice melts at 0°, the density increases from 0·917 g ml^{-1} to 0·99984 g ml^{-1}, and then to a maximum of 1·000 g ml^{-1} at 3·98°. This large increase in

[16] Holmes, R. R. (1972), *Accounts Chem. Research*, **5**, 289.

density between solid and liquid corresponds to a closer approach of oxygen atoms to one another in the less ordered liquid water structure. It has been calculated that if water consisted only of monomeric H_2O molecules in a random close-packed array, the density would be about $1 \cdot 8$ g ml^{-1}; cf. H_2S. The order in the ice structure is probably retained only in small domains in liquid water, interspersed and exchanging with domains containing monomers or small polymers of H_2O. The numerous theories on the structure of the liquid are summarized by Horne [17].

Apart from water, the dihydrides H_2A are smelly poisonous colourless gases. Their thermal stability decreases from H_2O to H_2Te. The latter is endo-thermic and quickly decomposed by light in the presence of moisture. It is also a strong reducing agent. The strength of the hydrides as acids increases from H_2O to H_2Te (Table 2.5). Electropositive metal sulphides, selenides, or tellurides are decomposed by water or dilute acids to liberate H_2S, H_2Se, or H_2Te. Direct combination of the elements can be used to form H_2S or H_2Se:

$$H_2(g) + Se(l) \xrightarrow{350°} H_2Se(g)$$

(ii)   *Halides of sulphur, selenium, and tellurium.*   From simple valency considerations it might be predicted that sulphur, selenium, and tellurium would each form stable dihalides with tetra- and hexa-halides representing possible higher oxidation states. In practice, the dihalides are not particularly stable; SBr_2, SI_2, and SeI_2 are not known and seem to be unstable with respect to the elements; the difluorides rapidly disproportionate to the free elements and the corresponding tetrafluoride. Selenium dichloride is well known as a gaseous decomposition product of $SeCl_4$ at high temperatures and has been stabilized as a 1:1 complex with $(NMe_2)_2C=S$:.

The most stable of the dihalides are SCl_2, which is a red liquid, and $TeCl_2$ which is a black solid. The former gives 1:1 complexes with strong Lewis acids, e.g. $AlCl_3$ or $SbCl_5$, and also with Lewis bases such as pyridine, but its most important reactions are with sulphur to give polysulphanes Cl_2S_n (p. 205) and with unsaturated organic compounds, e.g.

$$SCl_2 + C_2H_4 \longrightarrow ClC_2H_4SCl \xrightarrow{C_2H_4} (ClC_2H_4)_2S$$

[17] Horne, R. A. (1968), *Survey of Progress in Chemistry*, Vol. 4, Academic Press, New York. Review of structure of ice and water.

The product of this last reaction is the notorious 'mustard gas', but related compounds containing two chlorine atoms β to sulphur or nitrogen include some very promising anti-cancer drugs. Tellurium dichloride is a stronger Lewis acid than SCl_2 and forms a stable 2:1 *cis* square planar complex with thiourea.

The tetrafluorides are well characterized; SF_4 and SeF_4 are gases, the former being difficult to obtain completely free of SOF_2; TeF_4 is a crystalline solid with a fluorine bridged structure in which there is square pyramidal co-ordination about tellurium. Both SF_4 and SeF_4 are powerful fluorinating agents, and SF_4 is particularly useful for converting oxides into fluorides (p. 43), e.g.

$$SeO_2 + SF_4 \rightarrow SeF_4 + SOF_2$$

All the tetrafluorides complex with BF_3, and an X-ray structure determination on the SF_4 complex has shown it to be $SF_3^+ BF_4^-$. The SF_3^+ ion is pyramidal with FSF angles of 97° [18]. The compounds also complex with strong Lewis bases, e.g. pyridine or trimethylamine, and with CsF to give the square pyramidal ions SF_5^-, SeF_5^-, and TeF_5^-.

Other tetrahalides are less stable. Thus, SCl_4 decomposes below 0° and $SeBr_4$ decomposes at room temperature. $TeCl_4$ in benzene forms Te_4Cl_{16} which may have a cubane-like structure. Complex anions, e.g. $SeCl_6^{2-}$, TeI_6^{2-} (p. 38), and $Te_3Cl_{13}^-$ are more stable.

Only fluorine-rich hexahalides are known. The chemical reactivity of the gaseous hexafluorides increases from SF_6 to TeF_6, although TeF_6 has the highest heat of formation. Sulphur hexafluoride is exceptionally inert and is unaffected by almost all aqueous reagents under normal conditions. It is used as filler gas for transformers and switchgear because it inhibits electrical break-down. It has an electron affinity of about 100 kJ mol^{-1} and thus reacts with alkali metals and with solvated electrons. It is also attacked by sulphur trioxide:

$$8\,Cs + SF_6 \xrightarrow[\text{liq. } NH_3]{-60°} 4\,Cs_2S + 6\,NaF$$

$$H_2O \xrightarrow{\text{pulse radiolysis}} e^-(aq.) \xrightarrow{SF_6, H_2O} F^- + SO_4^{2-} + H_3O^+$$

$$2\,SO_3 + SF_6 \longrightarrow 3\,SO_2F_2$$

[18] Gibler, D. D., Adams, C. J., Fischer, M., Zalkin, A. and Bartlett, N. (1972), *Inorg. Chem.*, 11, 2325.

Selenium hexafluoride oxidizes aqueous sulphites to sulphate, and TeF_6 is slowly hydrolysed by water to telluric acid $Te(OH)_6$. Unlike SF_6 or SeF_6, TeF_6 behaves as a weak Lewis acid. With CsF it forms $2\,CsF.TeF_6$, but it is not certain if this contains TeF_7^- or TeF_8^{2-}; it forms a 2:1 complex with trimethylamine. This shows the possibility of higher coordination numbers for halides of the heavier non-metals.

Oxidation of SF_4 with chlorine in the presence of CsF gives SF_5Cl;

$$SF_4 + CsF + Cl_2 \rightarrow SF_5Cl + CsCl$$

SF_5Br can be prepared in a similar way. These compounds are much more reactive than SF_6; they are decomposed by dilute alkaline solutions and they add across olefinic bonds by a free radical mechanism involving $\cdot SF_5$, to give organic compounds containing SF_5 groups. Other inorganic groups of high electronegativity, but without too strong an affinity for fluorine, can replace Cl or Br, e.g. NF_2 and OF_2. The compounds TeF_5Cl and TeF_5Br have also been reported but they do not readily split out the TeF_5 radical.

2.10.5 *Group VII*

(i)   The hydrogen halides.   The thermal stability of the hydrogen halides decreases greatly from HF to HI. The first is so stable that a hydrogen–fluorine flame has a temperature of about 4000°, above the temperature of oxy-acetylene or oxy-hydrogen flames. The last is readily decomposed thermally or by light.

General features of the sequence of aqueous acid strengths $HF < HCl < HBr < HI$, and of hydrogen bonding in HF and HF_2^- have already been discussed (p. 26). Liquid HF is an excellent solvent for many inorganic and some organic compounds (particularly proteins, so that liquid HF causes instant serious burns in contact with skin). It is a powerful proton donor, e.g.

$$Fe(CO)_5 + 2\,HF \longrightarrow HF_2^- + [Fe(CO)_5H]^+$$

$$HNO_3 + 4\,HF \longrightarrow NO_2^+ + H_3O^+ + 2\,HF_2^-$$

It is also a fluorinating agent (p. 43) and dissolves many elements with formation of fluorides, e.g.

$$2\,HF(l) + Ge \xrightarrow[100°]{\text{sealed tube}} GeF_2 + H_2$$

61

Hydrogen bonding occurs with the other hydrogen halides but to a lesser extent than with HF. Measurements on the equilibrium:

$$Me_4N^+ HX_2^- \rightleftharpoons Me_4N^+ X^- + HX$$

have given heats of hydrogen bond formation (kJ mol^{-1}) in HX_2^- ions as: HF_2^- 155, HCl_2^- 50, HBr_2^- 38, and HI_2^- 29.

Structure determinations on salts of HCl_2^- and HBr_2^- indicate that in some compounds the hydrogen atom lies mid-way between the halogen atoms, but in others it lies closer to one halogen than the other. A similar effect is observed with polyhalide ions (p. 64).

Liquid hydrogen chloride and hydrogen bromide have limited use as ionizing solvents. For example, $(C_6H_5)_3CCl$ can be titrated with boron trichloride in HCl using conductance measurements to determine the end-point which which corresponds to the formation of a 1:1 complex; the equilibria involved are:

$$(C_6H_5)_3CCl + HCl \rightleftharpoons (C_6H_5)_3C^+ + HCl_2^-$$

$$(C_6H_5)_3C^+ + HCl_2^- \rightleftharpoons (C_6H_5)_3C^+ BCl_4^- + HCl$$

A number of anionic chlorides have been formed in HCl, e.g.

$$2\,Me_4NCl + B_2Cl_4 \xrightarrow{\text{liq. HCl}} (Me_4N)_2{}^{2+}B_2Cl_6{}^{2-}$$

(ii)   *Interhalogen compounds.*   The interhalogens are a varied group of compounds with reactivity comparable to or greater than that of the free halogens. We shall consider the range of neutral compounds, special properties of some of them, and the structures and bonding of the interhalogen anions and cations.

Simple valency rules predict 1:1 compounds between the halogens with the possibility of forming higher-valency compounds AX_3, AX_5, or AX_7, especially when X is fluorine. As shown in Table 2.1, this simple idea is only partly true. The compounds BrCl and IBr are in equilibrium with their elements at room temperature, and, as in Group VI, some low-valency compounds are unstable to disproportionation. Thus, BrF is in equilibrium with bromine and BrF_3 at room temperature:

$$BrF_3 + Br_2 \rightleftharpoons 3\,BrF$$

This equilibrium is displaced to the right at higher temperatures. Similarly, IF is completely unstable at room temperature:

$$IF_5 + 2I_2 \rightleftharpoons 5IF$$

but it is abundant in the gas phase equilibrium above $500°$. It can be isolated as a metastable solid below $-80°$. Iodine trifluoride is also unstable at room temperature with respect to iodine and IF_5, but it can be isolated from the reaction of iodine and fluorine at low temperatures [19].

The stability of the higher-valency compounds increases from chlorine to iodine. This is reflected in bond dissociation energies and in chemical reactivity which for the fluorides follows an approximate sequence $(ClF_5) > ClF_3 > BrF_5 > IF_7 > ClF > BrF_3 > IF_5$. The only stable trichloride is ICl_3. However, by spraying halogen atoms, produced in an electric discharge, on to a very cold surface, other trihalides including $BrCl_3$ are believed to have been formed.

The trihalides dimerize through halogen bridging; the stability of the dimers decreases in the series $ICl_3 > BrF_3 > ClF_3$. As shown in Fig. 2.9, the dimer of ICl_3 is planar, unlike, for example, Al_2Cl_6 or B_2H_6 in which the bridging atoms are in a plane at $90°$ to the terminal atoms. The boiling points of BrF_3 and ClF_3 are higher than those of the corresponding pentafluorides because of this association.

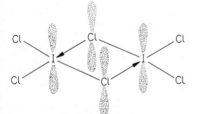

FIGURE 2.9
ICl_3 dimer

Liquid BrF_3, and to a lesser extent IF_5, BrF_5 and ClF_3 are electrical conductors. The ionization process in BrF_3 is believed to be:

$$2BrF_3 \rightarrow BrF_2^+ + BrF_4^-$$

[19] Schmeisser, M., Sartori, P. and Naumann, D. (1970), Chem. Ber., 103, 590, 880.

The liquid is an ionizing solvent for fluorine rich compounds. Thus, SbF_5 dissolves to a conducting solution containing SbF_6^- and BrF_2^+; NOF dissolves to give a solution containing NO^+ and BrF_4^- from which the stable salt $NOBrF_4$ can be isolated. Similarly, IF_5 dissolves SbF_5 to give IF_4^+ and SbF_6^-, and HF in IF_5 forms HF_2^- and IF_4^+.

The oxidizing power of the halogen fluorides, particularly ClF_3, is enormous. Many compounds inflame in contact with ClF_3. Above 200° all metals are attacked except a few which form adherent fluoride coatings.

(iii) *Polyhalide anions and cations* [20].   A very large number of poly-halide anions is known. Some of these have the general formula XYZ^- and result from the addition of a halide ion to a halogen or to an interhalogen. Table 2.9 lists some examples with bond lengths determined by X-ray studies. It is seen that both symmetric and asymmetric ions are found depending on the cation. Large cations, with a weak polarizing influence, favour symmetric ions. The bonding in these compounds can be represented in a very similar way to that used for hydrogen bonding in HF_2^- (p. 27). The bonding is weak and the ions are readily dissociated in solution.

TABLE 2.9

Polyhalide anions

	Bond lengths (pm) X---Y---Z		Compound
I—I—I	290	290	$Me_4N^+\ I_3^-$
I—I—I	283	304	$Cs^+\ I_3^-$
Br—I—I	278	291	$Cs^+\ I_2Br^-$
Br—I—Br	272	278	$Cs^+\ IBr_2^-$
Br—Br—Br	253	253	$[Me_3NH^+]_2\ Br^-\ Br_3^-$
Br—Br—Br	244	270	$Cs^+\ Br_3^-$
Cl—I—Cl	236	236	$Me_4N^+\ ICl_2^-$

More complex polyiodide ions can arise by weak interactions between I_2 molecules and I^- or I_3^- ions. Thus, in $Me_4N^+\ I_5^-$ the anion is V-shaped with two I_2 molecules weakly bonded to an I^- ion and I—I distances of 314 and 281 pm.

[20] Gillespie, R. J. and Morton, M. J. (1971), *Quart. Rev.*, **25,** 553. Halogen and interhalogen cations.

Strong Lewis acids and oxidizing agents are used to prepare and stabilize cationic species. Chlorine monofluoride reacts with AsF_5 to form complexes of the Cl_2F^+ and Cl_3^+ ions:

$$2\,ClF\ +\ AsF_5\ \rightarrow\ Cl_2F^+\,AsF_6^-$$
$$Cl_2F^+\,AsF_6^-\ +\ Cl_2\ \rightarrow\ Cl_3^+\,AsF_6^-\ +\ ClF$$

These ions have bent structures unlike the anions, X_3^- (Cl_3^+ is isoelectronic with SCl_2). Derivatives of ClF_4^+ are formed from Lewis acids and ClF_5, but the formation of ClF_6^+ requires the use of a powerful oxidizing agent:

$$2\,ClF_5\ +\ 2\,PtF_6\ \xrightarrow{\;h\nu\;}\ ClF_4^+\,PtF_6^-\ +\ ClF_6^+\,PtF_6^-$$

(or $ClF_2^+\,PtF_6^-$ + F_2 depending on the irradiating frequency)

Cationic species of the bromine and iodine fluorides are formed by similar methods.

2.10.6 *The noble gas halides* [21, 22]. For many years it was supposed that no noble gas compounds could exist but it is now known that xenon fluorides can be made with surprising ease. Xenon difluoride is formed by heating a 1:1 mixture of Xe and F_2 to 300° at 1 atm or exposing the gas mixture to sunlight for a few hours in a Pyrex flask. It can also be made by exposing a mixture of Xe and OF_2 to sunlight, or less efficiently by quenching the products of an electric discharge in a mixture of Xe and CF_4. Synthesis of XeF_4 and XeF_6 requires more vigorous conditions, using an excess of fluorine and higher pressures at temperatures of 300–400°.

Radon difluoride RnF_2 has been made by the reaction of radon with F_2 or ClF_3. Investigation of the compound has been hampered by the intense radio-activity of radon ([222]Rn has a half-life of 3·8 days). Unlike XeF_2 or KrF_2, RnF_2 is not volatile; it dissolves in BrF_3 to give solutions which may contain the ion RnF^+. Krypton difluoride has been made by the action of an electrical discharge on a mixture of Kr and F_2 at low pressure at $-185°$. The KrF_2 formed condensed out immediately on the cold walls of the surrounding vessel. There has been no reliable report of KrF_4. No fluorides of the lighter noble gases have yet been isolated.

[21] Holloway, J. H. (1968), *Noble Gas Chemistry*, Methuen, London.
[22] Bartlett, N. (1971), *The Chemistry of the Noble Gases*, Elsevier, New York.

Two xenon chlorides are known, $XeCl_2$ and $XeCl_4$. The latter has been characterized only by Mössbauer spectroscopy. Decay of ^{129}I in labelled $KICl_4.4\,H_2O$ yielded $^{129}Xe^*Cl_4$, the xenon being formed in a short-lived excited state. The Mössbauer effect, providing evidence for the identity and chemical environment of the xenon atom, was measured on the *gamma*-photon emitted by decay of the excited xenon to the stable form of ^{129}Xe. Xenon dichloride has been detected mass spectrometrically but its structure has been demonstrated by matrix infrared spectroscopy. A mixture of xenon and chlorine in a 200:1 mole ratio was passed through a microwave discharge and the gases were condensed under vacuum on a caesium iodide window cooled at 20 K. A structured absorption band was observed around 313 cm^{-1} as shown in Fig. 2.10. A complex absorption band was expected from a xenon chloride; xenon has seven natural isotopes of significant abundance and chlorine has two, so that each of the different mass combinations would have

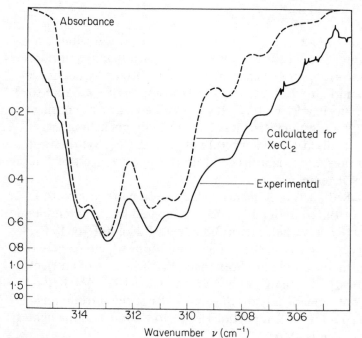

FIGURE 2.10

Infrared spectrum obtained on condensing the products of a discharge in Xe and Cl_2 at 20 K [Nelson, L. Y. and Pimentel, G.C. (1967), *Inorg. Chem.*, 6, 1758]

its own Xe—Cl stretching frequency. By making the assumption that the band was due to the asymmetric stretching mode of a linear Cl—Xe—Cl molecule (analogous to linear F—Xe—F), it was possible to calculate the expected infrared absorption band shape. The exact agreement between the calculated and experimental spectrum is good evidence for the presence of $XeCl_2$. The compound is very unstable, and may be completely decomposed below $-100°$.

The xenon fluorides XeF_2, XeF_4, and XeF_6 are white crystalline solids at room temperature, melting at $129°$, $117°$, and $49.6°$ respectively. The hexa-fluoride is the most volatile with a vapour pressure of about 25 mm at $25°$ but it begins to decompose above its melting point. (Krypton difluoride is appreciably more volatile than XeF_2 and has a vapour pressure of about 30 mm at $0°$.) They are exothermic compounds with heats of formation ranging from about -110 kJ mol^{-1} for gaseous XeF_2 to about -320 kJ mol^{-1} for gaseous XeF_6, although the exact values are at present in dispute.

Xenon difluoride is slightly soluble in cold water. The solution contains XeF_2 molecules but slow hydrolysis occurs which is rapid in alkaline solution, i.e.

$$XeF_2 + 2\,OH^- \rightarrow Xe + \tfrac{1}{2}O_2 + 2\,F^- + H_2O$$

Both XeF_4 and XeF_6 are hydrolysed more rapidly, particularly the latter, and yield solutions containing the explosive XeO_3 (p. 146). Although XeF_2 and XeF_4 can be handled in dry quartz apparatus, XeF_6 attacks glass forming oxo-fluorides.

The xenon halides form a range of complexes particularly with fluoride ion acceptors. In many of its complexes, XeF_2 tends towards XeF^+ but some fluoride bridging may still occur (p. 39). The first known xenon compound, $XePtF_6$, made by Bartlett in 1962, probably contains XeF^+. Xenon tetra-fluoride is a much weaker Lewis base or fluoride ion donor than XeF_2, and its complexes are less well characterized. However, XeF_6 forms complexes containing the XeF_5^+ ion with fluoride ion acceptors, e.g. $XeF_5^+\,PtF_6^-$ and $XeF_5^+\,SbF_6^-$. It also combines with CsF to give salts containing the XeF_7^- and XeF_8^{2-} ions; Cs_2XeF_8 is stable to $400°$ although the corresponding sodium salt decomposes at $100°$ liberating XeF_6. An X-ray structure determination on $(NO)_2XeF_8$ has shown that the XeF_8^{2-} is a slightly distorted Archimedean antiprism [23].

[23] Peterson, S. W., Holloway, J. H., Coyle, B. A. and Williams, J. M. (1971), *Science*, **173**, 1238.

The xenon fluorides are not as powerful fluorinating agents as some of the halogen fluorides. In a few cases, specific uses for their oxidizing power have been found, notably the conversion of BrO_3^- into BrO_4^- by XeF_2, one of the first preparations of the elusive perbromate ion (p. 124). The krypton compound $KrF^+ Sb_2F_{11}^-$ is a very much stronger fluorinating agent [24]; for example, it converts IF_5 into IF_6^+ and $XeOF_4$ into $XeOF_5^+$.

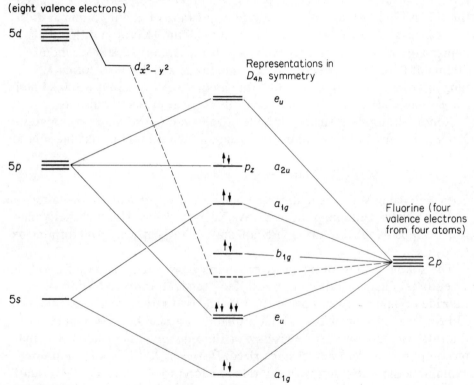

FIGURE 2.11
Qualitative molecular orbital energy diagram for σ bonding in XeF_4

Bonding in each of the xenon fluorides has been described by molecular orbital schemes involving only $5s$ and $5p$ orbitals of xenon. The possibility that $5d$, $6s$, or $6p$ orbitals of xenon participate in bonding cannot be ruled

[24] McKee, D. E., Adams, C. J., Zalkin, A. and Bartlett, N. (1973), *Chem. Comm.*, 26.

out, especially for XeF_4 and XeF_6. Figure 2.11 shows how mixing with $5d$ orbitals could improve bonding in XeF_4.

The range of noble gas compounds which can be made seems to be quite limited. The main requirement for stability is that the group attached to the noble gas atom be very electronegative. Thus, stability for xenon compounds falls in the sequence, fluorides > oxofluorides (p. 147) > oxides > chlorides. The instability of $XeCl_2$ suggests that neither $KrCl_2$ nor $XeBr_2$ is likely to be made. Some derivatives of XeF_2 have been prepared in which the fluorine is replaced by strongly electronegative groups e.g. $FXeOTeF_5$ [which forms a complex $(XeOTeF_5)^+AsF_6^-$] and $Xe(O_2CCF_3)_2$, but few groups are sufficiently electronegative. Gaseous diatomic cations containing noble gas atoms have been made by ion–molecule reactions, e.g. ArH^+ which is isoelectronic with HCl. There is a faint chance that the ArF^+ ion could be successfully stabilized in a crystal lattice by a large and very electronegative anion.

2.11 The pseudo-halides

In closing the chapter we shall look briefly at a series of groups which resemble halide groups to some extent in their properties. The term pseudo-halide was first applied to a series of nitrogen-containing groups, particularly CN, OCN, SCN, SeCN, and N_3 (see Table 2.10), but other groups such as $(CF_3)_2NO$ [25], NSF_2 [26], and FSO_3 are sometimes classed with the pseudo-halides.

The pseudo-halides resemble the halides for three main reasons:

(1) Although the groups may not be thermodynamically stable with respect to their elements, they contain strong bonds and have a considerable degree of kinetic stability enabling them to retain their identity as mono-valent groups in a variety of chemical environments.

(2) The ease of oxidation of the pseudo-halides to free pseudo-halogens (or their decomposition or polymerization products) is similar to the ease of oxidation of halides to halogens [approximate sequence F < Cl, NSF_2 < $(CF_3)_2NO$ < Br < CN < SCN < SeCN].

[25] Spaziante, P. M. (1972), *M.T.P. Internat. Review of Science*, Series 1, Vol. 3 (Series Ed., Eméleus, H. J.; Vol. Ed., Gutmann, V.).

[26] Glemser, O. and Mews, R. (1972), *Adv. Inorg. Chem. Radiochem.*, **14**, 333.

(3) The size, charge, and polarizability of the pseudo-halide ions and groups is sufficiently similar to that of bromide or iodide to make physical properties such as the solubility of metal salts or the volatility of covalent compounds quite comparable.

TABLE 2.10
Some pseudo-halides

Group	Structure		Parent compound
	Covalent	*Ionic*	
Cyanide	115 pm H—C≡N	105 pm (C≡N)⁻	N≡C—C≡N
Isocyanide	117 pm ∕N≡C		dicyanogen
Cyanate	∕O—C≡N		(OCN)₂
Isocyanate	118 pm ∕N≡C≡O	(O≡C≡N)⁻	(unknown)
Fulminate		(O≡N≡C)⁻	(ONC)₂ (unknown)
Thiocyanate	161 pm ⌐122 pm ∕S—C≡N		N≡C—S—S—C≡N
Isothiocyanate	122 pm ⌐156 pm ∕N≡C≡S	(S≡C≡N)⁻	thiocyanogen
Selenocyanate	∕Se—C≡N		
Isoselenocyanate	∕N≡C≡Se	(Se≡C≡N)⁻	(SeCN)₂ (unstable)
Azide	124 pm 113 pm ∕N≡N≡N	115 pm (N≡N≡N)⁻	(N₃)₂ (unknown)

The groups CN, OCN, SCN, and SeCN may bond either through nitrogen or through the other terminal atom. The CN group most commonly bonds through carbon, but OCN, SCN, and SeCN most commonly bond through nitrogen; in compounds with heavy, polarizable B-Group elements and some transition metals, SCN and SeCN may bond through S and Se respectively. There is evidence of strong $(p–d)\pi$ interactions between pseudo-halides and attached silicon atoms. Thus, CH_3NCO is bent but SiH_3NCO is linear (Chapter 6).

Many pseudo-halide derivatives of the non-metals are stable liquids or solids which can be boiled without decomposition, e.g.

$$Si[(CF_3)_2NO]_4 \text{ b.p. } 135° \qquad cf. \ SiBr_4 \text{ b.p. } 155°$$
$$Si(NCO)_4 \qquad \text{b.p. } 185°$$
$$Si(OCN)_4 \qquad \text{b.p. } 247°$$

However, like the halides, such compounds are sensitive to hydrolysis. The hydrogen compounds of the pseudo-halogens are acids. An approximate sequence of acid strengths is $HSO_3F \approx HCl > HNCS > HF > HNCO > HN_3 > HCN \approx (CF_3)_2NOH$ (v. weak).

The most important of the pseudo-halides are the cyanides. Sodium cyanide is manufactured from calcium carbide,

$$CaC_2 + N_2 \xrightarrow{1100°} CaNCN + C$$
$$\text{calcium cyanamide}$$
$$CaNCN + C + Na_2CO_3 \xrightarrow{\text{fuse}} CaCO_3 + 2\,NaCN$$

Although HCN is readily formed from NaCN, it is also made directly by catalytic oxidation of methane and ammonia:

$$2\,CH_4 + 3\,O_2 + 2\,NH_3 \xrightarrow[1000°]{\text{catalyst}} 2\,HCN + 6\,H_2O$$

Organic cyanides, e.g. adiponitrile $NC(CH_2)_4CN$ and acrylonitrile $CH_2{=}CHCN$, are used in the manufacture of artificial fibres.

Pure HCN, b.p. 26°, is liable to polymerize violently. It is a liquid of high dielectric constant and is a good ionizing solvent for some metal salts and protonic acids. The parent pseudo-halogen, cyanogen, $N{\equiv}C{-}C{\equiv}N$, can be formed from mercuric cyanide:

$$Hg(CN)_2 + HgCl_2 \xrightarrow{300°} Hg_2Cl_2 + (CN)_2$$

or, like iodine from iodides, by oxidation of CN^- with Cu^{2+}:

$$2\,Cu^{2+} + 4\,CN^- \rightarrow 2\,CuCN + (CN)_2$$

It is a gas, b.p. $-21°$, which is quite stable at ordinary temperatures when pure although it is highly endothermic ($\Delta H_f°$ 296 kJ mol^{-1}); impure cyanogen

71

will polymerize at 300–500° to paracyanogen (CN)$_n$ which may have the structure:

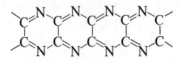

A mixture of oxygen and cyanogen burns to yield the two most stable molecules CO and N_2; the flame temperature of about 4800° is only exceeded at atmospheric pressure by using ozone in place of oxygen, or dicyanoacetylene $N{\equiv}C{-}C{\equiv}C{-}C{\equiv}N$ in place of cyanogen.

The reaction of cyanogen with dilute alkali is analogous to that of the halogens:

$$C_2N_2 + 2\,OH^- \rightarrow CNO^- + CN^- + H_2O$$

All the cyanogen halides XCN have been prepared as volatile compounds; they are linear molecules which polymerize to cyclic trimers (p. 256).

Soluble cyanides, HCN, C_2N_2, and the cyanogen halides, are very poisonous.

Cyanates, thiocyanates, and selenocyanates are easily prepared from cyanides:

$$OCN^- \xleftarrow[\text{heat}]{\text{PbO}} CN^- \quad \begin{array}{l} \xrightarrow[\text{heat}]{\text{Se}} SeCN^- \\[1em] \xrightarrow[\text{heat}]{\text{S}} SCN^- \end{array}$$

The azide group $-N_3$ is endothermic; the enthalpy of formation of gaseous HN_3 is 290 kJ mol^{-1} but unlike cyanogen or HCN (see above) it is violently explosive as are many other covalent azides.

Sodium azide is formed from sodamide and nitrous oxide; as isotopic labelling has shown, the reaction is not simple:

$$2\,NaNH_2 + O^{15}NN \xrightarrow{180°} Na^+[N^{15}NN]\ (78\%) + Na^+[NN^{15}N]\ (22\%)$$

The halogen azides are chemically very reactive compounds; toxic, dangerously explosive, gaseous ClN_3 is formed from chlorine and sodium azide:

$$N_3^-\ (aq.) + Cl_2\,(g) \xrightarrow{N_2\ \text{diluent}} ClN_3 + Cl^-$$

There is no evidence that $(N_3)_2$ is formed either by oxidation or thermal decomposition of azides; N_2 is the product.

Since their discovery in 1964, bistrifluoromethyl nitroxide radicals have been formed by a variety of routes one of which is:

$$CF_3I + NO \xrightarrow{\text{Hg}} CF_3NO \xrightarrow{\text{NH}_3} (CF_3)_2NOH \xrightarrow{\text{Ag(II) oxide}} (CF_3)_2NO$$

Unlike other pseudo-halogens, $(CF_3)_2NO$ is more stable as a monomeric radical than as a dimer, but in other respects it mimics the properties of a halogen fairly closely.

Non-metal oxides, sulphides and their derivatives

3

3.1   Introduction

Structurally there are many points of contrast between the oxides and sulphides of the non-metallic elements and their corresponding halides. This is often due to the 2-valence of oxygen and sulphur, which can lead to the formation of two covalent bonds by these elements. Thus oxygen may bond either to one other atom through a double bond [Fig. 3.1(a)] or to two other atoms through single bonds [Fig. 3.1(b)]. Situation (a) is apparently different from that in Fig. 3.1(c), where oxygen accepts a lone pair of electrons from a donor group M. Bonds to terminal oxygen atoms, however, generally possess

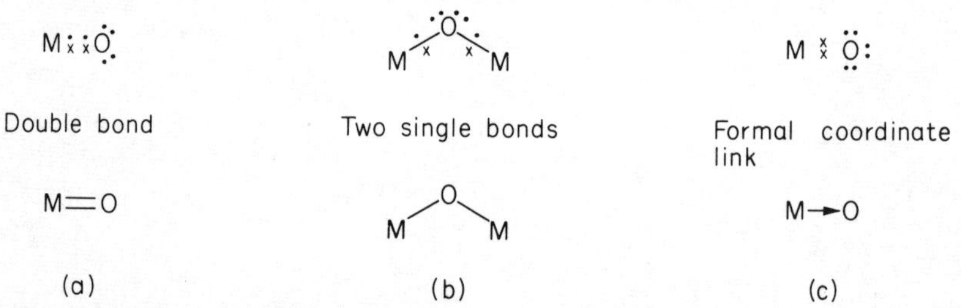

Double bond

$M = O$

(a)

Two single bonds

(b)

Formal coordinate link

$M \rightarrow O$

(c)

FIGURE 3.1
Representations of bonding in oxides

some double bond character, whether of the $(p–p)\pi$ or $(p–d)\pi$ type, and in any case such formal distinctions can be unhelpful, and tend to disappear when a delocalized rather than a localized bond model is used. Bonding as in (b), in which oxygen is linked to two other atoms M, can lead to the formation of ring or chain structures. The incidence of these bonding forms thus grossly affects the structures and physical properties such as volatility of the oxides.

74

3.2 Range of compounds

In Table 3.1 are listed the oxides and sulphides of the non-metals which exist as isolable species at room temperature. In a few cases, species which are stable only at high temperatures or as ligands in transition metal complexes are also included. At first sight this table may present a complicated and perhaps puzzling picture, since some formulae (e.g. NO, ClO_2, P_4S_3) apparently do not fit simple valency rules. This is a result of special structural and electronic factors discussed below.

TABLE 3.1
Non-metal oxides and sulphides

(BO)		CO	(CS)	N_2O	N_4S_4		F_2O	
(BO_2)		CO_2	CS_2	NO	etc.		F_2O_2	
B_2O_3	B_2S_3	C_3O_2		N_2O_3	(Ch. 6)		F_2O_4	
				$NO_2 \rightleftharpoons N_2O_4$				
				N_2O_5				
		(SiO)		P_4O_6	P_4S_3	(S_2O)	Cl_2O	
		SiO_2	SiS_2	P_4O_7	P_4S_5	(SO)	Cl_2O_3	
				P_4O_8	P_4S_7	SO_2	ClO_2	
							Cl_2O_4	
				P_4O_9	P_4S_9	SO_3	Cl_2O_6	
				P_4O_{10}	P_4S_{10}		Cl_2O_7	
		GeO	GeS	As_4O_6	As_4S_3	SeO_2	Br_2O	
		GeO_2	GeS_2	As_2O_5	As_4S_4	SeO_3	BrO_2	
				As_2S_3			BrO_3 or Br_3O_8	
				As_2S_5			Br_2O_7?	
				Sb_2O_3	Sb_2S_3	TeO_2	I_2O_4	XeO_3
				Sb_2O_5		TeO_3	I_4O_9	XeO_4
							I_2O_5	

3.3 Structures and physical properties

The physical properties of the non-metal oxides reflect the extent of aggregation within their structures, and the ease with which these aggregates are broken down, for example by heat. Very approximately, one may recognize three classes (Table 3.2). The oxides of C, N, F, and Cl (except for NO_2 and ClO_3 which are odd-electron molecules and dimerize to some extent to N_2O_4

75

and Cl_2O_6 respectively; see p. 124) exist as low-boiling monomers which are gases or volatile liquids at ordinary temperatures. Their boiling points are comparable with those of covalent, unassociated halides such as NF_3.

TABLE 3.2
Boiling points of some non-metal oxides

	Compound	B.p. (°C)	Compound	B.p. (°C)
Monomeric	CO	−191·5	NO	−151·8
	CO_2	−78·5 subl.	N_2O	−88·5
	cf. CS_2	46·3	cf. NF_3	−128.8
	F_2O	−144·8	Cl_2O	3·8 extrap.
	SO_2	−10	ClO_2	9.9 extrap.
Partly or weakly	SO_3	44·8	SeO_2	340–350 subl.
polymerized	P_4O_6	175·4	I_2O_5	dec. above 300°
	P_4O_{10}	300 subl.		
	As_4O_6	457·2		
Polymerized; giant	SiO_2	2230[a]	GeO_2	2100[a]
lattices	B_2O_3	2300		

[a] 1 atm of AO + $\frac{1}{2}$ O_2 at this temperature.

Down any Group (IV–VII), the oxides show an increasing tendency to polymerize. The most striking example of this occurs in the compounds CO_2 and SiO_2. Whereas carbon dioxide is a volatile species, monomeric in condensed states as well as in the gas phase, silicon dioxide forms a three-dimensional network, which is rather hard, infusible (m.p. 1710°), and involatile. Some oxides (e.g. SO_3 and SeO_2), however, are fairly weakly polymerized in the solid and are relatively easily volatilized by breakdown of the structure. Others crystallize as discrete units (e.g. P_4O_6, As_4O_6) which volatilize unchanged.

3.3.1 *Gas phase structures of monomeric compounds*

The shapes of simple covalent halides can often be predicted approximately by considering electron pair repulsions within a molecule (p. 6). The Gillespie–Nyholm rules can be applied successfully to oxides and sulphides also, provided that the limitations of this approach are recognized; for instance, the rules give no indication whether a monomeric, oligomeric, or polymeric structure is to be expected. The bonding in compounds such as NO, CO_2, and SO_2 involves both a σ bond skeleton and π bonding. The question of multiple bonding must first be considered in relation to the Gillespie method.

The shapes of the molecules CO_2 (linear) and SO_2 (bent; angle OSO = 120°) are illustrated below:

2 σ electron pairs   3 σ electron pairs

This indicates that the presence of multiple bonding may, to a first approximation, be ignored in applying the repulsion ideas. The following series of compounds shows this well:

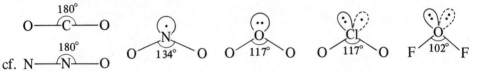

cf. N——N——O

Note how the odd-electron molecules NO_2 and ClO_2 fit into the series. The bond angle in NO_2 lies between that predicted for two (180°) and three (120°) σ electron pairs, since the repulsions between the bonding electrons and the orbital containing the odd electron are less than when this orbital is filled as in ozone or sulphur dioxide. The bond angle in triplet methylene is explained in a similar way on p. 23.

The shapes of oxo-halide molecules can generally be predicted successfully using the concept of electron pair repulsions. It is a convenient formalism to think of the bond between a central atom A and oxygen as a coordinate linkage A→O. The structures of halides and oxo-halides are therefore closely related; oxygen atoms in the latter replace lone pairs in the former. Some illustrations are given in Fig. 3.2. This does not mean that the A—O bonds possess no double bond character. As already noted above, any π character of bonds to terminal oxygen often does not, to a first approximation, affect the general shapes of molecules in which it occurs. The repulsive effects of a lone pair and of the electrons bonding an oxygen atom in this way are apparently much the same, since the XAX angles in halides AX_n and the corresponding oxo-halides $O_m AX_n$ are usually rather similar.

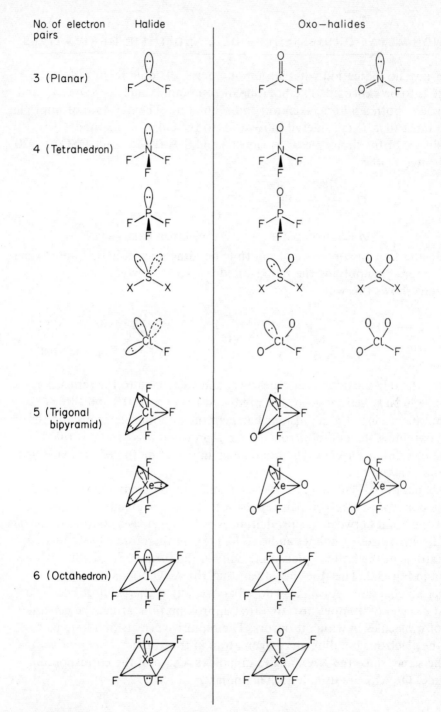

FIGURE 3.2
Structures of some oxo-halides

Although the concept of spatial distribution of electron pairs is useful in predicting the shapes of simple molecular oxides and oxo-halides, it tells us little about the nature of bonding within the molecules. The molecular orbital approach described in Chapter 1 in relation to diatomic and triatomic species is more informative, especially when accurate calculations and measurements of molecular energy levels have been carried out. Thus, in volatile oxides part of the bonding arises from electrons in π molecular orbitals which are formed from $2p$ (or for S and Cl $3p$) atomic orbitals. This may in part explain the occurrence of odd-electron molecules such as NO and ClO_2 in which the unpaired electron is present in a π molecular orbital and is delocalized to some extent over the molecule. Hence their resistance to dimerization compared with radicals such as $\cdot CH_3$ can be understood.

3.3.2 Polymerized oxides

(i)   *Some features of bonding.*   The contrast between the structures of carbon dioxide and silica is noted above. In silica, each silicon atom is tetrahedrally surrounded by four oxygen atoms, which is consistent with the formation by silicon of four single bonds. Carbon, however, prefers to form two *double* bonds to oxygen in carbon dioxide.

Consider the relative energies of single and double bonds between oxygen and carbon and silicon respectively:

$$E(C-O) \ 358 \ kJ \ mol^{-1} \quad E(Si-O) \ 464 \ kJ \ mol^{-1}$$
$$E(C=O) \ 803 \ kJ \ mol^{-1} \quad E(Si=O) \ 640 \ kJ \ mol^{-1}$$

The bond energy $E(C=O)$ in carbon dioxide is more than twice that of a single bond; $2 \ E(C-O) = 716 \ kJ \ mol^{-1}$. Therefore a three-dimensional silica-like structure for carbon dioxide is thermodynamically unstable with respect to monomeric CO_2. These and related bond energy values (Table 3.3) suggest that, whereas strong $(2p-2p)\pi$ overlap can occur, $(3p-2p)\pi$ or $(3p-3p)\pi$ overlap is significantly weaker. This agrees with calculations of overlap integrals for these combinations of orbitals. The poorer overlap of $3p$ orbitals may arise first on account of the greater size and hence diffuseness of $3p$ relative to $2p$ orbitals. Secondly, the lateral extension of the p orbitals may be sufficient to give good overlap only at the short bond distances which are observed in oxides of first-row elements, and not at the greater distances obtaining in compounds of the elements of the second and subsequent rows.

In addition, formal single bonds between second-row elements (e.g. Si, P) and atoms which carry lone pairs of electrons (e.g. F, O, N) can, it is thought, be strengthened through $(2p-3d)\pi$ bonding (cf. halides, p. 52; nitrogen compounds, p. 257). Thus, the Si—O bond, as in silica, probably possesses some double bond character. The 'SiOSi angle in various polymorphic forms of silica has been shown by X-ray diffraction to be considerably wider than the approximately tetrahedral angle expected for pure σ bonding. In β-cristobalite the 'SiOSi angle is 150° and in α-quartz 142°. This is consistent with appreciable delocalization of oxygen p electrons into the empty $3d$ orbitals of silicon. The planar skeleton of trisilylamine $(H_3Si)_3N$ provides better evidence for such delocalization (see Chapter 6, p. 258).

Whereas formal single bonds are favoured in oxides of silicon and phosphorus over formal double bonds, it is likely that considerable $(3p-3p)\pi$ bonding occurs in sulphur dioxide and perhaps in the chlorine oxides. Here the competition from formal single bonds, strengthened by $(2p-3d)\pi$ overlap is probably less than in silica.

Association in oxides increases as the electronegativity of the central atom decreases, that is, with increasing A—O charge separation. This is consistent with the Pauling electroneutrality principle. There is a tendency for this charge separation to be reduced, and this can be achieved by association (cf. halides, p. 27). This is illustrated by the following facts. While SO_2 is monomeric, SeO_2 and SO_3, in both of which the formal positive charge on the central atom is greater than in SO_2, show polymerization.

(ii)   Coordination number and structure.   Another trend in the structures of oxides and sulphides is the increase in coordination number of the central atom down a Group. This is summarized in Fig. 3.3. This may be partly a size effect, but is also associated with the increase in ionic character of oxides down a Group. Thus, the rutile structure (6:3 coordination) appears in GeO_2 and TeO_2, although this does not necessarily imply truly ionic bonding in these compounds, in which a high degree of covalency is likely to persist.

Most of the oxide structures can be understood in terms of tetrahedral geometry. Those in which the central atom is 4-coordinate arise from linking of AO_4 tetrahedra. With 3-coordinate atoms such as P(III) or Se(IV) one lone

80

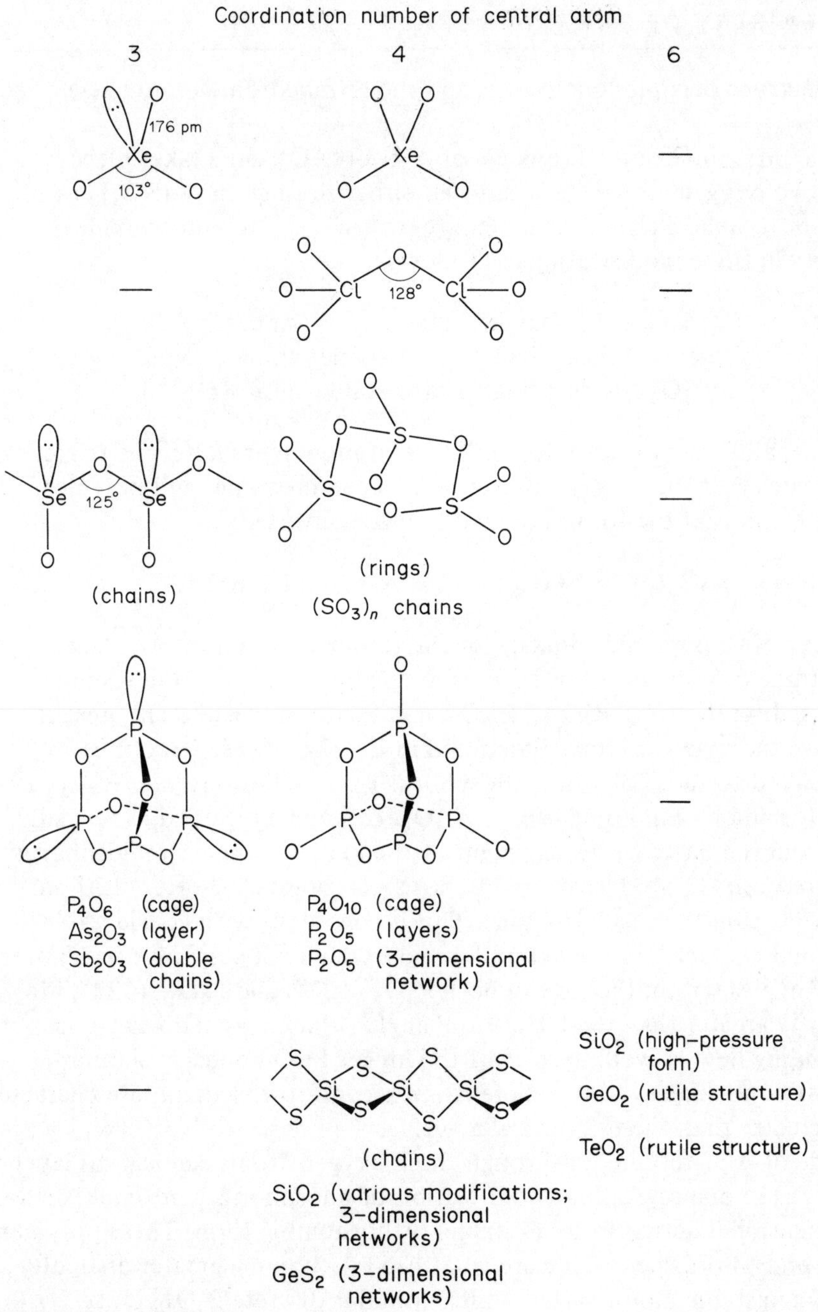

Coordination number of central atom

3	4	6

FIGURE 3.3
Structures of some oxides and sulphides

pair of electrons occupies one position in the tetrahedron, i.e. : AO_3 (see Fig. 3.3).

In the oxides of Group VI, linkage of AO_4 or : AO_3 units takes place through two oxygen atoms. This can lead either to rings, as in $(SO_3)_3$ or $(SeO_3)_4$, or to helical chains, as in $SeO_2(c)$ or $(SO_3)_n$. Sulphur trioxide crystallizes in three modifications as follows:

α-SO_3 helical chains   stable   m.p. 62·3
β-SO_3 helical chains   metastable   m.p. 32·5
γ-SO_3 trimer; rings   metastable   m.p. 16·8

On heating, all forms vaporize to a mixture of monomer and cyclic trimer. This indicates that the energy difference between monomer and polymer is only small, and that the forms are readily interconverted:

$$\beta\text{-}SO_3(c) \rightarrow SO_3(g) \quad (\Delta H = +57 \cdot 5 \text{ kJ mol}^{-1})$$

In Group VB compounds, linkage of the tetrahedral units takes place through three oxygen atoms of each. In the vapour phase, and in some crystalline forms, discrete P_4O_6, P_4O_{10}, As_4O_6, and Sb_4O_6 molecules are present, which have the cage structures illustrated in Fig. 3.3. These structures are closely related to those of white phosphorus P_4 or yellow arsenic As_4 (p. 174). P_4O_{10} is formed by mild oxidation of P_4O_6. It may be regarded as formally derived from the latter by replacement of the lone pair on each phosphorus atom by oxygen. The external P—O bonds are very much shorter (130 pm) than those within the cage (164 pm). This is consistent with considerable double bond character in the external bonds, which could involve (p–d) overlap. The ′POP angles within the cage in both P_4O_6 (127°) and P_4O_{10} (124°) are significantly greater than the tetrahedral angle, which may indicate some (p–d) bonding here as well, in spite of the longer P—O bonds. It should be noted that bond angles ′AOA, where A is a second-row element, are characteristically greater than the tetrahedral angle.

Linkage of AO_4 tetrahedra through three oxygen atoms can lead to layer structures as in one crystalline modification of phosphorus pentoxide, or to three-dimensional networks in its stable, orthorhombic form. These polymeric forms of phosphorus pentoxide are volatilized with much greater difficulty than the metastable modification which contains discrete P_4O_{10} units.

82

The number of crystalline modifications of silica is large. Most of these are made up by linking SiO_4 tetrahedra through all four oxygen atoms. The three main forms – quartz, tridymite, and cristobalite – are built up from SiO_4 tetrahedral units joined in such a way that every oxygen atom is common to two tetrahedra, but the arrangement of the tetrahedra in the crystal varies from one form to another. The forms stable at higher temperatures have more open structures and lower densities than the low-temperature forms α- and β-quartz.

	Temp. range	Density at room temp.
α-Quartz	up to 573°	2·655 g/cm³
β-Quartz	573–870°	2·655 g/cm³
Tridymite	870–1470°	2·30 g/cm³
Cristobalite	1470–1710° (m.p.)	2·27 g/cm³

Germania is known in the silica form, but this is metastable, the stable form being the rutile modification, in which the germanium atoms have 6-coordination of oxygen atoms. It is interesting that silica can be converted into a 6-coordinate rutile modification named stishovite by heating to 1300° under high pressure. This high-pressure form has a more compact structure than the normal 4-coordinate ones, and a high density.

$$\text{Quartz} \xrightarrow[\text{35 kbar}]{750°} \text{Coesite} \xrightarrow[\text{120 kbar}]{1300°} \text{Stishovite}$$

	density	density
	3·0 g/cm³	4·3 g/cm³
4-coordinate	4-coordinate	6-coordinated

The structure of silicon disulphide (Fig. 3.3) shows yet another way in which the tetrahedra may be linked, i.e. to form infinite chains. Germanium disulphide, however, forms three-dimensional networks, analogous to silica.

3.4 Thermochemistry; bond strengths

The standard heats of formation of some common non-metal oxides, expressed per g-atom of oxygen, are plotted in Fig. 3.4. This figure emphasizes that there is a general decrease in thermodynamic stability of the oxides across any

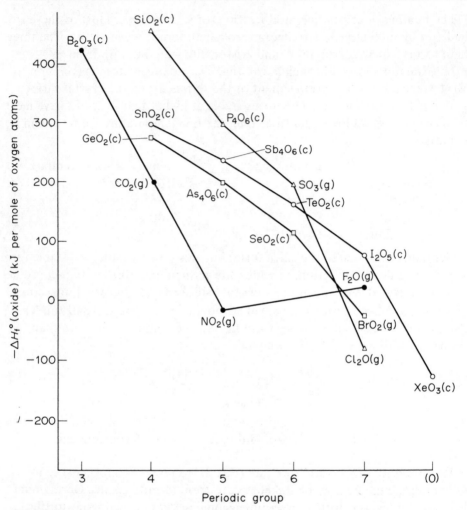

FIGURE 3.4
Heats of formation of some oxides of non-metallic elements

row of the Periodic Table, which is consistent with the decrease in polar character of the A—O bonds. F_2O is apparently out of line, but here there is a polar contribution in the sense $F(\delta-)$—$O(\delta+)$.

The oxides of the most electronegative elements, especially of nitrogen and the halogens, are thermodynamically unstable or only just stable (F_2O) with

84

respect to their constituent elements in their standard states. A similar pattern is observed for the halides. The rather low thermodynamic stability of the carbon and nitrogen compounds is associated with the strong bonding of the elements C, N, and O in their standard states, rather than in any inherent weakness of the C=O or N=O bonds (see p. 149 and Table 3.3). Oxides of chlorine, bromine, and xenon, however, are both kinetically and thermodynamically unstable. This is associated with the rather weak bonds which these elements form with oxygen.

TABLE 3.3
Bond energy term values (kJ mol^{-1}) for A–O bonds

Bond	E(A–O)	Compound	Bond	E(A–O)	Compound
C–O	362	Organic ethers	N–O	163	H_2NOH
C=O	803	CO_2	N=O	594	FNO
C≡O	1076	CO	N≡O	631	NO
Si–O	464	$SiO_2(c)$	P–O	368	P_4O_6
Si=O	640	$SiO_2(g)$	P–O	385	$(RO)_3P$
			P=O	~580	P_4O_{10}, R_3PO
O–O	146	H_2O_2	P=S	385	R_3PS
O=O	498	O_2	As–O	330	As_4O_6
S=O	523	SO			
S=O	635	SO_2			
F–O	213	F_2O			
Cl–O	205	Cl_2O			

Formation of the oxides of Si, Ge, P, and As from the elements is very favoured thermodynamically, compared with the compounds of the first-row elements C and N. This trend also occurs for the halides. This can be understood in terms of the occurrence of associated covalent structures for the first group of compounds, and perhaps the strengthening of formal single bonds such as Si–O and P–O by multiple bonding. It is worth noting that the bond energy term values lie in the same order as for the fluorides:

$$E(N{-}O) < E(P{-}O) > E(As{-}O)$$

$$E(N{-}F) < E(P{-}F) > E(As{-}F)$$

3.4.1 *Oxidation of non-metals; industrial aspects*

In this section the thermodynamics of the oxidation of carbon, nitrogen, and sulphur are illustrated by reference to some industrial processes.

(i)   The oxidation of carbon [1].   Either carbon monoxide or carbon dioxide can be formed on oxidation of carbon, depending on the conditions. For the reaction:

$$C(\text{graphite}) + O_2(g) \rightleftharpoons CO_2(g) \quad (\Delta H = -393 \text{ kJ mol}^{-1}$$
$$\Delta S = +2 \cdot 8 \text{ J K}^{-1} \text{ mol}^{-1} \text{ at } 25°)$$

there is a favourable heat change, but the entropy change is very small, as the number of gas molecules is unchanged. When carbon is converted into carbon monoxide, however, while the enthalpy change is not so favourable, there is an increase of entropy which arises mainly by the formation of two gas molecules of carbon monoxide from one of oxygen:

$$2\,C(\text{graphite}) + O_2(g) \rightleftharpoons 2\,CO(g) \quad (\Delta H = -221 \text{ kJ mol}^{-1}$$
$$\Delta S = +179 \text{ J K}^{-1} \text{ mol}^{-1} \text{ at } 25°)$$

This means that, while the free energy of the first reaction and hence its equilibrium constant is nearly independent of temperature, the formation of carbon monoxide is favoured by rise of temperature.

In Fig. 3.5 the free energies of formation of carbon dioxide and of carbon monoxide per mole of oxygen are plotted as functions of temperature. The lines corresponding to CO_2 and CO formation intersect at 710°. Below this temperature the oxidation of carbon to CO_2 is favoured, but above it, carbon monoxide is the more stable product. It also indicates that CO is thermodynamically unstable with respect to CO_2 and graphite below 710°, although this disproportionation occurs immeasurably slowly at ordinary temperatures.

Diagrams such as Fig. 3.5 (known as Ellingham diagrams after their originator) are useful in summarizing thermochemical data relevant to the reduction of oxides to the elements. In contrast to the formation of carbon

[1] Ives, D. J. G. (1960), *Principles of the Extraction of Metals*, Monographs for Teachers No. 3, Royal Institute of Chemistry, London.

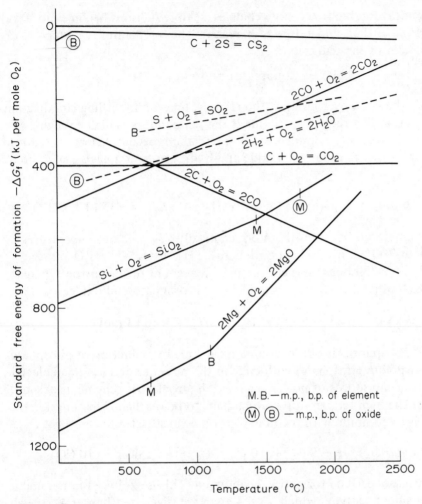

FIGURE 3.5
Standard free energies of formation (ΔG_f°) of oxides; variation with temperature

monoxide from carbon and oxygen, the oxidation of most other elements is accompanied by an entropy decrease, e.g.

$$2\,Mg(s) \;+\; O_2(g) \;\rightarrow\; 2\,MgO(s)$$

Thus, although very few oxides can be reduced by carbon at room temperature

87

owing to unfavourable free energy changes, such reductions become more and more feasible as the temperature is increased. The temperature at which $\Delta G°$ becomes zero for the reduction:

$$MO + C(graphite) \rightleftharpoons CO(g) + M$$

is given by the cross-over point of the relevant lines on the Ellingham diagram. Graphite can in fact reduce any oxide if the temperature is high enough. Figure 3.5 shows some examples of commercial importance. Steam is reduced to give a mixture of carbon monoxide and hydrogen (water gas). The desired reaction:

$$C(graphite) + H_2O(g) \rightleftharpoons CO(g) + H_2(g) \quad (\Delta H = +134 \text{ kJ mol}^{-1})$$

is endothermic, but becomes thermodynamically favoured at temperatures above about 700° (the crossing point of the $2 H_2 + O_2 \rightleftharpoons 2 H_2O$ and the $2 C + O_2 \rightleftharpoons 2 CO$ lines on the diagram), on account of the entropy increase. Below this temperature there is a tendency to form carbon dioxide, e.g. via

$$CO + H_2O \rightleftharpoons CO_2 + H_2 \quad (\Delta H° = +46 \text{ kJ mol}^{-1})$$

Elemental phosphorus is obtained on a large scale by reduction of phosphate rock (e.g. calcium phosphate) with coke in the presence of silica in an electric furnace. A cheap source of power, such as a hydroelectric scheme, is desirable because of the high temperatures which have to be reached. The function of the silica is to combine with the lime to form a silicate slag:

$$2 Ca_3(PO_4)_2 + 6 SiO_2 + 10 C \rightarrow P_4 + 6 CaSiO_3 + 10 CO$$

In some cases carbide formation is observed. This is exploited in the manufacture of silicon carbide, which is used as an abrasive (see Chapter 4) (see also p. 92, where the reduction of calcium sulphate is discussed).

The formation of carbon disulphide from its elements is slightly unfavourable thermodynamically over a wide range of temperature. Consequently carbon does not act as a reducing agent for metal and non-metal sulphides. Sulphide ores such as zinc blende ZnS are therefore first roasted in air to convert them into oxide, which is subsequently reduced by carbon. The sulphur dioxide which is a by-product of the roasting is converted into sulphuric acid.

(ii)   *Oxidation of nitrogen and ammonia.*   The reaction:

$$N_2(g) + O_2(g) \rightleftharpoons 2\,NO(g) \quad (\Delta H = +181 \text{ kJ mol}^{-1})$$

is endothermic, and therefore nitric oxide formation should be favoured at high temperatures. Even at 3200°, however, the equilibrium concentration of NO is only about 4·4% by volume. The reaction was exploited commercially at one time in Norway (Birkeland–Eyde process) using an electric arc to attain the high temperatures required. A more recent approach has been to use a plasma torch giving more efficient use of power. In either case, rapid cooling is necessary to slow down the reversal of equilibrium. The process is not economical compared with the oxidation of ammonia (see below). Production of nitrogen oxides (e.g. NO) occurs whenever nitrogen and oxygen are heated together. They arise during thunderstorms and are present in exhausts from cars and aeroplanes unless catalysts are there to decompose them. Recently concern has been expressed in connection with the formation of NO by jet aircraft flying at high altitude. Nitric oxide catalyses the decomposition of ozone, the presence of which is important as it absorbs ultraviolet radiation from the sun:

$$NO + O_3 \rightarrow NO_2 + O_2$$
$$NO_2 + O \rightarrow NO + O_2$$

$$\overline{}$$

$$O_3 + O \rightarrow 2\,O_2$$

O_3 and O are both present in the upper atmosphere.

    Nitric oxide for nitric acid manufacture is prepared commercially by the oxidation of ammonia [2]. Ammonia can be burnt in air, and forms an explosive mixture with it (16–25% by volume NH_3). Under these conditions nitrogen and water are produced:

$$4\,NH_3 + 3\,O_2 \rightarrow 2\,N_2 + 6\,H_2O \quad (\Delta H = -1267 \text{ kJ mol}^{-1})$$

The oxidation to NO is not so exothermic:

$$4\,NH_3 + 5\,O_2 \rightarrow 4\,NO + 6\,H_2O \quad (\Delta H = -907 \text{ kJ mol}^{-1})$$

and other unwanted reactions such as:

$$4\,NH_3 + 4\,O_2 \rightarrow 2\,N_2O + 3\,H_2O \quad (\Delta H = -377 \text{ kJ mol}^{-1})$$

[2] Jones, D. G. (Ed.) (1967), *Chemistry and Industry*, Clarendon Press, Oxford.

and the decomposition of nitric oxide to its elements must be suppressed. The desired reaction can be obtained almost quantitatively using a catalyst (90% Pt, 10% Rh) in the form of fine gauze at about 800° with a contact time of 10^{-3} s. In Europe atmospheric pressure is usually used, although in the U.S.A. plant operating throughout at about 8 atm is favoured.

The next stage is the oxidation of NO to NO_2. The kinetics of this reaction follow a third-order law:

$$2\,NO + O_2 \underset{k_d}{\overset{k_f}{\rightleftharpoons}} 2\,NO_2 \quad ; \quad d[NO_2]/dt = k_f[NO]^2[O_2] - k_d[NO_2]^2$$

The second-order dependence on [NO] is also found in its reactions with Cl_2, Br_2, and H_2, and may be associated with the odd electron present, causing loose $(NO)_2$ dimers to be incorporated into the transition state. The reaction is remarkable in having a negative temperature coefficient, i.e. it gets faster as the temperature is lowered. This implies that association of NO molecules ('sticky collisions') is necessary for reaction, and that the lifetime of such associations diminishes with rise of temperature. For rapid oxidation nitric oxide and air are cooled and the gases absorbed in a countercurrent flow of water in an absorption tower. The reactions involved are complex, including at least the following stages:

$$2\,NO_2 \rightleftharpoons N_2O_4$$
$$N_2O_4 + H_2O \rightarrow HNO_3 + HNO_2$$
$$2\,HNO_2 \rightarrow NO + NO_2 + H_2O$$
$$3\,NO_2 + H_2O \rightarrow 2\,HNO_3 + NO$$
$$2\,NO + O_2 \rightarrow 2\,NO_2 \rightleftharpoons N_2O_4(g)$$

When the concentration of nitric oxide falls towards the end of the process its rate of oxidation becomes very slow. This can be increased by application of pressure, and this is an important reason for operating throughout at 8 atm, even though the conversion in the ammonia oxidation step is less complete under these conditions.

Nitric acid produced by absorption of NO_2 has a concentration of about 60%. It can be concentrated by distillation; this produces an azeotrope containing 68% HNO_3. Until recently 'high strength' nitric acid (i.e. above 98% HNO_3) has been made by dehydrating the concentrated acid with sulphuric acid or magnesium nitrate. Processes have now been developed in which the high-strength acid is obtained directly from ammonia oxidation. The final stage involves oxidation of N_2O_4 with oxygen or air under pressure in the presence of the calculated quantity of water:

$$2\,N_2O_4 \;+\; 2\,H_2O \;+\; O_2 \;\rightarrow\; 4\,HNO_3$$

(iii)   Oxidation of sulphur to sulphur dioxide and sulphur trioxide.   The inorganic chemical which is manufactured in the greatest bulk in the United States is sulphuric acid. In 1971 about 8 million tons of sulphur from various sources were converted into this compound. Of this about half was used to make fertilizers, mostly phosphates but also ammonium sulphate. While ammonium sulphate is no longer competitive in cost relative to ammonium nitrate (the main use of nitric acid) or urea as a nitrogenous fertilizer, and its production will probably remain static over the next few years, the demand for phosphate fertilizers is increasing.

In the U.S.A. about 75% of sulphur consumption in 1971 came from natural elemental sulphur (Frasch process). In other countries, such as the U.K., where elemental sulphur has to be imported, other sources such as crude petroleum, smelter gas, or pyrites are more widely used. A source which is being increasingly exploited in this country is calcium sulphate, either in the form of naturally occurring anhydrite or gypsum, or as a by-product from phosphoric acid manufacture (see below).

In modern sulphuric acid plants, the contact process is always used. This depends on the oxidation of sulphur dioxide to sulphur trioxide over a vanadium oxide catalyst:

$$SO_2 \;+\; \tfrac{1}{2}\,O_2 \;\rightleftharpoons\; SO_3$$

The rate of this reaction is increased by high temperatures and by high concentrations of oxygen. Vanadium catalysts in fact do not operate well below 420–430°. Increase of temperature, however, does not favour high conversion into SO_3, as there is an entropy decrease in the reaction. In the Bayer double catalysis system, conversions of SO_2 over 99·5% are obtained by removing some of the SO_3 after the gas mixture has passed over three of four catalyst beds in the reactor. To do this, partly converted gas is cooled in a heat exchanger, and the sulphur trioxide is absorbed in sulphuric acid. The effluent

91

is then heated up again and passed over the last catalyst bed before final absorption [3].

The reduction of calcium sulphate with carbon can lead to either of two sulphur end-products – calcium sulphide, which is usually not required, or sulphur dioxide:

$$CaSO_4 + 4C \rightarrow CaS + 4CO \qquad \text{(below } 1000°)$$

$$2CaSO_4 + 2C \rightarrow 2CaO + 2SO_2 + 2CO \qquad \text{(above } 1350°)$$

One way in which this process is carried out commercially is to combine the sulphuric acid plant with cement manufacture. Calcium sulphate, coke, and a mixture of silica, alumina (bauxite), and iron oxide are fired together in a kiln. The lime produced combines with the oxides to produce cement clinker, and the sulphur dioxide is converted into acid in an adjacent plant. By using some of the sulphuric acid directly for phosphoric acid and detergent manufacture, the process has no wasteful by-products.

Another way of utilizing calcium sulphate is to convert it directly into ammonium sulphate. This process depends on the reactions:

$$2NH_3 + H_2O + CO_2 \rightarrow (NH_4)_2CO_3$$

$$(NH_4)_2CO_3 + CaSO_4 \rightarrow (NH_4)_2SO_4 + CaCO_3\downarrow$$

For this purpose calcium sulphate produced as a by-product of phosphoric acid manufacture can also be employed. The chalk is a useful by-product for agricultural or other use.

3.5   Acid-base character of oxides

3.5.1   *Lewis acidity*

Non-metal oxides are not such strong Lewis acids in comparable valence states as are the corresponding fluorides or chlorides. This is perhaps surprising, in view of the comparable electronegativity of oxygen with the halogens. One reason for the low electron acceptor power of the oxides compared with the halides is the stronger ability of oxygen to donate electrons to the central atom. This can occur through association; for instance, B_2O_3 already contains

[3] Edwards, R. H. (1969), *British Chemical Engineering*, **14**, 795.

4-coordinate boron, whereas in BCl_3 boron is 3-coordinate. Another mechanism for reducing the electron acceptor character of the central atom is through π back-bonding from oxygen into empty orbitals [$(p-d)\pi$ for second- and third-row elements; $(p-p)\pi$ for boron]. Oxygen seems to be a better π donor than the halogen atoms.

In some cases the Lewis acidity of oxides is rather difficult to assess on the basis of available evidence. Phosphorus pentoxide interacts with a number of common donors such as water, ammonia, and ethers, but in all cases no simple complex is isolated, but rather the products of further reaction.

Sulphur dioxide forms a few 1:1 complexes, for example with amines (e.g. $Me_3N.SO_2$) and with halide ions of which the fluorosulphite ion, FSO_2^-, is the most stable. As might be expected, sulphur trioxide is a stronger Lewis acid than sulphur dioxide, and forms complexes with pyridine or dioxan, bases which it does not oxidize. These are useful sulphonating agents in organic chemistry. The Lewis acid properties of N_2O_4, which are significant in its solvent behaviour, are described on p. 131.

3.5.2 *Lewis basicity*

Carbon monoxide and related species. Although carbon monoxide is an extremely weak electron pair donor towards most Lewis bases, it forms complexes with certain boron acids (see p. 35) and a very wide range of transition metal compounds, the carbonyls. The bonding of carbon monoxide to transition metals involves (a) σ donation of electrons from the carbon atom to the metal, and (b) π back-donation from filled d orbitals on the metal to the π^* antibonding orbitals of carbon monoxide.

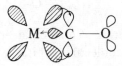

Some examples of metal carbonyl complexes are:

$$Cr(CO)_6 \quad (OC)_5Mn{-}Mn(CO)_5 \quad Fe(CO)_5 \quad Ni(CO)_4$$

Other molecules which have similar orbitals of suitable symmetry for forming transition metal complexes include NO, N_2, CS, and NS. Numerous transition metal complexes of NO, which can bind formally as NO^+ (linear M—N—O) or

93

NO⁻ (bent M—N̈—O), and of N_2 (first reported in 1964) are now being very actively studied (p. 171). A few complexes of CS, which incidentally is unstable in the free state, are known, but those of NS are not established. Some transition metal complexes of P_4O_6, e.g. $P_4O_6.Ni(CO)_3$, and of SO_2 in which the oxide acts as an electron pair donor are also known.

3.5.3 *Formation of oxo-acids and oxo-anions*

Many of the oxides of the non-metallic elements form oxo-acids or oxo-anions. The best known simple oxo-anions are listed in Fig. 3.6, where their structures are also indicated. Many polymeric oxo-anions are also formed. They are discussed on p. 109.

(i)   Oxo-anions; structural features.   The structures of the simple oxo-anions present rather regular trends in relation to the Periodic Table. Thus, the isoelectronic series of anions AO_3^{n-} (BO_3^{3-}, CO_3^{2-}, NO_3^-) of the first-row elements are planar (compare the isoelectronic molecule BF_3). This is consistent with the distribution of three σ electron pairs in space. In the nitrate ion, the negative charge is considered to be distributed over all three oxygen atoms equally; all three N—O bonds are exactly equivalent. This is not very clearly expressed in terms of resonance structures. It is necessary to write one bond as a coordinate link and one as a double bond to fulfil the requirements of the octet rule:

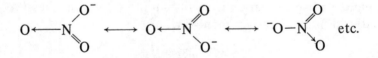

A better description is in terms of molecular orbital theory. Figure 3.7 shows the lowest lying bonding π molecular orbital, which is delocalized in a symmetrical fashion over the ion.

The nitrite ion NO_2^- is isoelectronic with ozone O_3, and likewise is bent, with a bond angle ′ONO of 115° (in crystalline sodium nitrite).

The structures of the oxo-anions of the second-row elements are all based on the tetrahedron (Fig. 3.6). The isoelectronic series AO_4^{m-} (SiO_4^{4-}, PO_4^{3-}, SO_4^{2-}, ClO_4^-) all possess regular tetrahedral symmetry. The bond lengths observed in typical compounds by X-ray diffraction are listed in Table 3.4.

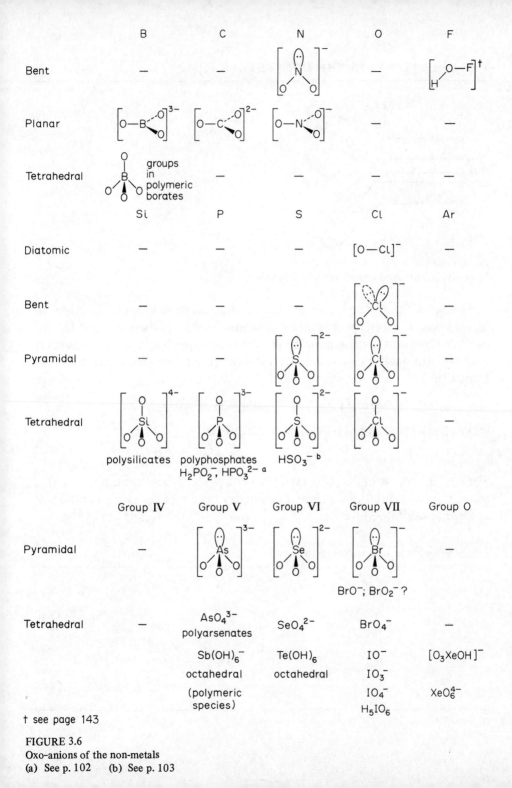

† see page 143

FIGURE 3.6
Oxo-anions of the non-metals
(a) See p. 102   (b) See p. 103

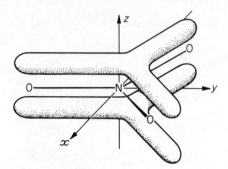

FIGURE 3.7
Lowest lying delocalized π molecular orbital in NO_3^-

The bonding in these ions may be considered, to a first approximation, to involve only the s and p orbitals of the central atom. Participation of the $3d$ orbitals is permitted on symmetry grounds, although for energetic reasons it may be only small. In T_d symmetry the valence orbitals of the central atom transform as:

$$A_1(s) + 2T_2(p_x,p_y,p_z; d_{xy},d_{yz},d_{zx}) + E(d_{z^2},d_{x^2-y^2})$$

while the twelve oxygen p orbitals transform as:

$$A_1 + 2T_2 + T_1 + E$$

The d_{xy}, d_{yz}, d_{zx} orbitals (t_2 set) of the central atom can thus interact with a set of oxygen orbitals with similar symmetry properties to give essentially σ molecular orbitals. Moreover, the $d_{x^2-y^2}$ and d_{z^2} orbitals (e set) are of the

TABLE 3.4
A—O bond lengths in some oxo-anions (pm)

BO_3^{3-}	CO_3^{2-}	NO_3^-		
138	129	122		
	SiO_4^{4-}	PO_4^{3-}	SO_4^{2-}	ClO_4^-
	163	154	149	146
		AsO_4^{3-}	SeO_4^{2-}	BrO_4^-
		176	161	161
				IO_4^-
				179

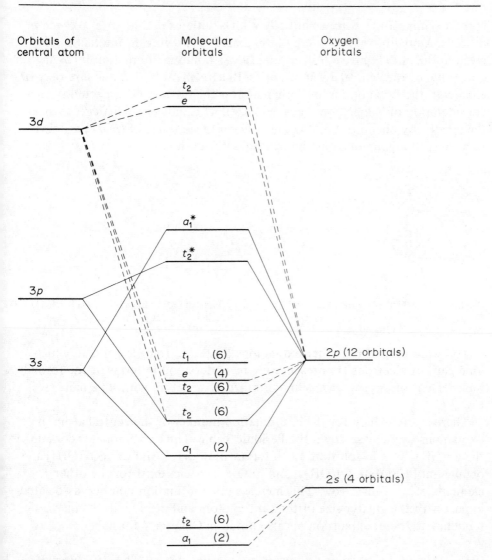

FIGURE 3.8

Qualitative molecular orbital energy level diagram for a tetrahedral anion XO_4^{n-}, where X = Si, P, S, Cl. The total number of valence electrons = $(8 - n) + 24 + n = 32$. The occupancy of the various MOs is indicated. All bonding and non-bonding orbitals are filled

correct symmetry to form essentially π MOs with a suitable set of oxygen p orbitals. A qualitative MO energy level diagram, showing $3d$ interaction, is given in Fig. 3.8. Figure 3.9 illustrates how a bonding interaction involving the d_{z^2} orbital of the central atom can arise. In agreement with a measure of $(p–d)$ character, the A—O bonds are rather shorter than would be expected from a consideration of 'single bond' covalent radii. It is, however, difficult to assess the length any chemical bond would have in the absence of $(p–d)$ participation, so such arguments must be treated with caution.

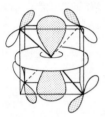

FIGURE 3.9
Overlap of d_{z^2} orbital of central atom X with oxygen p orbitals in tetrahedral anions XO_4^{n-} [Nickless, G. (Ed.) (1968), *Inorganic Sulphur Chemistry*, Elsevier, Amsterdam; Ch. 2, Cruickshank, D. W. J. and Webster, B. C., p. 29 (Fig. 2.11)]

The structures of the other oxo-anions of second-row elements in which lone pairs of electrons are present may be understood in terms of the formal replacement of oxygen atoms in a tetrahedral structure with lone pairs (see Fig. 3.6).

There is a tendency for the coordination number of the central atom in oxo-anions to increase down the Periodic Table. Thus, antimonates contain the $Sb(OH)_6^-$ ion in solution. Both tetrahedral [KIO_4 and $CsXeO_3(OH)$] and octahedral [$Te(OH)_6$, $OI(OH)_5$, and XeO_6^{4-}] species exist for the other elements of the fourth row. This increase in coordination number, associated in part with the greater size of the central atom and partly with its increased tendency to 'octet expansion', is also noted in Chapter 2 for halides.

(ii)   *Structures of some oxo-acids in the solid state.*   The structures of some crystalline oxo-acids have been studied by X-ray diffraction. Usually the hydrogen atom positions cannot be located by this technique, owing to the low scattering of hydrogen relative to all but the lightest of other atoms, and they must be inferred from the determined oxygen positions. In the case of

boric acid, however, it was possible to locate the hydrogen atoms also, and to show that they are involved in hydrogen bonds. Boric acid forms a hydrogen-bonded layer structure, and crystallizes as plates [Fig. 3.10(a)]. Crystalline orthophosphoric acid consists of molecules of approximately C_{3v} symmetry

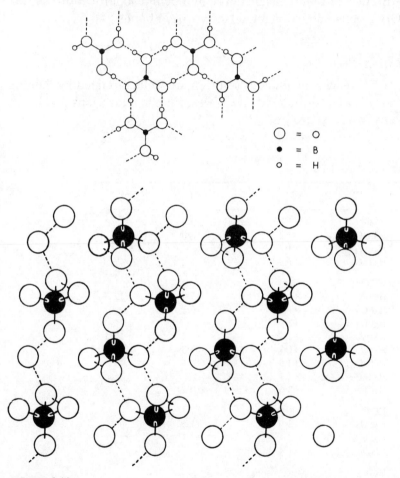

FIGURE 3.10

(a) Portion of a layer of H_3BO_3. Broken lines indicate O—H$\cdots$O hydrogen bonds

(b) The structure of orthophosphoric acid, H_3PO_4. Hydrogen-bond system shown with broken lines. The zigzag chains shown are linked by further hydrogen bonds to similar chains above and below the plane of the paper, giving a sheet structure

in which one P—O bond is significantly shorter than the other three. The molecules are linked together by hydrogen bonds into a continuous sheet structure [Fig. 3.10(b)]. Crystalline sulphuric acid and selenic acid have very similar structures, in which SO_4 or SeO_4 groups are linked in puckered layers. The crystal structure of telluric acid (in the monoclinic modification) shows discrete $Te(OH)_6$ octahedra connected by hydrogen bonds [4].

3.5.4 Acid strengths

The strengths of oxo-acids in aqueous solution are well correlated by Pauling's rules. Oxo-acids may be formulated $AO_n(OH)_m$, as the ionizations involve hydrogen atoms from OH groups.

TABLE 3.5
Dissociation constants of oxo-acids

		pK_1	pK_2	pK_3
$n = 0$	HClO	+7·2		
	H_3AsO_3	+9·2	+12·0	
	^{a} H_3BO_3	+9·2		
	H_6TeO_6	+7·8	+11·2	
$n = 1$	$HClO_2$	+2·0		
	H_3PO_4	+2·1	+7·4	+12.3
	^{a} H_3PO_3	+1·8	+6·2	
	^{a} H_3PO_2	+2		
	H_3AsO_4	+3·5	+7·2	+12·5
	^{a} H_2SO_3	+1·9	+7·3	
	H_2SeO_3	+2·6	+6·6	
	H_2TeO_3	+2·7		
	^{a} H_2CO_3	+3·6	+10·2	
$n = 2$	$HClO_3$	−1·0		
	H_2SO_4	−3·0	+1·5	
	H_2SeO_4	−3	+2·1	
	HNO_3	−1·4		
$n = 3$	$HClO_4$	very strong ca. −10		

^{a} See text.

[4] Lindquist, O. (1970), Acta Chem. Scand., 24, 3178.

The first rule states that successive dissociation constants for a polybasic acid are in the ratio:

$$K_1/K_2 \approx K_2/K_3 \approx 10^5$$

In other words, it becomes successively more difficult for a proton to ionize the greater the negative charge on the anion. This is expected on the basis of electrostatic attraction. The successive dissociation constants of orthophosphoric acid $(HO)_3PO$ given in Table 3.5 provide a good example of this rule.

The second rule relates n, the number of oxygen atoms which are not bound to hydrogen, to the strength of the acid. Thus:

$$n = 0, \text{ the acid is very weak,} \quad pK_1 \approx 7$$
$$n = 1, \text{ the acid is weak,} \quad pK_1 \approx 2$$
$$n = 2, \text{ the acid is strong,} \quad pK_1 \approx -3$$
$$n = 3, \text{ the acid is very strong,} \quad pK_1 \approx -8$$

The strength is, to a first approximation, independent of m, the number of OH groups.

The strengths of the oxo-acids of chlorine (Table 3.5) fit in very well with Pauling's second rule. Consider the ionization processes involved:

$$H-O-Cl + H_2O \rightleftharpoons H_3O^+ + {}^-O-Cl$$

$$H-O-Cl-O + H_2O \rightleftharpoons H_3O^+ + {}^{1/2}\,{}^-O-Cl-O^{1/2-}$$

$$H-O-Cl(-O)(O) + H_2O \rightleftharpoons H_3O^+ + {}^{1/3}\,{}^-O-Cl({}^{1/3}O^-)-O^{1/3-}$$

$$H-O-Cl(-O)(O)(O) + H_2O \rightleftharpoons H_3O^+ + {}^{1/4}\,{}^-O-Cl({}^{1/4}O^-)(-O^{1/4-})(O^{1/4-})$$

The increase in strength down the series may be understood as follows. First, the ionization of the proton in $HOClO_3$ is greater than in $HOCl$ on account of the inductive (electron attracting) effects of the oxygen atoms in the former. Secondly, in the anion ClO_4^- the negative charge is delocalized over four oxygen atoms, where as in ClO^- it is localized on only one. The charge density on the

101

oxygen atoms in ClO_4^- is thus much lower than in ClO^-, so that the former is less able to acquire a proton to re-form the undissociated acid.

It may appear that the predictions of Pauling's second rule do not correlate with the observed acid strengths of phosphorous acid H_3PO_3 and hypophosphorous acid H_3PO_2. The first dissociation constants of both of these acids are comparable to that of orthophosphoric acid, in which there is one oxygen atom ($n = 1$) not bound to hydrogen.

hypophosphorous acid (monobasic)   phosphorous acid (dibasic)   orthophosphoric acid (tribasic)

Hypophosphorous acid, however, is monobasic, and phosphorous acid dibasic. These facts suggest the structures shown above in which phosphorus has approximately tetrahedral coordination. The infrared and Raman spectra of various salts of these acids show sharp absorptions in the region 2280–2400 cm^{-1}, which are characteristic of P—H stretching vibrations. This is also supported by ^1H and ^{31}P ($I = \frac{1}{2}$) n.m.r. spectra and by a crystal structure determination of the anion. For example, the ^{31}P n.m.r. spectrum of phosphorous acid shows a doublet centred at -4.5 p.p.m. relative to 85% H_3PO_4 ($J_{PH} = 700$ Hz), which is consistent with (A) rather than the tautomeric form (B). The large value of the coupling constant is characteristic of hydrogen bonded directly to phosphorus.

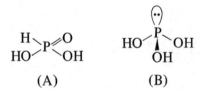

(A)   (B)

Since the infrared spectra of the esters of phosphorous acid show no evidence of P—H bonds, and the ^{31}P n.m.r. spectra exhibit single resonances in the region -125 to -140 p.p.m., chemical shifts characteristic of 3-coordinate phosphorus, they have the structure $P(OR)_3$. Phosphorous acid and hypophosphorous acid are, like phosphine, powerful reducing agents. It

102

should be noted that P—H bonds are too weakly acidic to ionize in aqueous solution to any measurable extent (cf. PH_3, p. 55).

The hydrogen sulphite ion is in tautomeric equilibrium in aqueous solution:

(at 3×10^{-3} M)

At higher concentrations these two forms associate by hydrogen bonding to give (C), which itself is in equilibrium with the pyrosulphite ion (D).

$K = \dfrac{[S_2O_5{}^{2-}]}{[HSO_3{}^-]^2} = 7 \times 10^{-2}$ mol^{-1}

The presence of S—H bonds is indicated by a band at 2532 cm^{-1} (S—H stretch) in the infrared spectrum.

Sulphur dioxide is present in aqueous solution largely in hydrated form $SO_2.xH_2O$ and only in very small amount as $(HO)_2SO$ itself. The acidity of sulphur dioxide solutions is due to the equilibrium:

$$SO_2.xH_2O \rightleftharpoons HSO_3{}^-(aq.) + H_3O^+ + (x-2)\,H_2O$$

giving the hydrogen sulphite ion, which, as we have seen, is itself involved in a series of equilibria. It is therefore pure chance that the observed acid dissociation constants for 'sulphurous acid' fit Pauling's rule.

Similarly carbon dioxide in aqueous solution is only partly present as carbonic acid $(HO)_2CO$. The rest is in loosely hydrated form. The apparent first dissociation constant of carbonic acid, assuming that all the carbon dioxide is in the form $(HO)_2CO$, is $4 \cdot 2 \times 10^{-7}$, but Pauling's rule predicts the acid to be much stronger (ca. 10^{-2}). When correction is made for the presence of loosely hydrated carbon dioxide, the true value is found to be 2×10^{-4}.

Boric acid in water acts as a Lewis acid (OH$^-$ acceptor) rather than as a proton donor:

$$B(OH)_3 + 2\,H_2O \rightleftharpoons B(OH)_4{}^- + H_3O^+ \quad (pK = 9\cdot0)$$

103

On complexing with poly-alcohols such as mannitol, the acid strength is increased. This reaction is used analytically for determination of boric acid by titration against standard sodium hydroxide or barium hydroxide solutions.

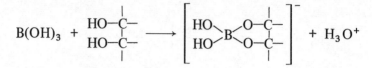

Polymeric species are also present in borate solutions (see p. 119).

As mentioned above (p. 98), the elements of the fourth row (Sb, Te, I, and Xe) show a marked tendency to form 6-coordinate species. 4-Coordinate ions such as IO_4^- and $XeO_3(OH)^-$ are known for iodine and xenon. Telluric acid is a weak dibasic acid which gives salts such as $KTeO(OH)_5$, H_2O and $K_2TeO_2(OH)_4$.

3.5.5 *Sulphuric acid as a solvent*

Sulphuric acid dissolves a wide variety of compounds which are able to ionize as electrolytes in this medium. Its good solvent properties may be attributed to its high dielectric constant, the polarity of its molecules, and its ability to form strong hydrogen bonds.

Sulphuric acid, like water or liquid ammonia, shows appreciable auto-protolysis:

$$2\ (HO)_2SO_2 \rightleftharpoons (HO)_3SO^+ + (HO)SO_3^-$$

or as usually written

$$2\ H_2SO_4 \rightleftharpoons H_3SO_4^+ + HSO_4^- \quad (pK_{ap} = 3\cdot6)$$

It also dissociates to some extent into water and sulphur trioxide. Water behaves as a base and is extensively protonated:

$$H_2O + (HO)_2SO_2 \rightleftharpoons H_3O^+ + HOSO_3^- \quad K_{H_2O} = \frac{[H_3O^+][HOSO_3^-]}{[H_2O]} = 1$$

and sulphur trioxide forms disulphuric acid, $H_2S_2O_7$ or $(HO)SO_2.O.SO_2(OH)$:

$$SO_3 + (HO)_2SO_2 \rightleftharpoons (HO)S\begin{smallmatrix}O\\ \\O\end{smallmatrix}\begin{smallmatrix}O\\ \\ \end{smallmatrix}\begin{smallmatrix}O\\ \\O\end{smallmatrix}S(OH)$$

Disulphuric acid behaves as a weak acid in sulphuric acid solution, and is partially ionized:

$$(HO)S \overset{O}{\underset{O}{\diagup}} \overset{O}{\diagdown} \overset{O}{\underset{O}{S(OH)}} + (HO)_2 SO_2 \rightleftharpoons$$

$$(HO)_3 SO^+ + \left[OS \overset{O}{\underset{O}{\diagup}} \overset{O}{\diagdown} \overset{O}{\underset{O}{S(OH)}} \right]^- \quad K = \frac{[HS_2 O_7^-][H_3 SO_4^+]}{[H_2 S_2 O_7]} = 1 \cdot 4 \times 10^{-2}$$

There are consequently several equilibria which must be considered in quantitative work in this solvent.

Owing to the high acidity of sulphuric acid most solutes behave as bases. Sulphuric acid has a levelling effect on the strengths of bases, in much the same way as liquid ammonia, acting as a strong base, levels the strengths of acids. Many substances which are acidic in aqueous solution, such as ortho-phosphoric acid, are protonated in sulphuric acid:

$$(HO)_3 PO + (HO)_2 SO_2 \rightleftharpoons HOSO_3^- + P(OH)_4^+$$

Note that bases form the hydrogen sulphate ion from the solvent. Many organic compounds (not aliphatic hydrocarbons or some aromatics) dissolve as bases but may be recovered unchanged by pouring on to ice, e.g.

$$(CH_3)_2 CO + (HO)_2 SO_2 \rightleftharpoons (CH_3)_2 \overset{+}{C}.OH + HOSO_3^-$$

Some substances behave as bases with dehydration. Thus, under more forcing conditions, dehydration of acetone, e.g. to mesitylene, can occur. Sulphuric acid is used as a solvent in studying reactive cations such as NO_2^+ and R_3C^+, which are unstable in the relatively basic solvent H_2O:

$$HONO_2 + (HO)_2 SO_2 \rightleftharpoons NO_2^+ + H_3O^+ + HOSO_3^-$$
$$Ph_3 C.OH + (HO)_2 SO_2 \rightleftharpoons Ph_3 C^+ + H_3 O^+ + HOSO_3^-$$

Boric acid dissolves in sulphuric acid, and it has been shown by cryoscopic and conductivity measurements that the reaction:

$$B(OH)_3 + 6 (HO)_2 SO_2 \rightleftharpoons [B(OSO_2 OH)_4]^- + 3 H_3 O^+ + 2 (HO)_3 SO^-$$

occurs. The acid $H[B(OSO_2.OH)_4]$ must therefore be a strong acid in the sulphuric acid system, as its anion is not solvolysed. Solutions of the acid can be obtained by using oleum, which removes H_3O^+:

$$H_3O^+ + SO_3 \rightleftharpoons (HO)_3SO^+$$

or

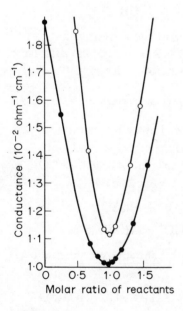

$$B(OH)_3 + 2(HO)S \overset{O}{\underset{O}{\diagdown}}\overset{O}{\diagup}\overset{O}{\underset{O}{\diagdown}}S(OH) \Longrightarrow$$

$$(HO)_3SO^+ + [B(OSO_2.OH)_4]^- + (HO)_2SO_2$$

These solutions be titrated conductimetrically with potassium hydrogen sulphate or benzoic acid, which behave as strong bases (Fig. 3.11). When electrolysed, nearly all the current in sulphuric acid solutions is carried by either the $(HO)_3SO^+$ or the $(HO)SO_3^-$ ion, both of which have very high mobilities compared with other ions. Conduction is thought to occur by a proton transfer mechanism (cf. H_3O^+ and OH^- in water).

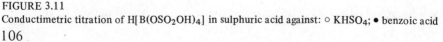

FIGURE 3.11
Conductimetric titration of H[B(OSO₂OH)₄] in sulphuric acid against: ○ KHSO₄; ● benzoic acid

3.5.6 *Fluorosulphuric acid; 'superacids'* [5]

Apart from disulphuric acid, pure fluorosulphuric acid is one of the most acidic (proton donating) media known. The electrical conductivity (κ = 1·085 x 10^{-4} ohm^{-1} cm^{-1} at 25°) is largely due to autoprotolysis:

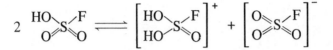

The extent of autoprotolysis is much lower than in sulphuric acid, which is an advantage when interpreting conductimetric or cryoscopic measurements. As with sulphuric acid, electrical conductivity occurs mainly by proton transfer involving the ions $(HO)_2S(O)F^+$ and O_3SF^-. A very wide variety of compounds behave as bases in this solvent; thus, nitrobenzene is a strong base while sulphuric acid is a weak base. Protonation of aromatic compounds, e.g. phenol and anisole, occurs on the ring (*para* to the oxygen substituent in the cases quoted). This is proved by the proton n.m.r. spectra of solutions of these compounds in fluorosulphuric acid (Fig. 3.12).

Addition of very strong Lewis acids such as antimony pentafluoride increases the acidity of fluorosulphuric acid even further. It is thought that the ionization:

$$SbF_5 + 2\,FSO_2(OH) \rightleftharpoons [F_5Sb(OSO_2F)]^- + [FSO_2(OH)_2]^+$$

is primarily responsible for the increased concentration of $FSO_2(OH)_2^+$, but other species are probably also present. If sulphur trioxide is added, a still stronger acid results, e.g.

$$SO_3 + SbF_5 \rightleftharpoons SbF_4(OSO_2F)$$
$$2\,SO_3 + SbF_5 \rightleftharpoons SbF_3(OSO_2F)_2$$
$$3\,SO_3 + SbF_5 \rightleftharpoons SbF_2(OSO_2F)_3 \text{ (a strong acid)}$$

$$SbF_2(OSO_2F)_3 + 2\,FSO_2(OH) \rightleftharpoons [FSO_2(OH)_2]^+ + [SbF_2(OSO_2F)_4]^-$$

The antimony pentafluoride–fluorosulphuric acid system has been widely used to study the protonation of organic compounds, especially using proton magnetic resonance spectroscopy. Sulphur dioxide is often added to reduce

[5] Gillespie, R. J. (1968), *Accounts Chem. Research*, **1**, 202; (1973), *Endeavour*, **53**, 3.

the viscosity of the medium. Another use is the formation of cationic species of the non-metallic elements, e.g. from sulphur, selenium, tellurium, and iodine, cf. p. 180.

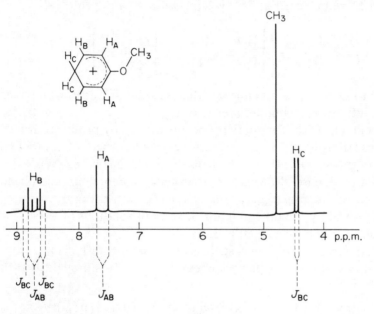

FIGURE 3.12
Proton magnetic resonance spectrum of anisole in fluorosulphuric acid–antimony pentafluoride (idealized)

3.5.7   *Basic properties of oxides*

The basic character of the oxides in aqueous solution increases down a Group while their acidic character tends to decrease. The oxides of Ge, As, Sb, and Te, for example, show some amphoteric properties; arsenious oxide dissolves in concentrated hydrochloric acid, and the volatile arsenic trichloride can be distilled from the solution in a stream of HCl, even though it is readily hydrolysed by water. Antimony(III) oxide is more basic than acidic. It dissolves in aqueous hydrochloric acid to form complex anions such as $SbCl_4^-$, which on dilution are partially hydrolysed to the insoluble oxochloride SbOCl. Similarly, solutions of tellurium dioxide in hydrochloric acid contain anions such as $TeCl_6^{2-}$. These trends are consistent with an increase in metallic character which occurs down these Groups.

3.6   Condensed oxo-acids and oxo-anions [6]

Many oxo-acids and oxo-anions polymerize to form condensed species. This is especially pronounced for weak acids such as boric, silicic, and phosphoric. In the series SiO_4^{4-}, PO_4^{3-}, SO_4^{2-}, ClO_4^{-}, the tendency to polymerization decreases. In the anions of weak acids, a high charge density would reside on the oxygen atoms. Polymerization can be considered as a means of reducing the overall charge density on the anion. For example, the dimerization of SiO_4^{4-} may formally be represented as:

$$\begin{array}{c}^-O\\{}^-O\end{array}\!\!Si\!\!\begin{array}{c}O^-\\O^-\end{array} + \begin{array}{c}^-O\\{}^-O\end{array}\!\!Si\!\!\begin{array}{c}O^-\\O^-\end{array} \longrightarrow \begin{array}{c}^-O\\{}^-O\end{array}\!\!Si\!\!-\!O\!-\!Si\!\!\begin{array}{c}O^-\\O^-\end{array} + O^{2-}$$

Further association reduces this charge density even more. It can be seen that the ways in which such condensations may occur are very numerous for silicates, where there are up to four possible sites per silicon atom. This can lead to rings or chains (SiO_4 tetrahedra sharing two corners), double chains, sheets, or three-dimensional networks. The polymerization of phosphates is less complex, since here there are three instead of four available sites per phosphorus atom. Only two of these are normally used in the formation of polyphosphates, however, perhaps because the first acid dissociation constant of phosphoric acid corresponds to a fairly strong acid, so that rings and chains result. Condensation of sulphate is unimportant. Polysulphates are broken down in aqueous solution, but disulphuric acid and trisulphuric acid are present in solutions of sulphur trioxide in sulphuric acid.

The oxo-acid species which polymerize in this way are indicated in Fig. 3.6. Further details of the chemistry of the condensed species are given in the sections which follow.

[6] Emeléus, H. J. and Anderson, J. S. (1960), *Modern Aspects of Inorganic Chemistry*, Routledge and Kegan Paul, London. Contains a useful account of polyacids and silicates.

3.6.1 *Condensed phosphates*

The structures of condensed polyphosphates are derived by the linkage of PO_4 tetrahedra through two oxygen atoms (sharing two corners). When acid monophosphates are heated, water is eliminated (condensation polymerization). The simplest example of such a process occurs when disodium hydrogen phosphate is heated and sodium pyrophosphate (sometimes called diphosphate) is formed:

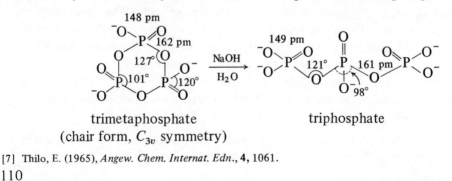

Three types of condensed phosphates [7] have been recognized:

(a) Metaphosphates; these have ring structures of composition $M^I_x(P_xO_{3x})$ where x is 3 up to at least 8.

(b) Polyphosphates; these have chain structures of composition $M^I_n H_2 P_n O_{3n+1}$ or $M^I_{n+2} P_n O_{3n+1}$, e.g. $Na_5 P_3 O_{10}$.

(c) Ultraphosphates; these contain cross-links. Unlike meta- and polyphosphates they are readily hydrolysed in neutral solution, and consequently have been much less studied. Cross-links are introduced by heating mixtures of $P_4 O_{10}$ and $NaH_2 PO_4$ above 300°.

The variety of products which are formed by heating sodium dihydrogen phosphate $NaH_2 PO_4$ is very complicated indeed. Under suitable conditions of heating, or of tempering the glasses which result on melting at above 625°, sodium trimetaphosphate is formed. This salt dissolves in water to give a neutral solution, showing that no acid groups remain. It is quantitatively converted by 2M-sodium hydroxide at room temperature into triphosphate:

trimetaphosphate
(chair form, C_{3v} symmetry)

triphosphate

[7] Thilo, E. (1965), *Angew. Chem. Internat. Edn.*, **4**, 1061.

These observations are consistent with a cyclic structure for the trimetaphos-phate anion, which is confirmed by single-crystal X-ray diffraction studies of alkali metal salts.

The reaction of copper nitrate with phosphoric acid at 400° leads selectively to copper tetrametaphosphate which is converted into the sodium salt by treatment with sodium sulphide. P_4O_{10} is hydrolysed very largely to tetra-metaphosphoric acid by ice–water, with retention of the basic structural skeleton:

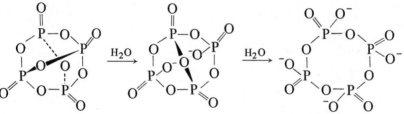

The eight-membered cyclic anion $P_4O_{12}^{4-}$ can exist in both chair and boat forms [8]. Cyclic species up to at least $P_8O_{24}^{8-}$ have been characterized [9]. The bonding in these and related systems is discussed in Chapter 6. Consider-able $(p-d)\pi$ bonding both within the ring and to terminal oxygen atoms is likely. The exocyclic P=O bonds in metaphosphates (ca. 148 pm) are shorter than those within the ring (162 pm), but both are less than the estimated P—O single bond length (172 pm).

Chain polyphosphates are formed by heating mixtures of Na_2HPO_4 and NaH_2PO_4. The individual species can be separated by paper or ion-exchange chromatography. They are rather stable in neutral solution but are slowly broken down in a stepwise fashion in acid. In addition, chains longer than $n = 5$ can degrade via formation of tri- or tetra-metaphosphate. The chain length of a polyphosphate (or the average chain length in a mixture) can be determined by titration of the residual strong acid groups:

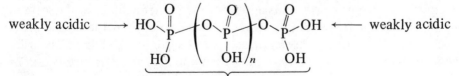

strongly acidic groups

[8] Koster, D. A. and Wagner, A. J. (1970), *J. Chem. Soc.* (A), 435.
[9] Schulke, U. (1968), *Z. Anorg. Chem.*, **360**, 231.

Polyphosphates with infinite chains are also known and have been investigated by X-ray diffraction. Figure 3.13 shows some of the ways in which the PO_4 tetrahedra are arranged in these chains. In $(NaPO_3)_z$ (Kurrol salt), for example, the chains have a helical form.

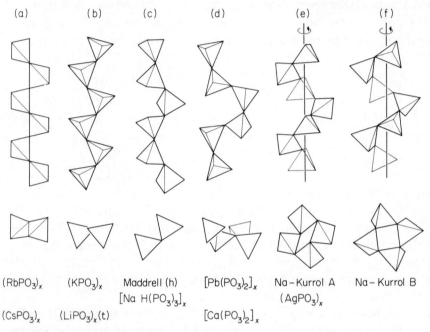

| (a) | (b) | (c) | (d) | (e) | (f) |

$(RbPO_3)_x$ $(KPO_3)_x$ Maddrell (h) $[Pb(PO_3)_2]_x$ Na–Kurrol A   Na–Kurrol B

$[Na\ H(PO_3)_3]_x$ $(AgPO_3)_x$

$(CsPO_3)_x$ $(LiPO_3)_x(t)$ $[Ca(PO_3)_2]_x$

FIGURE 3.13

The six known types of anion chains present in high-molecular weight crystalline polyphosphates. Above: vertical projections; below: projections along the chain axis [Thilo, E. (1965), *Angew. Chem. Internat. Edn.*, **4**, 1061]

Oligo- and high molecular weight polyphosphates are able to bind cations such as Mg^{2+} and Ca^{2+} and thus keep them in solution in the presence of precipitants. This property finds application commercially in water softening and in detergents. Heavy-duty powder detergents contain at least one-third in weight of sodium tripolyphosphate as a water softening and dirt dispersal agent. It has been suggested that more than one PO_4 group is involved in binding a cation, possibly forming stable chelates. The excessive discharge of phosphates into water can lead to extremely active algal growth which has proved a serious pollution hazard in certain lakes.

Phosphate esters play an essential role in many biological processes [10]. During the oxidation of foodstuffs in the cell, some of the energy produced is conserved as adenosine triphosphate (ATP), which is formed from adenosine diphosphate via enzyme catalysed pathways. Adenosine triphosphate is involved, for example, in the biosynthesis of macromolecules such as fats, proteins, polysaccharides, and nucleic acids, in transport of solutes *in vivo* against concentration gradients, and in muscle contraction. The net chemical change which it undergoes in such processes corresponds to a hydrolysis:

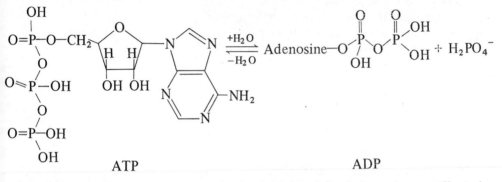

ATP   ADP

but this equation represents merely the initial and final stages in complicated cycles. The maximum work available from such a process is related to the standard free energy change ΔG° and the activities of the various reactants and products, but is thought to be at least 28 kJ mol^{-1} and could be as much as 50 kJ mol^{-1}.

The way in which ATP is involved in muscular contraction, for example, is not yet understood in detail. Muscle contains principally two contractile proteins myosin and actin which, when activated by Ca^{2+} and Mg^{2+} ions respectively, catalyse the hydrolysis of ATP. In the course of the reaction cycle, one or other of these proteins is considered to become phosphorylated. The regeneration of ATP from ADP and monophosphate in muscle is catalysed by the enzyme creatine kinase. The phosphate transfer reaction:

$$ADP + PCr \rightleftharpoons ATP + Cr$$

has an equilibrium constant of 20 or more, and is complete within 60 ms. Thus, during mild exercise the ATP concentration hardly falls.

[10] Lehninger, A. L. (1965), *Bioenergetics*, Benjamin, New York.

Nucleic acids RNA and DNA consist of a large number of nucleotide units linked through phosphate ester bonds. Discussion of these aspects of phosphate chemistry can be found in textbooks of biochemistry or organic chemistry.

3.6.2 *Polyarsenates and polyarsenites*

Polyarsenates, analogous to polyphosphates, are formed on heating $NaH_2AsO_4.H_2O$. Diarsenates, triarsenates, and polyarsenates have been recognized, but they all are hydrolysed to orthoarsenate in water. Mixed arsenatophosphates are formed by heating NaH_2AsO_4 and NaH_2PO_4 together. The products can be studied by hydrolysis. As—O—As and As—O—P links are rapidly destroyed, whereas P— -P links are stable:

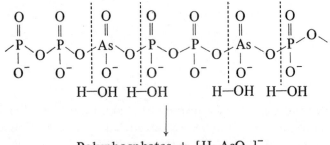

$$\text{Polyphosphates} + [H_2AsO_4]^-$$

Polymetaarsenites such as $(NaAsO_2)_n$ contain long chains of pyramidal $:AsO_3$ groups sharing two corners.

3.6.3 *Silicates*

A very large part of silicon–oxygen chemistry is concerned with the chemistry of the silicates. This is such a wide and specialized topic that it is not possible, through lack of space, to discuss it in any detail. The structures of metal silicates can be classified, like those of the phosphates, in terms of the linkage of SiO_4 tetrahedra through vertices. In Fig. 3.14 some basic silicate structures are summarized.

Silicate minerals are seldom really homogeneous. Moreover, isomorphous replacement of one element by others of similar size is widespread. This may occur between species of the same formal charge (e.g. Fe^{2+} or Ca^{2+} for Mg^{2+};

114

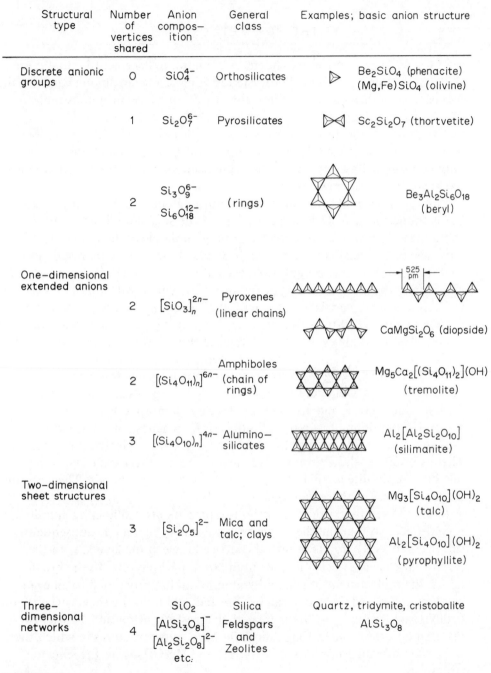

Structural type	Number of vertices shared	Anion composition	General class	Examples; basic anion structure
Discrete anionic groups	0	SiO_4^{4-}	Orthosilicates	Be_2SiO_4 (phenacite) $(Mg,Fe)SiO_4$ (olivine)
	1	$Si_2O_7^{6-}$	Pyrosilicates	$Sc_2Si_2O_7$ (thortvetite)
	2	$Si_3O_9^{6-}$ $Si_6O_{18}^{12-}$	(rings)	$Be_3Al_2Si_6O_{18}$ (beryl)
One-dimensional extended anions	2	$[SiO_3]_n^{2n-}$	Pyroxenes (linear chains)	525 pm $CaMgSi_2O_6$ (diopside)
	2	$[(Si_4O_{11})_n]^{6n-}$	Amphiboles (chain of rings)	$Mg_5Ca_2[(Si_4O_{11})_2](OH)$ (tremolite)
	3	$[(Si_4O_{10})_n]^{4n-}$	Alumino-silicates	$Al_2[Al_2Si_2O_{10}]$ (silimanite)
Two-dimensional sheet structures	3	$[Si_2O_5]^{2-}$	Mica and talc; clays	$Mg_3[Si_4O_{10}](OH)_2$ (talc) $Al_2[Si_4O_{10}](OH)_2$ (pyrophyllite)
Three-dimensional networks	4	SiO_2 $[AlSi_3O_8]^-$ $[Al_2Si_2O_8]^{2-}$ etc.	Silica; Feldspars and Zeolites	Quartz, tridymite, cristobalite $AlSi_3O_8$

FIGURE 3.14
Basic structures of silicates

Fe^{3+} for Al^{3+}) or of different charge. A common replacement is aluminium for silicon. Compensation is made for the resulting change in anion charge by the inclusion of additional cations into the lattice, or by isomorphous replacement of cations by others of higher charge, e.g. Ca^{2+} for Na^+.

The simplest silicate structures are orthosilicates, in which discrete SiO_4 units may be recognized. In olivine $(Mg,Fe)SiO_4$, the metal atoms are octahedrally coordinated by oxygen, while in phenacite Be_2SiO_4 the beryllium atoms are in a tetrahedral environment.

Linkage of two SiO_4 tetrahedral units through one corner is rather rare, but is found in the $Si_2O_7^{6-}$ ion which occurs in $Sc_2Si_2O_7$ (thortvetite). Further condensations can lead either to linear polyanions, as in the pyroxene minerals, or to rings, as in benitoite or beryl. These species are respectively analogous to the linear polyphosphates and to the cyclic metaphosphates. In amphiboles there is a doubling of the pyroxene chain. All amphiboles contain OH^- groups, which are associated with the cations in the crystal. Some of these minerals are fibrous, i.e. cleavage along the length of the chains occurs easily. This is not always so, however, since the interionic attraction of the chain anions and the metal cations situated between them is often appreciable.

Further cross-linking leads to two-dimensional sheets; this is found in the micas and in talc. Generally two of these $Si_2O_5^{2-}$ sheets are superimposed to form a double layer, and are held together by isomorphous replacement of silicon by aluminium (as in pyrophillite) or by magnesium (as in talc). OH^- ions also replace O^{2-}, so that the double layers achieve electrical neutrality. These substances show pronounced cleavage parallel to the sheets, which in talc or pyrophyllite are held together only by hydrogen bonds. This accounts for the softness of these materials.

In micas the process of isomorphous replacement of silicon by aluminium is continued, so that the sheets here are anionic in character. Consequently cations such as K^+ are taken into the lattice between the layers, with the result that cleavage occurs less readily than in pyrophyllite. In the brittle micas, the replacement of silicon by aluminium has proceeded to an even greater extent, and Ca^{2+} ions can be inserted, and hold the sheets even more firmly together owing to the increased electrostatic attraction, so that the material becomes brittle. Clays similarly have layer structures in which there is considerable incorporation of $Al(OH)_3$ and $Mg(OH)_2$ into the silicate structures.

116

   Three-dimensional networks are found in the feldspars and the zeolites. These are again aluminosilicates, the anions of which have ideal compositions such as $AlSi_3O_8^-$ (orthoclase) and $Al_2Si_2O_8^{2-}$ (celsian and anorthite). Large cations such as Na^+, K^+, and Ca^{2+} are present in the holes in the lattices in order to reach electrical neutrality. The zeolites have more open structures than the feldspars. The channels through some zeolite structures are wide enough to accommodate small molecules such as CO_2, H_2O, N_2, or the noble gases. They can be used to separate them chromatographically; these zeolites are thus sometimes called 'molecular sieves' [11]. They can be used to separate straight chain paraffin hydrocarbons from their branched isomers. The former can enter the channels in a suitable 'molecular sieve' and are retained, whereas the bulkier branched chain hydrocarbons are not.

   It has been suggested that the original crystallization of silicate minerals from the melt or magma followed the order of increasing structural complexity of the silicate ions described above. This is summarized in Table 3.6. Basic

TABLE 3.6
Crystallization of silicate minerals

Temperature	Minerals crystallizing	Comments
above 1200°	Refractory oxides, Fe_3O_4, spinels	Silica content of fluid melt increasing
ca. 1200°	Orthosilicates e.g. olivine	
ca. 1000°	Pyroxenes	
	Amphiboles	Viscosity of melt rises and water content
	Granites (containing feldspars and micas)	(above critical point) rises; pressure rises
ca. 500°	Zeolites	Aqueous solution
	(Hydrothermal crystallization)	

[11] Breck, D. W. (1964), *J. Chem. Educ.*, **41**, 678.

117

oxides such as MgO and FeO were concentrated in the early crystalline fractions. Consequently the silica content of the melt increased as crystallization proceeded and successive polymerization to linear and then to sheet structures occurred. Water vapour assisted condensation of the silicate groups, and many rocks such as micas deposited at this stage contain OH groups. In the final stages of the crystallization a supercritical aqueous phase was present (hydrothermal crystallization) and the open-work structures of the zeolites resulted through interaction between this aqueous solution and crystals previously deposited [12].

3.6.4 *Borate structures* [13]

The range of structures adopted by borates in the solid state includes both trigonal planar (BO_3) and tetrahedral (BO_4) units, and they often occur together within a single structure. As expected, the mean B—O bond length in trigonal units (137 pm) is less than that in tetrahedral units (148 pm).

The most abundant boron mineral is the borosilicate tourmaline. The bulk of commercial boron, however, is obtained from minerals deposited by the evaporation of salt lakes. Boron becomes concentrated in the aqueous phase in the weathering of rocks. Moreover, boric acid is volatile in steam, and is present in vapours emerging from volcanos and from hot springs.

The most important deposits of borates in the United States are in California and consist mainly of tincal $Na_2B_4O_7.10\ H_2O$ together with some kernite $Na_2B_4O_7,4\ H_2O$. In Europe, colemanite $Ca_2B_6O_{11}.5\ H_2O$, found in Turkey, is the main source.

The thermal dehydration of orthoboric acid leads successively to three forms of metaboric acid (III, II, and I) and finally to boric oxide itself. Forms III and II are metastable with respect to I, but the rates of interconversion are rather slow. Their structures are all based on B_3O_3 rings. In form III planar $B_3O_3(OH)_3$ units are held together by hydrogen bonds. Form II has one tetrahedral boron atom per ring through which the cyclic units are linked into chains, and in form I all three boron atoms are tetrahedrally coordinated.

In a few metal borates only triangular BO_3 units are present. Discrete

[12] Barrer, R. M. (1966), *Chem. in Britain*, **2**, 380.
[13] Muetterties, E. L. (Ed.) (1967), *The Chemistry of Boron and its Compounds*, Wiley, New York.

planar BO_3^{3-} ions are found in borates of the lanthanides MBO_3. These compounds are isostructural with calcite or aragonite $CaCO_3$. In the pyroborate ion, which occurs in $Mg_2B_2O_5$ and $Co_2B_2O_5$, two triangular BO_3 units share a corner. Chains of BO_3 units, similarly linked, are found in calcium metaborate (see Fig. 3.15). A common feature of most of the structures of metal borates is the six-membered B_3O_3 ring. This unit is found in potassium metaborate. In the borax anion, two such rings are linked through a common B—O—B unit. Another way in which two rings can join, through a tetrahedrally coordinated boron atom, is illustrated by the structure of the pentaborate anion. Considerable distortion of the rings from planarity occurs when they contain tetrahedrally coordinated boron atoms. Linkage of rings through BO_4 groups in this way can lead to extended structures. There may be one, two, or sometimes three tetrahedral sites within any ring, so that chains, sheets, or three-dimensional networks can be built up. In crystalline boron phosphate BPO_4, which is isomorphous with cristobalite, a form of silica, all the boron and phosphorus atoms have tetrahedral coordination of oxygen. An amorphous low-temperature form of boron phosphate finds application as a heterogeneous acid catalyst for the hydration of alkenes to alcohols or for the dehydration of amides to nitriles.

Borates are used extensively in the production of borosilicate glass (e.g. Pyrex) [14, 15]. Another major consumption is in the manufacture of sodium peroxoborate for the detergent industry (see p. 218). At present about 300 000 tons per annum are consumed in this latter way [16].

In strongly basic aqueous borate solutions the principal species is the tetrahedral anion $B(OH)_4^-$. As the pH is lowered, polymeric species are formed, especially in concentrated solutions. A cyclic trimer is thought to be an important component in these mixtures:

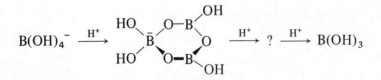

[14] Dislich, H. (1971), *Angew. Chem. Internat. Edn.*, **10**, 363. Production of glasses by hydrolysis and condensation of metal alkoxide complexes.

[15] Jones, G. O. (Ed.) (1969), *Glass*, Methuen, London.

[16] Thompson, R. (1971), *Chem. in Britain*, **7**, 140. Industrial aspects of boron chemistry.

Trigonal planar BO₃ units only

Discrete BO_3^{3-} ions: LaBO₃

Two BO₃ groups linked: pyroborates

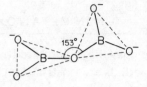

Chains

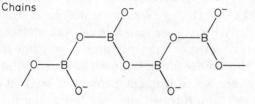

e.g. calcium metaborate

Rings

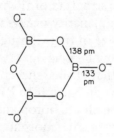

e.g. potassium metaborate

Rings linked through tetrahedral BO₄ groups

One tetrahedrally coordinated B atom

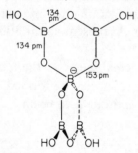

Pentaborate ion as in $K[B_5O_6(OH)_4]2H_2O$

Two tetrahedrally coordinated B atoms

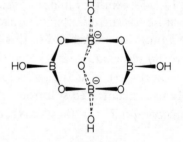

Borax $[B_4O_5(OH)_4]^{2-}$

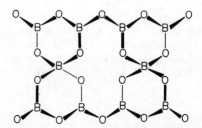

further condensation

FIGURE 3.15
Some borate structures

3.7   Redox reactions of oxo-acids and oxo-anions [17]

Reference to Fig. 3.4 shows that there is an alternation in oxide stability on descending Groups V–VII. Especially marked is the variation in the stability of the Group valence oxide species relative to the (Group $-$ 2) valence species. A thermodynamic measure of these relative stabilities in aqueous solution is given by the redox potentials for couples such as $SO_4^{2-},4H^+/H_2SO_3.H_2O$ or $SeO_4^{2-},4H^+/H_2SeO_3.H_2O$. These (referred to acid solution, $a_{H^+} = 1$), are plotted in Fig. 3.16 against the row of the Periodic Table for the Groups VB to VIIB. The more positive the value of the redox potential the more strongly oxidizing is the Group valence oxo-acid species.

First, across any Period the stability of the oxo-acid species decreases with the decrease in polarity of the A—O bonds. Secondly, the higher valence oxo-acids of the third-row elements, viz. arsenic, selenic, and perbromic, are very much stronger oxidizing agents than the corresponding oxo-acids of the second-row elements, phosphoric, sulphuric, and perchloric. Thus, phosphoric acid and phosphates have no oxidizing properties, whereas arsenic acid and arsenates are moderately effective. Again, while sulphuric acid and sulphates do not generally act as oxidizing agents (except sometimes the concentrated acid), selenic acid is quite powerfully oxidizing. Tetrahedral species such as AsO_4^{3-}, SeO_4^{2-}, or ClO_4^-, however, react rather slowly relative to species which contain lone pairs of electrons such as $:ClO_3^-$.

3.7.1   *Redox equilibria of halogen oxo-acids*

Much of the chemistry of halogen–oxygen compounds relates to redox equilibria in aqueous solution. The data are well summarized in terms of oxidation state diagrams. Figure 3.17 shows the oxidation state diagram for the halogens in basic ($a_{OH^-} = 1$) solution. This diagram is constructed by plotting the volt equivalent of a compound or ion against the formal oxidation state of the element in that species. The volt equivalent is defined as the product of the oxidation state and the redox potential relative to the element in its standard state.

[17] Phillips, C. S. G. and Williams, R. J. P. (1965), *Inorganic Chemistry*, Vol. I, Clarendon Press, Oxford. Several relevant sections on oxygen and oxides (Ch. 13, 14), oxidation state diagrams (Ch. 9), etc.

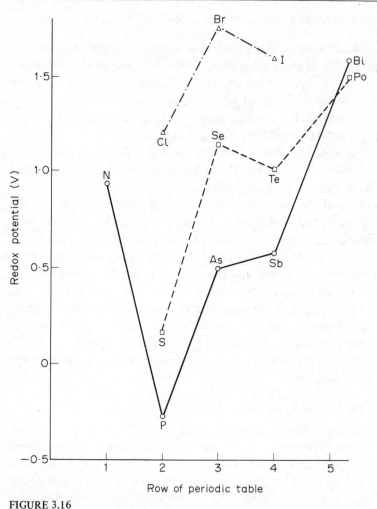

FIGURE 3.16
Redox potentials for couples
(Group valence oxo-acid)/(Group $-$ 2 valence oxo-acid) in acid solution, $a_{H^+} = 1$

The gradient of the line joining any two points on the diagram is equal to the redox potential of the couple formed by the species which the points represent. Thus, any couple will oxidize any other couple for which the slope is *less* than that of the first. By comparing the relevant slopes, therefore, it is possible to predict the direction of a reaction involving any two species. Of course, this will tell us nothing about the rate of the reaction, but only if it is thermodynamically feasible. Perchloric acid and perchlorates, for example, are quite strong oxidizing agents, but their reactions are often sluggish compared with those of chlorate or hypochlorite.

When three oxidation states of an element lie approximately on a straight line, an equilibrium involving all three species will be set up. When the middle

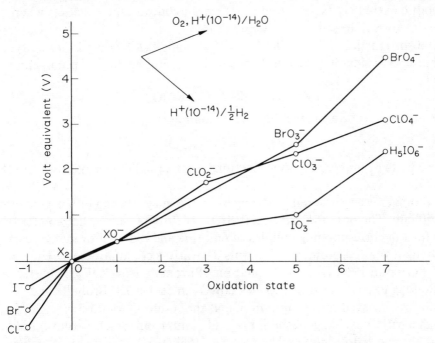

FIGURE 3.17
Oxidation state diagram for the halogens in basic solution, $a_{OH^-} = 1$

component in the diagram lies below the line joining the outer two, it is stable with respect to disproportionation, while if it lies above this line it is expected to disproportionate. Thus, in alkaline solution, X_2 disproportionates to X^- and XO^-, and this reaction is especially favoured for chlorine. The equilibrium constants for the reactions:

$$X_2 + 2\, OH^- \rightleftharpoons X^- + XO^- + H_2O$$

are X = Cl, 7.5×10^{15}; X = Br, 2×10^8; and X = I, 30.

123

The diagram also shows that XO^- lies above the lines joining X^- and XO_3^- for all three halogens. Hypohalites should therefore disproportionate to halide and halate. This reaction is slow at room temperature for OCl^-, and alkaline hypochlorite solutions can be stored for long periods; they are used as bleaches and disinfectants. Chlorates are produced in good yield, however, by heating to about 75°. The disproportionation of hypobromite is faster, and that of hypoiodite extremely fast, so that iodate and iodide are the products when iodine dissolves in base at room temperature.

The disproportionation of ClO_3^- to ClO_4^- and Cl^- is favoured thermodynamically, but is very slow in solution. It occurs on careful heating of potassium chlorate:

$$4 \, KClO_3 \rightarrow KCl + 3 \, KClO_4$$

At higher temperature the perchlorate decomposes:

$$KClO_4 \rightarrow KCl + 2 \, O_2$$

The products of numerous other reactions can be predicted similarly from the diagram.

Perbromate is a considerably stronger oxidizing agent than either perchlorate or periodate. The potential $BrO_4, 2H^+/BrO_3^-$ (1·76 V) is somewhat greater than those for the corresponding couples of chlorine and iodine. For many years it was thought that perbromic acid and its derivatives could not exist. They were first reported in 1968 from the oxidation of bromate with XeF_2. A better procedure is to pass fluorine into 1M-NaBrO$_3$ in 5M-NaOH. Bromate and fluoride are removed by precipitation, and the resulting solution is passed through a cation exchange resin in the acid form, from which a solution of perbromic acid $HBrO_4$ elutes. The 6M-acid (55% $HBrO_4$) seems to be stable indefinitely at room temperature [18].

In spite of the high redox potential of perbromate, it is a sluggish oxidant at room temperature in dilute solution, reacting only very slowly, for example, with bromide or iodide.

Potassium perbromate is thermally remarkably stable. It decomposes in two stages as follows:

$$KBrO_4 \xrightarrow[\text{exothermic}]{275-285°} KBrO_3 \longrightarrow KBr + \tfrac{3}{2} O_2$$
$$+ \tfrac{1}{2} O_2$$

[18] Appleman, E. H. (1969), *Inorg. Chem.*, 8, 223.

Its resistance to thermal decomposition indicates that, once formed, the ion has an appreciable kinetic stability. The difficulty in synthesizing perbromate also seems to be associated with a high activation energy for its formation.

Periodic acid is used in organic chemistry for the specific oxidative cleavage of 1,2-diols and related compounds. It has proved valuable in structure determination of natural products, particularly carbohydrates and nucleic acids. The oxidation of 1,2-diols to form aldehydes or ketones is considered to go through a cyclic intermediate:

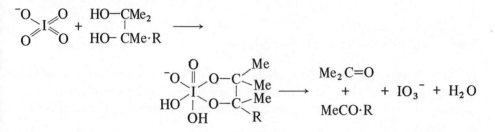

Knowledge of the aqueous solution chemistry of astatine [19] is based almost entirely on tracer studies, owing to the instability of all isotopes of this element; the longest lived, ^{210}At, has a half-life of only 8·3 hours. The following species have been detected:

$$AtO_4^- \longrightarrow AtO_3^- \xrightarrow{1\cdot5\,V} HOAt \xrightarrow{1\cdot0\,V} At \xrightarrow{0\cdot3\,V} At^-$$

The potentials of the various couples have been estimated by observing whether or not reagents of known oxidizing power effect oxidation. For example, HOAt or AtO$^-$ is produced by oxidizing astatine with bromine. Oxidation of the element with hypochlorite yields an ion which is probably AtO_3^-, as it is carried by IO_3^-. Formation of perastatate AtO_4^- by oxidation of astatine with XeF_2 or anodically has recently been reported.

Xenates and perxenates (see p. 146) are very powerful oxidizing agents indeed. They are both thermodynamically unstable to reduction through the oxidation of water. Perxenates oxidize water fairly rapidly, but the reaction of xenate is very slow, presumably owing to a high activation energy barrier,

[19] Nefedov, V. D., Norseyev, Yu. V., Toropuva, M. A. and Khalkin, V. A. (1968), *Russ. Chem. Rev.*, **37**, 87.

which arises because there are no stable intermediate oxidation states of xenon between Xe(VI) and Xe, through which the reaction can pass. Oxidation potentials for xenon couples are:

$$Xe \xrightarrow{\text{2·10} \pm \text{0·01 V}} XeO_3 \xrightarrow{\text{2·3 V}} H_4XeO_6 \quad \text{(acid solution)}$$

$$Xe \xrightarrow{\text{1·24} \pm \text{0·01 V}} HOXeO_3^- \xrightarrow{\text{0·9 V}} HXeO_6{}^{3-} \quad \text{(basic solution)}$$

$$\qquad\qquad\quad \text{xenate} \qquad\qquad \text{perxenate}$$

3.8 Volatile oxides and their derivatives

In this section, aspects of oxide chemistry which are not covered in preceding general sections of this chapter are discussed. Many of these topics concern monomeric or low molecular weight oxides and sulphides and their simple derivatives.

3.8.1 *Vapour phase oxide species of boron and silicon*

The predominant species in the vapour of boric oxide is the molecule B_2O_3, which probably has a V-shaped structure. Reduction of boric oxide with boron at high temperatures yields B_2O_2 (p. 241).

It has been suggested that the green colour which is characteristic of flames which contain boron is due to a radical species BO_2.

When a mixture of silicon and silica is heated to above 1200°, gaseous silicon monoxide is formed. It has been shown by mass spectrometry that, in addition to SiO, dimeric and higher polymeric species are present in the vapour. The vapours over heated silica also contain these species. Infrared spectra of the gaseous species trapped in an argon matrix at 15 K show the presence of monomeric SiO and oligomeric molecules $(SiO)_n$ (where n = 2 to 4). The dimers probably have a cyclic structure. Condensed silicon monoxide is metastable and disproportionates slowly above 100° to silicon and silica. It may contain Si—Si bonds, since it yields catenated silanes (see p. 192) on treatment with aqueous hydrofluoric acid.

When silica is heated using a plasma gas containing hydrogen, silicon monoxide volatilizes rapidly at temperatures above 2000 K. The vapours leaving the furnace are reoxidized with jets of air, and the very fine powder is rapidly cooled and collected. Such powders have a very high surface area, each particle being only about 10 nm across. A layer of Si—OH groups on the surface gives the particles useful thixotropic properties. In dispersion in a non-polar liquid the silica particles aggregate by hydrogen bonding to form a gel, which is broken down by stirring. This finds application in paints and polishes.

3.8.2 Nitrogen oxides

The oxides of nitrogen, together with the structures of the most stable forms, are listed in Fig. 3.18. Other isomers, where they exist, are mentioned in the text.

Representations of the bonding in compounds containing N—O bonds are often confusing. The octet rule suggests that only $2s$ and $2p$ orbitals of nitrogen can be used in bonding (to any significant extent), and that eight electrons in the valence shell of nitrogen are the maximum. Attempts to depict the bonding using valence bond structures lead in most cases to several resonance forms. For example, N_2O_3 may be represented as:

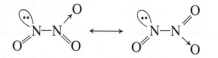

This accounts qualitatively for the slightly longer N—O bond in the NO_2 part of the molecule, but the difference seems too small. Also, the very long N—N central bonds in N_2O_3 and N_2O_4 are difficult to explain (cf. N—N 147 pm in hydrazine). Molecular orbital calculations have been performed on some of these molecules, but the bonding is still not clearly understood.

The concept of formal oxidation state, although useful when discussing redox potentials between different oxide species, is often a source of confusion when bonding is considered. Oxidation, in the sense of addition of oxygen, is, of course, involved across the series:

$$N_2O_3 \xrightarrow{\hat{O}} N_2O_4 \xrightarrow{\hat{O}} N_2O_5$$
$$\quad 3 \qquad\qquad 4 \qquad\qquad 5 \quad \text{(formal oxidation state of nitrogen)}$$

The bonding of the NO_2 group, however, in all three compounds is very similar, and there is therefore no reason at all to find '5-valent' nitrogen a problem in N_2O_5.

127

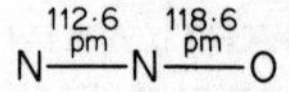

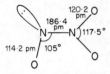

N—N—O N_2O Nitrous oxide   Linear; isoelectronic with N_3^-, CO_2 etc.

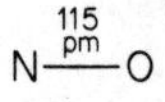

N—O   NO   Nitric oxide   odd–electron molecule

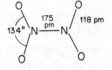

N_2O_3 Dinitrogen trioxide   anhydride of nitrous acid

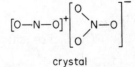

Nitrogen dioxide   Dinitrogen tetroxide

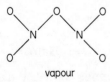

vapour   crystal   anhydride of nitric acid

Dinitrogen pentoxide

FIGURE 3.18
Oxides of nitrogen

(i)   *Nitrous oxide.*   Nitrous oxide is usually prepared by thermal decomposition of molten ammonium nitrate at 200–300°. Kinetic studies give an activation energy of 206 kJ mol^{-1} for the uncatalysed decomposition. The mechanism is complex but involves NO_2^+, formed by the autoprotolysis of nitric acid, as a key intermediate, viz.

$$NH_4NO_3 \rightleftharpoons NH_3 + HNO_3$$

$$2\,HNO_3 \rightleftharpoons NO_2^+ + H_2O + NO_3^-$$

$$NO_2^+ + NH_3 \rightarrow [H_3N.NO_2]^+ \rightarrow N{-}N{-}O + H_2O$$

nitramide
cation

It is thought that the N—N bond of N_2O is formed via nitramide as an intermediate.

Nitrous oxide can support combustion, and is used as an anaesthetic. It has a linear structure and is isoelectronic with carbon dioxide. Recently it has been shown to form a complex $[Ru(NH_3)_5N_2O]^{2+}$ analogous to $[Ru(NH_3)_5N_2]^{2+}$. This aspect of its chemistry has been little investigated, but may prove to be a fruitful field of research.

Nitrous oxide is *formally* the anhydride of hyponitrous acid [20] $HO.N{=}N.OH$; cf. CO as the formal anhydride of formic acid, $NaOH + CO \rightarrow Na(HCO_2)$. The equilibrium is very unfavourable to acid formation; a pressure of 10^{27} atm N_2O is necessary to form 0.001M-hyponitrous acid solution. Isotopic labelling by ^{18}O indicates that the reaction of nitrous oxide with water is very slow indeed. The hydrogen hyponitrite ion, however, decomposes to nitrous oxide in the pH range 4–14.

(ii)   *Nitric oxide.*   Nitric oxide is an odd-electron molecule. Molecular orbital calculations and the photoelectron spectrum show that the bonding is similar to that in N_2 (p. 13) with the additional electron occupying a π^* orbital. The magnetic moment varies appreciably with temperature. The ground state of the molecule ($^2\Pi_{1/2}$) lies only about 1.5 kJ mol^{-1} below an excited state ($^2\Pi_{3/2}$), which is thus significantly populated even well below room temperature (kT at 300 K is about 2.5 kJ mol^{-1}).

[20] Hughes, M. N. (1968), *Quart. Rev.*, **22**, 1.

Studies of the vibrational spectra of nitric oxide trapped in noble gas matrices at ca. 15 K have shown the presence of dimeric species. The most stable form is *cis*-ONNO, with C_{2v} symmetry, but a *trans* form is also found [21]. Similar association probably occurs in pure solid NO. There is some evidence for the presence of loose dimers (dissociation energy ~8 kJ mol^{-1}) in low concentration in the vapour at the boiling point.

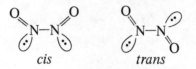

cis   *trans*

Nitric oxide fairly readily loses an electron (I.P. 9·23 eV), e.g. under photo-ionization, to give NO$^+$. Salts of this cation can be formed by treating nitrosyl halides with Lewis acids, e.g.

$$ClNO + SbCl_5 \rightarrow NO^+ SbCl_6^-$$

The NO stretching frequency in nitrosonium salts is much higher (ν_{NO} 2150–2400 cm^{-1}) than in free nitric oxide (ν_{NO} 1840 cm^{-1}), consistent with the formation of a stronger bond in NO$^+$ on removal of the electron from an anti-bonding orbital.

The industrial preparation of nitric oxide by oxidation of ammonia is discussed on p. 89. In the laboratory it can be made by reduction of acidified nitrite by iodide or by ferrous ion in aqueous solution:

$$NO_2^- + 2 H^+ + Fe^{2+} \rightarrow Fe^{3+} + H_2O + NO$$

(iii)   *Dinitrogen trioxide.*   This oxide is prepared by mixing NO and NO$_2$ (N$_2$O$_4$) at low temperatures. The liquid (m.p. $-100°$) has an intense cobalt blue colour. It dissociates in the liquid and gas phases to NO and NO$_2$; in fact, only 0·5% N$_2$O$_3$ is present in the vapour at $-78°/10$ torr, conditions under which its structure was determined by microwave spectroscopy [22].

$$N_2O_3 \rightleftharpoons NO + NO_2 \quad (\Delta H_{diss} = 39·7 \text{ kJ mol}^{-1})$$

Although the N—N bond is weak, and even longer than in N$_2$O$_4$ (Fig. 3.18), there is a barrier to internal rotation of about 30 kJ mol^{-1}. An unstable form

[21] Guillory, W. A. and Hunter, C. E. (1969), *J. Chem. Phys.*, **50**, 3516.
[22] Brattain, A. H., Cox, A. P. and Kuczkowski, R. L. (1969), *Trans. Faraday Soc.*, **65**, 1963.

ONONO is thought to be present in the solid. It may also be an intermediate in the rapid exchange of labelled nitrogen which occurs when NO and NO_2 are mixed in the gas phase:

$$NO + {}^{15}NO_2 \rightleftharpoons ON{-}O{-}{}^{15}NO \rightleftharpoons NO_2 + {}^{15}NO$$

N_2O_3 is the anhydride of nitrous acid. Nitrite ion is the sole product when it is neutralized with aqueous alkali.

(iv)   Dinitrogen tetroxide.   This oxide exists in a dimeric and an odd-electron monomeric form:

$$N_2O_4 \rightleftharpoons 2\,NO_2$$
colourless, diamagnetic   brown, paramagnetic

At $100°$ the vapour contains 90% NO_2 and 10% N_2O_4. At the boiling point, $21·15°$, there is only $0·1\%$ NO_2 in the liquid, but $16·1\%$ in the vapour. The equilibrium in the vapour may be followed using pressure measurements. In the liquid phase it has been studied photometrically, by magnetic susceptibility, and by electron spin resonance. At low temperatures (ca. $-80°$), a triplet in the e.s.r. spectrum of nitrogen dioxide arises by coupling of the spin of the unpaired electron, which is chiefly in a σ orbital (a_1) on nitrogen, with the nuclear spin of nitrogen ($I = 1$). As the temperature is raised, the dimerization becomes faster, so that the e.s.r. signal loses its fine structure. From an analysis of the temperature dependence $\Delta H_{diss}[N_2O_4(liq)]$ has been found to be 65 kJ mol^{-1}.

The stable form of N_2O_4 is planar; in addition, two unstable isomeric forms have been found by matrix isolation at ca. 4 K:

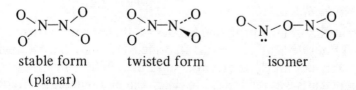

stable form   twisted form   isomer
(planar)

Dinitrogen tetroxide is quite a useful solvent for many reactions, especially for the preparation of anhydrous metal nitrates and in organic chemistry for

131

various nitrations [23]. It has a slight electrical conductivity which may be attributed to a dissociation:

$$N_2O_4 \rightleftharpoons NO^+ + NO_3^-$$

Electron donors such as amines, ethers, and esters form 2:1 complexes. With strong donors such as amines, these complexes are often ionic, whereas with weak donors they are essentially covalent:

$$D_2NO^+ + NO_3^- \xrightleftharpoons[]{N_2O_4} 2D + N_2O_4 \rightleftharpoons O_2N-NO_2 \begin{matrix} D \\ | \\ | \\ D \end{matrix}$$

ionic, D a strong donor   covalent, D a weak donor

Many metals, metal oxides, or metal halides react with dinitrogen tetroxide to form nitrates; the reactions are aided by addition of donor solvents such as ethyl acetate, e.g.

$$Cu + 2N_2O_4.D_2 \rightarrow Cu(NO_3)_2 + 2NO + 2D$$
$$ZnO + 3N_2O_4 \rightarrow Zn(NO_3)_2.2N_2O_4 + 2N_2O_3$$

Dinitrogen tetroxide is a strong oxidizing agent. It has been used, with hydrazine or methylhydrazine, as a fuel for rockets; this mixture is autoigniting (hypergolic).

(v)   Dinitrogen pentoxide.   Dinitrogen pentoxide is the anhydride of nitric acid, and is prepared by dehydration of the latter, e.g. with phosphorus pentoxide. In the solid it is ionic, $NO_2^+ NO_3^-$. The NO_2^+ ion is linear, being isoelectronic with N_2O and CO_2. In the vapour the structure of dinitrogen pentoxide is $O_2N.O.NO_2$ (see Fig. 3.18).

3.8.3   *Oxo-halides of nitrogen*

The structures of some of the oxo-halides of nitrogen are shown in Figure 3.19.

Nitrosyl fluoride NOF and nitryl fluoride NO_2F have been known for many years but were not much investigated until the 1960s, when their potential as rocket propellants was realized [24]. They can be prepared by fluorination of

[23] Addison, C. C. (1967), *Chemistry in Non-aqueous Ionising Solvents*, Vol. III, Part I, Pergamon, Oxford. Chemistry of dinitrogen tetroxide.
[24] Schmutzler, R. (1968), *Angew. Chem. Internat. Edn.*, 7, 440.

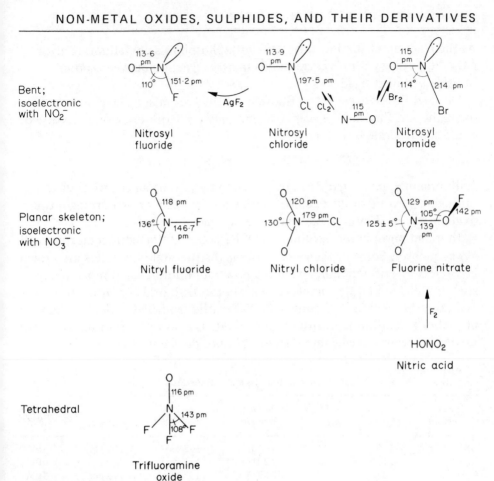

FIGURE 3.19
Oxo-halides of nitrogen

NO and NO_2 respectively. Lewis acidic fluorides form salts of the NO^+ or NO_2^+ ions, e.g.

$$NO_2F + BF_3 \rightarrow NO_2^+ BF_4^-$$

The reverse type of reaction, heating a nitryl salt with an alkali metal fluoride, can be used to prepare nitryl fluoride, e.g.

$$NO_2^+ PF_6^- \xrightarrow[\text{NaF}]{\text{Heat/}} NaPF_6 + NO_2F$$
$$\searrow NaF + PF_5$$

133

As the reaction of fuming nitric acid with phosphorus pentafluoride gives $NO_2^+ PF_6^-$, the synthesis corresponds to a net reaction between sodium fluoride and nitric acid.

Nitrosyl fluoride and nitryl fluoride act towards many elements both as oxidizing and fluorinating agents. Commonly an oxofluoride or a mixture of oxide and fluoride is obtained, e.g.

$$Cr + 2 O_2NF \rightarrow CrO_2F_2 + 2 NO$$

Trifluoramine oxide ONF_3 can be prepared by passing an electrical discharge through a mixture of nitrogen trifluoride and oxygen, or by burning nitric oxide in excess fluorine followed by rapid quenching to $-125°$ [25]. Both it and phosphorus oxofluoride OPF_3 possess tetrahedral molecules with C_{3v} symmetry. Some of their properties and structural parameters are shown in Table 3.7. Trifluoramine oxide is a powerful fluoride ion donor. X-Ray studies indicate that its complexes with boron trifluoride or with antimony pentafluoride should be formulated $ONF_2^+ BF_4^-$ and $ONF_2^+ SbF_6^-$. Unlike phosphorus oxofluoride, trifluoramine oxide is a powerful fluorinating agent. Loss of oxygen to regenerate nitrogen trifluoride is not observed.

TABLE 3.7
Properties of nitrogen and phosphorus oxofluorides and trifluorides

Compound	M.p.	B.p.	Dipole moment	d(A—F)	d(A—O)	Angle 'FAF
ONF_3	$-160°$	$-88°$	0·04 D	143 pm	116 pm	108°
NF_3	$-216°$	$-120°$	0·2 D	137 pm		102°
OPF_3	$-39°$	$-40°$	1·69 D	152 pm	148 pm	106°
PF_3	$-160°$	$-95°$	1·03 D	153 pm		100°

3.8.4 Oxides and sulphides of phosphorus and arsenic

The structures of phosphorus oxides and sulphides form a regular pattern. We saw above that, in the vapour phase and in certain crystalline modifications, P_4O_6 and P_4O_{10} form discrete units based structurally on the P_4 tetrahedron. Although these are the most important phosphorus oxides, the complete series P_4O_n (n = 6 to 10) is known. The structures are closely related by the stepwise addition of oxygen to the four phosphorus atoms in P_4O_6 (Fig. 3.20).

[25] Fox, W. B. et al. (1970), J. Amer. Chem. Soc., 92, 9240.

The structures of some phosphorus sulphides are also shown in Fig. 3.20. Note the basic P_4 tetrahedron in each. The 'PSP angle in phosphorus sulphides is usually about the tetrahedral angle (109°), whereas the 'POP angle in the oxides is much wider. This may indicate that $(p-d)\pi$ bonding is unimportant in the former compounds. P_4S_3, P_4S_7, and P_4S_{10} have congruent melting points

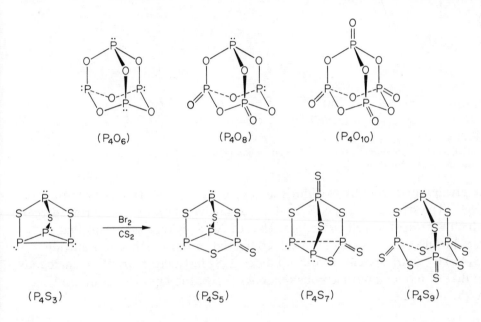

(P_4O_6) (P_4O_8) (P_4O_{10})

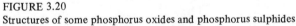

(P_4S_3) (P_4S_5) (P_4S_7) (P_4S_9)

FIGURE 3.20
Structures of some phosphorus oxides and phosphorus sulphides

in the phase diagram phosphorus–sulphur (Fig. 3.21). P_4S_5 and P_4S_9, however, are well characterized in the solid state by X-ray diffraction. The latter disproportionates readily in carbon disulphide solution to P_4S_7 and P_4S_{10}. The ^{31}P n.m.r. spectrum of P_4S_3 provides further evidence for its structure. It shows three equivalent phosphorus nuclei coupled to a single phosphorus nucleus in a different environment (I ^{31}P = $\frac{1}{2}$) (Fig. 3.22). P_4S_3 is a component of 'red' match heads.

Arsenic forms four sulphides (Fig. 3.23), which can all be made by direct union of the elements in the correct proportions. As_2S_3 and As_2S_5 can also

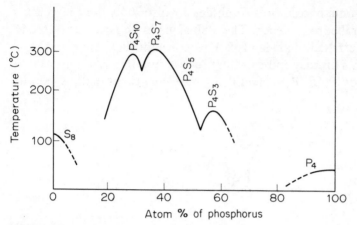

FIGURE 3.21
Melting point–composition diagram for the system phosphorus–sulphur, after reaction has occurred
(After van Wazer, Vol. I, p. 42)

be precipitated from hydrochloric acid solutions of As(III) or As(V) respectively. The structures of As_4S_3 and As_4S_4 are based on the As_4 tetrahedron which is present in yellow arsenic. That of As_4S_3 is very similar to that of P_4S_3, while that of As_4S_4 has been compared to tetrasulphur tetranitride (S_4N_4) (p. 270). Arsenic sesquisulphide As_2S_3 has a layer structure analogous to that of monoclinic arsenious oxide As_2O_3, but it vaporizes as discrete As_4S_6 molecules.

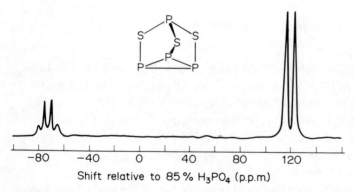

FIGURE 3.22
^{31}P nuclear magnetic resonance spectrum of phosphorus sesquisulphide at 12·3 Hz

The scarlet realgar and golden-yellow orpiment were used as pigments in ancient Egypt, e.g. in frescoes, and later in ancient Greece. Black antimony sulphide Sb_2S_3 was also known to these civilizations; it was used by women to blacken their eyelashes and eyebrows.

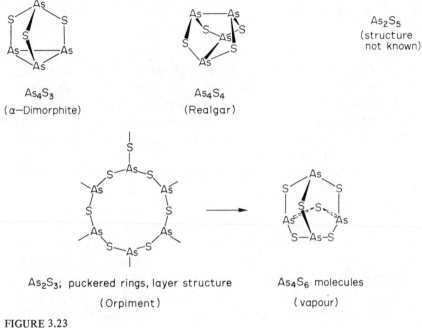

As$_4$S$_3$
(α–Dimorphite)

As$_4$S$_4$
(Realgar)

As$_2$S$_5$
(structure
not known)

As$_2$S$_3$; puckered rings, layer structure

(Orpiment)

As$_4$S$_6$ molecules

(vapour)

FIGURE 3.23
Arsenic sulphides

3.8.5 Oxides of Group VI

In addition to the stable oxides SO_2 and SO_3, sulphur forms two well character-ized but short-lived oxide species. The first, sulphur monoxide, is obtained by the action of a glow discharge on a mixture of sulphur dioxide and sulphur vapour at 120°/0·5 torr. Sulphur monoxide is paramagnetic, and like the oxygen molecule O_2, it has a triplet ground state ($^3\Pi$). The S—O bond is quite strong [$\bar{D}$(S—O) = 516 kJ mol^{-1}] but the molecule is slightly endothermic (ΔH_f° = 6·7 kJ mol^{-1}). It disproportionates readily:

$$\tfrac{1}{3}\,S_2O(g) + \tfrac{1}{3}\,SO_2(g) \leftarrow SO(g) \rightarrow \tfrac{1}{16}\,S_8 + \tfrac{1}{2}\,SO_2$$

137

to sulphur or sulphur suboxide and sulphur dioxide. S_2O is better prepared by passing thionyl chloride over silver sulphide at $160°/0·5$ torr. The molecule has a bent structure, analogous to that of ozone. It polymerizes at pressures above 1 torr, with elimination of sulphur dioxide:

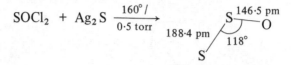

The formation of $1:1$ complexes between sulphur dioxide and amines or halide ions was mentioned on p. 93. Many of these complexes are thought to be of the charge transfer type. The interaction of halide ions Cl^-, Br^-, or I^- with sulphur dioxide in solvents such as acetonitrile or water has been studied spectrophotometrically. By plotting the absorbance against mole fraction of halide ion (Job's method) the composition of the adducts can be deduced. Thionyl chloride $SOCl_2$ and sulphuryl chloride SO_2Cl_2 form similar charge transfer complexes with halide ions.

Liquid sulphur dioxide is a useful solvent, especially for organic compounds. It also dissolves some salts such as the alkali metal halides, although in general the solubility of ionic compounds in it is rather low. It is, somewhat surprisingly in view of its low dielectric constant ($15·4$ at $0°$), rather a good ionizing solvent for compounds such as Ph_3CCl which is as strongly dissociated as potassium chloride in liquid sulphur dioxide, although it is virtually undissociated in nitrobenzene (dielectric constant $34·5$). It is now believed that autoionization of liquid sulphur dioxide, viz. $2\,SO_2 \rightleftharpoons SO^{2+} + SO_3^{2-}$, is negligible, on the grounds of the lack of radioisotope exchange, for example between labelled $*SO_2$ and $SOCl_2$. If autoionization were occurring $SOCl_2$ should form the SO^{2+} ion and thus lead to exchange of labelled sulphur. Charge transfer interaction of the type mentioned above is probably an important feature of the solvent action of liquid sulphur dioxide, since many solutes are also potential electron donors, e.g. Cl^- from Ph_3CCl.

Liquid sulphur dioxide is used in large quantities by the petroleum industry for the refining of lubricating oils, and in the tanning and textile industries.

Oxygen-free dithionite solutions (p. 207) give a strong e.s.r. signal owing to dissociation into radicals:

$$S_2O_4{}^{2-} \rightleftharpoons 2 \cdot SO_2^-$$

The $SO_2^-\cdot$ radical ion is isoelectronic with $ClO_2\cdot$ (p. 143), which shows little tendency to dimerize. The infrared spectrum of $SO_2^-\cdot$ has been observed in an argon matrix over the temperature range 4–14 K. The species $SO_2^-\cdot$ were produced by reaction of sulphur dioxide with alkali metal atoms within the matrix. From the infrared absorptions arising from various isotopically substituted $SO_2^-\cdot$ species (e.g. $^{32}S^{16}O_2^-\cdot$, $^{34}S^{16}O_2^-\cdot$, $^{32}S^{16}O^{18}O^-\cdot$) it was shown that the bond angle OSO is approximately $110°$, less than in SO_2 ($120°$), in agreement with Gillespie–Nyholm theory. The S—O stretching force constant is also lower than in SO_2, which is consistent with the unpaired electron being in an antibonding π molecular orbital [26].

3.8.6 *Some oxofluorides of sulphur, selenium, and tellurium*

The oxofluorides of sulphur, selenium, and tellurium are:

SOF_2	$SeOF_2$	
SO_2F_2	SeO_2F_2	
SOF_4		
$FOSF_5$	$FOSeF_5$	$XOTeF_5$ (X = e.g. H, OSO_2Cl, TeF_5)
$F_5S.OO.SF_5$	$F_5Se.OO.SeF_5$	
$FSO_2O.OSO_2F$		

This field has developed very considerably over the past few years [27], and only a few aspects can be mentioned briefly. Some reactions connecting the sulphur oxofluorides are illustrated. Note the formation of the hypofluorite $F_5S.OF$, and the production from it of $F_5SO\cdot$ radicals on irradiation, which combine with other radicals such as $\cdot NF_2$, $CF_3O\cdot$, or $FSO_2O\cdot$ (Fig. 3.24).

Anodic oxidation of solutions of alkali fluorosulphates yields peroxydisulphuryl difluoride $FSO_2O.OSO_2F$. This dissociates reversibly at $120–200°$ to $FSO_2O\cdot$ radicals:

$$FSO_2O.OSO_2F \rightleftharpoons 2\,FSO_2O\cdot \quad (\Delta H = 91\ kJ\ mol^{-1})$$

[26] Milligan, D. E. and Jacox, M. E. (1971), *J. Chem. Phys.*, **55**, 1003.
[27] Cohen, B. and Peacock, R. D. (1970), *Advances in Fluorine Chem.*, Vol. 6, Butterworths, London, p. 343.

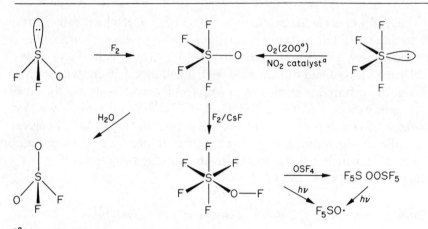

(^{a}Cf lead chamber oxidation of SO_2 to SO_3)

FIGURE 3.24
Some oxofluorides of sulphur

The compound reacts with various halides to form fluorosulphates. These reactions show that the FSO_2O group behaves as a very electronegative pseudohalogen (see p. 71):

$$KBr + 2\ FSO_2O.OSO_2F \rightarrow K^+\ Br(OSO_2F)_4^-$$
$$Cl_2 + FSO_2O.OSO_2F \rightarrow ClOSO_2F \text{ (see p. 144)}$$
$$I_2 + \tfrac{3}{2}\ FSO_2O.OSO_2F \rightarrow I(OSO_2F)_3$$

Treatment of barium selenate with fluorosulphuric acid gives SeO_2F_2, a useful fluorinating agent. Barium tellurate, however, gives the unusual, volatile acid F_5TeOH which is a strong acid and is slowly decomposed by water yielding other fluorotelluric acids:

$$BaTeO_2(OH)_4 \xrightarrow{FSO_2OH} \underset{\text{(b.p. 66°)}}{F_5TeOH} \xrightarrow[\text{slow}]{H_2O} F_nTe(OH)_{6-n}$$

$$\uparrow\ \text{HF, 40\% aq.}$$

$$Te(OH)_6$$

Note that, once again, tellurium is 6-coordinate in these compounds.

3.8.7 *Oxides and oxo-acids of the halogens*

The oxides of the halogens are listed in Table 3.1. Apart from oxygen difluoride OF_2 and the iodine oxides, all these compounds are endothermic with respect to their constituent elements (see Fig. 3.4). Chlorine oxides are explosive; bromine oxides also are all very unstable compounds, and decompose below room temperature. Iodine oxides exist as polymeric species at room temperature, and the solids possess appreciable ionic character. Their thermal stability is considerably greater than that of chlorine or bromine oxides.

(i) Bonding in halogen oxides.   Fluorine forms the oxide OF_2; two other oxides F_2O_2 and F_2O_4, which contain oxygen–oxygen bonds, are discussed in Chapter 5, p. 214. Chlorine, however, forms a large number of oxides, ranging from Cl_2O in which chlorine is formally monovalent, to Cl_2O_7 in which it is formally in the VII oxidation state. As with nitrogen oxides, it is possible to write structures for chlorine oxides in which the octet rule is obeyed, that is, neither octet expansion nor the use of orbitals other than Cl ($3s$ and $3p$) is invoked, e.g.

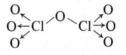

Appreciable double bond character in the Cl—O bonds in ClO_2, ClO_3, and Cl_2O_7, however, is possible. This is supported by the short Cl—O bond distance in ClO_2 (147 pm) and in the anions ClO_3^- and ClO_4^- (see p. 96), compared with the sum of single bond radii (165 pm) or the Cl—O distance in Cl_2O (170 pm). Evidence as to whether d orbitals are involved in the bonding in these species is very conflicting. Nuclear quadrupole resonance studies, for instance, suggest that such participation is unimportant.

In Fig. 3.25 the oxides of fluorine and chlorine and their relationship to the oxo-acids and oxo-anions are summarized.

(ii) Fluorine monoxide (oxygen difluoride) and hypofluorous acid.   The reaction of fluorine with dilute aqueous sodium hydroxide gives fluorine monoxide F_2O, a pale yellow gas, b.p. $-145°$. It decomposes by a unimolecular

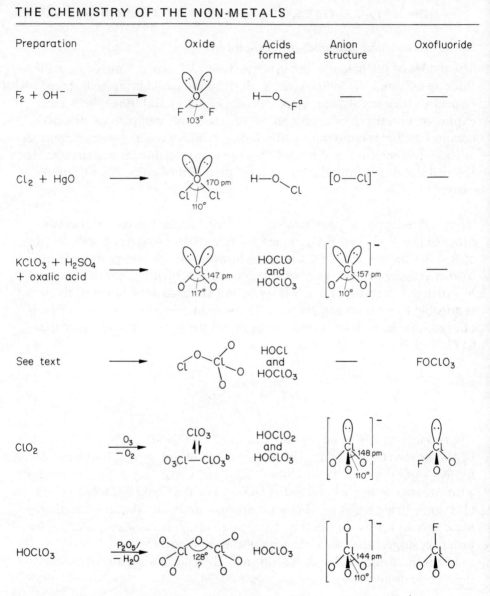

| Preparation | Oxide | Acids formed | Anion structure | Oxofluoride |

(Cl$_2$O$_3$ is possibly an unstable intermediate in the decomposition of ClO$_2$)

FIGURE 3.25
Oxides of fluorine and chlorine
[a] See text. [b] I.R./Raman spectroscopy indicates ionic structure ClO$_2^+$ClO$_4^-$ in solid at 87 K)

reaction at 250–280° to the elements. Prolonged contact with aqueous alkalis yields oxygen:

$$OF_2 + 2\,OH^- \rightarrow O_2 + 2\,F^- + H_2O$$

Fluorine monoxide is formally the anhydride of hypofluorous acid HOF. There is no evidence, however, that it reacts with water to form this compound. Hypofluorous acid and hypofluorite salts have been sought for many years without success, although organic hypofluorites such as CF_3OF (p. 215) are well known. Very recently the formation of HOF from the incomplete reaction of fluorine with water has been proved by its isolation at low temperature (m.p. $-117°$) and its characterization by mass spectrometry [28] as the parent ion $HOF^+\cdot$ at m/e 36. When D_2O was used in place of H_2O for the preparation, the corresponding ion in the mass spectrum appeared at m/e 37 ($DOF^+\cdot$). Hypofluorous acid decomposes with the elimination of HF in the gas phase at room temperature ($t_{1/2}$ is of the order of 30 min). It reacts with water to give hydrogen fluoride, oxygen, and hydrogen peroxide.

(iii) *Oxides of chlorine* (Fig. 3.25). Chlorine dioxide ClO_2 is a paramagnetic, odd-electron molecule. It is best prepared by reaction of sodium chlorate with 4M-sulphuric acid and oxalic acid. The oxalic acid acts as a reducing agent, and the carbon dioxide produced forms a diluent for ClO_2 which can be violently explosive especially if its partial pressure rises above about 50 mm. Chlorine dioxide is used commercially as a bleach in paper manufacture.

Photolysis of ClO_2 in an argon matrix at 4 K produces the isomeric $ClOO\cdot$ radical. This radical was postulated as an intermediate in the flash photolysis of chlorine–oxygen mixtures, and recently its ultraviolet spectrum has been observed in the gas phase in such reactions. The radical $ClO\cdot$ was also found in these experiments, and has a considerably longer lifetime than $ClOO\cdot$

$$Cl_2 + h\nu \rightarrow Cl\cdot + Cl\cdot$$
$$Cl\cdot + O_2 + M \rightarrow ClOO\cdot + M$$
$$Cl\cdot + ClOO\cdot \rightarrow ClO\cdot + ClO\cdot$$
$$Cl\cdot + ClOO\cdot \rightarrow Cl_2 + O_2$$
$$ClO\cdot + ClO\cdot \rightarrow Cl_2 + O_2$$

[28] Studier, H. M. and Appleman, E. H. (1971), *J. Amer. Chem. Soc.*, **93**, 2349.

$ClO\cdot$ is of interest since it is formally analogous to NO. As with the latter, evidence for a loose dimeric species $(ClO)_2$ at very low temperatures has been obtained by the matrix isolation technique.

Chlorine dioxide reacts with alkali to form a mixture of chlorate and chlorite (see Fig. 3.25) (cf. NO_2).

The oxofluorides $FClO_2$ and $FClO_3$, especially the latter, are extremely resistant to thermal decomposition and to chemical attack, in comparison with chlorine oxides. Chloryl fluoride $FClO_2$ is fairly readily hydrolysed by alkali to chlorate and fluoride, but perchloryl fluoride $FClO_3$ requires heating to over 200° with concentrated aqueous sodium hydroxide in a sealed tube for hydrolysis to occur. It thus behaves as a 'saturated' compound like CF_4 or SF_6, that is, there are apparently no available orbitals for nucleophilic attack, and its hydrolysis requires a high activation energy. It is also thermally stable to 300° in quartz apparatus.

Perchloryl fluoride and the analogous compound perbromyl fluoride are best prepared by solvolysis of $KClO_4$ or $KBrO_4$ with a mixture of HF and SbF_5:

$$KClO_4 + 2\,HF + SbF_5 \rightarrow FClO_3 + KSbF_6 + H_2O$$

Their structures (tetrahedral molecules, C_{3v} symmetry) have been confirmed by vibrational spectroscopy. The Raman spectra of the two compounds are extremely similar.

Quite recently a new oxide of chlorine, chlorine perchlorate, has been prepared by the following route:

$$ClF + SO_3 \longrightarrow ClO.SO_2F \xrightarrow[-45°\ \text{several days}]{Cs^+ClO_4^-} Cs^+\,FSO_3^- + ClO.ClO_3$$

Its structure was determined by vibrational spectroscopy. Analogous compounds $FOClO_3$ and $BrOClO_3$ have also been prepared.

Chlorine trifluoride oxide $OClF_3$ has been obtained by direct photochemical synthesis from the elements Cl_2, F_2, and O_2 at $-60°$. Fluorination of liquid dichlorine oxide or of chlorine nitrate can also be used:

$$Cl_2O + 3\,F_2 \xrightarrow{NaF} OClF_3 + ClF_3$$

$$ClONO_2 + 2\,F_2 \longrightarrow OClF_3 + FNO_2$$

The last method is preferred, as it gives yields of about 65% and avoids the use of the dangerously explosive compound dichlorine oxide. Chlorine trifluoride oxide, like ClF, ClF_3, and ClO_2F, forms adducts both with strong Lewis acids and with fluoride ion, e.g.

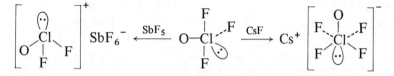

The vibrational spectra of the solid adducts are consistent with the essentially ionic structures shown [29].

(iv) *Oxides of bromine and iodine.* The lower stability of bromine oxides compared with chlorine oxides is in line with a general trend for the oxo-compounds of third-row compared with second-row elements. Bromine dioxide BrO_2 is made by the action of a glow discharge on a mixture of bromine and oxygen at liquid–air temperature. Its slow decomposition in vacuum gives bromine monoxide Br_2O among other products.

Iodine oxides are poorly characterized structurally. I_2O_5 is the anhydride of iodic acid, and is obtained by dehydrating it thermally at 240°. Its infrared and Raman spectra indicate a polymeric structure such as the following, and this conclusion is supported by X-ray diffraction results:

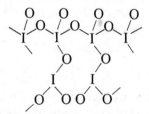

3.8.8 *Xenon–oxygen compounds* [30]

Two oxides of xenon are known, XeO_3 and XeO_4. Xenon trioxide is obtained

[29] Pilopovich, D., Lindahl, C. B., Schack, C. J., Wilson, R. D. and Christe, K. O. (1972), *Inorg. Chem.*, **11**, 2189, and following papers.
[30] Holloway, J. H. (1968), *Noble Gas Compounds*, Methuen, London.

by hydrolysis of XeF_4 or XeF_6 in neutral or acid solution:

$$3\,XeF_4 + 6\,H_2O \rightarrow XeO_3 + 2\,Xe + 1\tfrac{1}{2}\,O_2 + 12\,HF$$

$$XeF_6 + 3\,H_2O \rightarrow XeO_3 + 6\,HF \text{ (violent reaction)}$$

The oxide can be isolated by evaporation. The compound can explode without warning with a violence comparable to that of TNT. This instability is consistent with its heat of formation ($\Delta H_f^\circ = +401$ kJ mol^{-1}) and also explains the failure to prepare xenon oxides by direct combination of the elements.

X-Ray diffraction and vibrational spectra of solid XeO_3 indicate that the molecule has a pyramidal structure (C_{3v} symmetry), similar to the isoelectronic iodate ion IO_3^-. In acid or neutral aqueous solution, the major species are un-ionized XeO_3 molecules. On addition of alkali, the xenate ion $HOXeO_3^-$ is formed:

$$XeO_3 + OH^- \rightarrow HOXeO_3^-$$

Thus, xenon trioxide behaves as a weak monobasic acid. Like boric acid (p. 103) it acts as a Lewis acid (OH^- acceptor) in aqueous solution. Similarly, by addition of fluoride ion, salts of the $FXeO_3^-$ ion are formed:

$$XeO_3 + F^- \rightarrow FXeO_3^-$$

The crystal structure of $K^+\,FXeO_3^-$, determined by X-ray diffraction, shows that the anion is polymeric, the units being held together by bridging fluorine atoms (Fig. 3.26). The coordination about xenon is thus a distorted octahedron, with the xenon lone pair occupying one coordination position. Xenate ions are unstable in alkaline solution, and slowly disproportionate to xenon and perxenate:

$$2\,HOXeO_3 + 2\,OH^- \rightarrow XeO_6^{4-} + Xe + O_2 + 2\,H_2O$$

Perxenates are better prepared by oxidation of xenate with ozone. Salts such as $Na_4XeO_6.6H_2O$ can be crystallized from alkaline solutions (pH $>$ 12). At lower pH, $HXeO_6^{3-}$ (pH 10–12) and $H_2XeO_6^{2-}$ (pH 7–10) are the predominant species. We see here that the preference of Xe(VIII) is for octahedral coordination, cf. I(VII), whereas for Xe(VI) and I(V) tetrahedral coordination is favoured (see p. 98).

The oxidizing properties of xenate and perxenate are mentioned above (p. 125).

Xenon tetroxide XeO_4 is rather a volatile compound, having a vapour pressure of 25 mm at $0°$. Like xenon trioxide, it is liable to explosive decomposition. Vibrational spectra suggest a tetrahedral structure, as expected by analogy with the isoelectronic ion IO_4^-. The compound is made by treating barium perxenate with concentrated sulphuric acid.

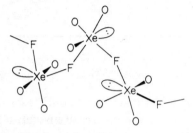

FIGURE 3.26
Structure of the ion $FXeO_3^-$ in crystalline $K^+.FXeO_3^-$

3.8.9 *Xenon oxofluorides*

The structures of the oxofluorides of xenon, XeO_2F_2, $XeOF_4$, and XeO_3F_2, are shown in Fig. 3.2. The first two are formed by partial hydrolysis of XeF_6. XeO_3F_2 has been prepared by the reaction:

$$XeF_6 + XeO_4 \rightarrow XeO_3F_2 + XeOF_4$$

The D_{3h} symmetry of the molecule was established by vibrational spectroscopy [31].

[31] Claasen, H. H. and Huston, J. L. (1971), *J. Chem. Phys.*, **55**, 1505.

The elements

4

4.1   Introduction

It is well known that the non-metals range from colourless 'permanent' gases to metallic looking, hard refractory solids, and from good electrical insulators to semi-conductors or conductors. These properties are controlled by the bonding and structure of the elements, and an understanding of these provides a useful guide to various other aspects of the chemistry of the non-metals. In addition, many of the non-metals are of practical importance in synthesis and as special materials. Thus, we devote a chapter to the elements and to certain compounds which have a structural relationship with them.

4.2   The elements in the condensed phase

Table 4.1 shows the melting and boiling points of common forms of the elements. It will be seen that, in terms of volatility, the elements can be roughly divided into three groups, gases at room temperature, condensed phases of intermediate boiling points (25–1000°), and condensed phases of high boiling point. This is a useful sub-division because of the simple relationship between volatility and structure for the elements. If a solid contains atoms strongly bonded to each other in an infinite lattice, then a high energy will be required to destroy the lattice and the solid will be relatively involatile. On the other hand, if the solid contains discrete atoms or molecules bonded to one another by van der Waals forces, little energy will be required to destroy the lattice and the solid will be relatively volatile. Volatility is more easily related to bonding than are melting points which are strongly affected by quite small changes in symmetry and packing efficiency within a solid.

148

TABLE 4.1
Melting points and boiling points of the elements

	B	C		N	O	F	Ne	H	He
M.p.	2150°	–		−210°	−218°	−223°	−249°	−259°	−272° (25 atm.)
B.p.	3680°	3860° (subl.)		−196°	−183°	−188°	−246°	−252°	−269°
		Si	P		S	Cl	Ar		
		1415°	44°		113°	−101°	−189°		
		3145°	280°		445°	−34°	−186°		
Solids of		Ge	As		Se	Br	Kr		Gases
low		958°	817°		217°	−7°	−157°		
volatility		2830°	613° (subl.)		680°	58°	−152°		
		Sn	Sb		Te	I	Xe		
		232°	630°		452°	113°	−112°		
		2518°	1440°		1087°	183°	−108°		

4.2.1   Infinite lattices and molecular solids

All structural evidence shows that, with first-row elements in their solid states, boron and carbon contain infinite lattices while nitrogen, oxygen, and fluorine exist as discrete diatomic molecules held together by van der Waals forces. This abrupt change is a consequence of the relative stabilities of single and multiple bonds for carbon on the one hand, and nitrogen and oxygen on the other, which can be seen in Table 4.2.

A solid containing a lattice of C—C single bonds, in which each carbon is joined tetrahedrally to four other carbon atoms, will have a binding energy of 2 x 354 kJ per mole of carbon atoms, while the binding energy per carbon atom in a C_2 molecule is less than 400 kJ. Thus, carbon is thermodynamically stable in an infinite lattice and does not vaporize except at very high temperatures. Conversely, a solid containing a lattice of N—N single bonds would have a binding energy of $1\frac{1}{2}$ x 159 kJ per nitrogen atom compared with 472 kJ in the N_2 molecule. The molecular state is strongly preferred and there is no evidence for polymerization of N_2 in the condensed phase. A similar argument applies to oxygen.

In the second row, silicon has a diamond-like tetrahedrally bonded structure. It is less refractory than diamond since the Si—Si bond energy is less than the C—C bond energy. Phosphorus and sulphur are more complicated. Inspection

149

of the values in Table 4.2 shows that the bonding energy per phosphorus and sulphur atom will be greater in singly bonded structures than in discrete molecules P_2 or S_2. What does not emerge from Table 4.2 is that singly bonded molecular forms of phosphorus and sulphur may be as stable as infinite structures. The choice with phosphorus lies between a molecular solid containing tetrahedral P_4 molecules and numerous different infinite structures in which the PPP bond angles are greater than in P_4 (see p. 172). The molecular solid (white phosphorus) is less stable by about 10 kJ per phosphorus atom than the most stable polymerized form (black phosphorus), but this energy is a small fraction of the total binding energy. The most stable form of solid sulphur contains S_8 rings. The difference in stability between this molecular form and other molecular forms with different ring sizes or infinite chains is 0·4–6·0 kJ per sulphur atom. The result is a vast range of allotropes differing only slightly in stability (p. 176).

TABLE 4.2
Single and multiple dissociation energies (kJ mol^{-1}) for the non-metals

C≡C	836	N≡N[a]	945						
C=C[a]	602			O=O[a]	513				
C—C	356	N—N	167	O—O	144	F—F[a]	158	H—H[a]	436
Si=Si[a]	~310	P≡P[a]	493	S=S[a]	430				
Si—Si	226	P—P	209	S—S	226	Cl=Cl[a]	242		
Ge=Ge[a]	~270	As≡As[a]	380	Se=Se[a]	~290				
Ge—Ge	188	As—As	180	Se—Se	172	Br—Br[a]	193		
Sn=Sn[a]	~190	Sb≡Sb[a]	293	Te=Te[a]	218				
Sn—Sn	151	Sb—Sb	142	Te—Te	149	I—I[a]	151		

[a] Heats of dissociation determined on discrete molecules in the gas phase; other values are obtained from the heats of atomization of the elements or from bond energies in compounds of the elements.

Among the third- and fourth-row elements, we find a steady weakening of the bonds in Group IV which allows increasing volatility, but in the other Groups the stability of polymerized forms relative to molecular forms is growing and the volatility decreases. With the heavier elements electrons are less thoroughly localized in bonding orbitals and new, more delocalized bonding forms become possible, contributing to the stability of the polymerized structures. It is found that, although bond length increases among the heavier elements, the 'non-bonding' distance between atoms increases less rapidly, giving the possibility of further bonding interactions. For example, such an effect contributes to the bonding in solid iodine. This is mainly a molecular solid with I_2 molecules, but the $I_2 \ldots I_2$ distances in the crystal are less than expected from the van der Waals radius of iodine (p. 182).

The divisions in Table 4.1 also give some guide to the hardness of the non-metals. Hardness is controlled in part by the binding energy in the solid (thus following volatility trends) but also by the structure of the solids. Boron, diamond, silicon, and germanium are the hardest of the non-metals, the hardness decreasing with binding energy. However, graphite with a layer structure [Fig. 4.3(a)] is very soft although the binding energy per carbon atom in the solid is equal to that in diamond.

None of the molecular solids is as hard as the solids containing infinite structures.

4.2.2 Electrical properties

One of the most important distinctions between metals and non-metals is in terms of electrical conductivity. The metals are conductors, the non-metals insulators or semi-conductors. A semi-conductor generally has a much lower conductivity than a metal but its conductivity increases with temperature in contrast to that of most metals.

Theoretical treatments of the electronic structure of solids, which explain electrical conductivity, are well developed [1]. Two approaches are used, one considering the energy levels created by the free motion of electrons within a crystal lattice, and the other considering the development of molecular orbitals over the whole lattice. The latter is more suited to our needs in non-metal chemistry where there are strong covalent bonds, but we shall consider it only in the most qualitative form as an extension of the molecular orbital approximation for isolated bonds.

We can compare, for example, the bonding in silane SiH_4 with that in solid silicon. The qualitative molecular orbital picture for silane is shown in Fig. 4.1. There are four filled bonding orbitals and four unfilled antibonding orbitals. This picture will be little different between solid SiH_4 and gaseous SiH_4 since interaction between SiH_4 molecules in the solid involves only weak

[1] A useful account for chemists is given in Ch. 6 of Phillips, C. S. G. and Williams, R. J. P. (1965), *Inorganic Chemistry*, Clarendon Press, Oxford.

151

forces. However, in solid silicon, although there is tetrahedral geometry around the silicon atoms as in SiH_4, each of the $Si(Si)_4$ units is itself part of a giant lattice. The $2n$ bonding molecular orbitals arising from n silicon atoms do not have discrete energies as in SiH_4, but form a band of energy levels. The result is shown in Fig. 4.1. Some mixing of d orbitals with p orbitals in silicon is possible and may influence the spread of the bands and help to reduce the energy gap between the 'bonding' and empty 'antibonding' bands.

When the bonding levels are completely filled and the antibonding levels completely empty, the material is an insulator. With silicon the energy gap, called the 'band gap', is such that at ordinary temperatures some electrons are in the higher-energy band, and there are, in consequence, also vacancies in the bonding levels. Under these conditions electrons can move through the solid under the influence of an applied voltage. The number of electrons in the upper band and the number of vacancies in the lower band is very sensitive to temperature, so that the conductivity of silicon (and other semi-conductors) increases very rapidly with temperature; hence these materials are used in temperature measurement and control. Electrons can also be excited from the filled lower band to the upper vacant band by light absorption. Table 4.3 shows the band gaps, determined experimentally by electrical and photoconductivity measurements, for some of the non-metals. Elements with band gaps less than about 150 kJ will be electronically excited by all wavelengths of light across the visible spectrum, and hence they will have a rather silvery, metallic appearance. However, silicon and germanium have some transparency in the infrared and are used as windows in spectroscopic work. Diamond, with a much larger band gap, is transparent in the visible region but absorbs in the ultraviolet region.

TABLE 4.3
Band gaps in non-metals (values in $kJ\ mol^{-1}$)

B	100	C	580 (diamond) 0 (graphite)						
		Si	115	P	250 (white) 155 (red) 30 (black)	S	230		
		Ge	70	As	115	Se	240 (red) 160 (grey)		
		Sn	10 (grey)	Sb	0	Te	40	I	130

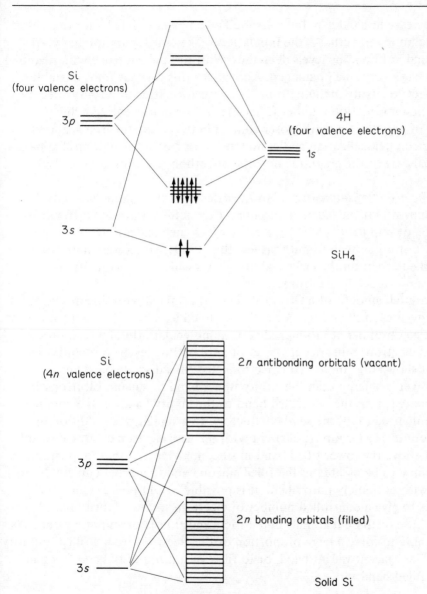

Si
(four valence electrons)

3p

3s

4H
(four valence electrons)

1s

SiH₄

Si
(4n valence electrons)

3p

3s

2n antibonding orbitals (vacant)

2n bonding orbitals (filled)

Solid Si

FIGURE 4.1
Comparison of bonding in SiH₄ and solid silicon.

153

The decrease in band gap down Group IV can be correlated with the decreasing bond strength. As the bonds get weaker the separation between bonding and antibonding levels decreases. With tin, the allotrope with diamond structure has a very small band gap. Above 13°, this form of tin is unstable with respect to a truly metallic form. The transformation is accompanied by a change in coordination number from 4 to 8. The body-centred cubic structure of metallic tin, with closer contact between the tin atoms, allows more electron delocalization and complete overlap of filled and unfilled bands. The special case of the graphite allotrope of carbon is discussed on p. 164.

(i)   The effect of impurities.   In the discussion of bonding in solid silicon it was assumed that the element was pure. In practice, it is quite difficult to free silicon of impurities (p. 170) because of its chemical affinity for many elements, but it has been found that less than 0·001% of certain impurities has a marked effect on the electrical properties which are of the utmost practical importance in electronics.

When a small amount of a Group V element is mixed with silicon, the atoms will occupy sites in the lattice normally occupied by silicon but will contribute one more electron per atom than silicon. In molecular orbital terms, these additional electrons must occupy a set of antibonding levels. A quantitative treatment shows that these extra electrons just fill a discrete band very slightly lower in energy than the empty upper band of silicon. Electrons are readily excited from the new filled band to the empty band, so the conductivity is enhanced (a *n*-type semi-conductor). In a similar way, addition of small amounts of a Group III element with one less electron creates a vacant band just above the lower filled band in silicon, giving increased opportunities for a vacancy to be created in the filled silicon band (a *p*-type semi-conductor). Starting with extremely pure silicon it is possible to add precise amounts of impurities to give a controlled number of electrons in the impurity bands. The successful use of these materials in rectifiers and transistor amplifiers depends on being able to force a large proportion of the electrons from a filled impurity band to the adjacent vacant band, or to fill a vacant impurity band from an adjacent filled band.

(ii)   The effect of pressure.   Pressures in excess of 10 000 atmospheres (10 kbar) have very marked effects on the non-metals. In some cases transfor-

mations to new phases occur under the influence of pressure at room temperature; in other cases, notably in the formation of diamond from graphite (p. 166), high pressures and high temperatures are required. The graphite–diamond conversion has been termed a 'reconstructive transformation' in which destruction of one crystal lattice and re-formation of another involves a large kinetic barrier which is overcome only at high temperatures.

The new phases formed under high pressures will have closer packing of atoms in the lattice. This may involve an increase in coordination number or a distortion of the original form of lattice. The effect will be to reduce the band gap and increase the electrical conductivity. For example, metallic forms of silicon, germanium, selenium, and iodine have been made at room temperature at pressures of 200, 120, 120, and 160 kbar respectively, although they revert to semi-conducting forms when the pressure is released. At extremely high pressures not yet attainable in the laboratory, all the non-metals including hydrogen and the noble gases may show metallic conductivity.

4.3   The elements as gases

The vapours of the non-metals include a wide range of species from atoms to quite complex molecules. Table 4.4 indicates the range of species for each element and the species most commonly found in the vapour. As is obvious by reference to the volatilities in Table 4.1, the vapour species of some of the elements are stable only at very high temperatures, whereas others are gases at room temperature. The main analytical tool for demonstrating the

TABLE 4.4

Vapour forms of the elements; the most common forms are shown in bold type

B, B_2	C, C_2, C_3, C_4–C_7	N, N_2	O, O_2, O_3	F, F_2
	Si, Si_2	P, P_2, P_4	S–S_{12} S_8	Cl, Cl_2
	Ge, Ge_2–Ge_7^a	As, As_2, As_4	Se–Se_8 Se_6	Br, Br_2
	Sn, Sn_2–Sn_7	Sb, Sb_2, Sb_4	Te, Te_2	I, I_2

[a] Polymers form up to 20 mol% of the vapour at the boiling point.

presence of species like C_7 or S_{12} in the vapour state is mass spectrometry, although many of the smaller molecules have been detected by emission and absorption spectroscopy.

4.3.1 *The atoms*

Atomic forms of all the non-metals can be obtained under sufficiently energetic conditions, e.g. at high temperatures, under the influence of an electric discharge, or on photolysis. Apart from the noble gases, the atoms are unstable at ordinary temperatures with respect to condensation to solid elements or to dimerization to stable molecules. However, recombination of atoms to form diatomic molecules requires the presence of other molecules to remove the heat of reaction and it may be inhibited by a large change in the electron spins (cf. N_2 p. 170). Both atomic nitrogen and hydrogen are sufficiently long-lived in the gas phase to be pumped around a vacuum system at a pressure of a few torr or even bubbled through aqueous solutions.

4.3.2 *The diatomic molecules*

Diatomic gaseous species have been detected for all the non-metals except the noble gases. With nitrogen, oxygen, hydrogen and the halogens the diatomic molecules are the normal forms of the elements in the gas phase. For the other elements, diatomic molecules appear to some extent during vaporization or dissociation of more complex vapours.

Bonding in the diatomic molecules has been studied by a variety of spectroscopic techniques some of which are discussed in Chapter 1. As a result the relative energies of the molecular orbitals and their electron occupancy is well established. The occupancy for the lowest energy state of the molecules is shown in Fig. 4.2.

Mixing of $2s$ and $2p$ orbitals becomes less favoured across the row as the energy separation increases, so the σp molecular orbital becomes more strongly bonding than the πp orbitals. The difference between the number of electrons in bonding and anti-bonding orbitals, is the same for B_2 and F_2, and for C_2 and O_2. However, for reasons discussed on p. 9, B_2 and C_2 have dissociation energies which are higher than dissociation energies of F_2 and O_2 respectively.

In the second row most of the bonds are weaker and a changed sequence of energies is observed. There Si_2 is much less stable than S_2. The lowest energy state of the Si_2 molecule is believed to have the sequence of molecular orbitals

156

$\sigma(3p_x)^2\pi(3p_y)^1\pi(3p_z)^1$. The π_p orbitals are much more weakly bonding and the σ_p orbitals is lower in energy than in C_2, so the bond in Si_2 is closer to a single than a double bond. The electronic structure of S_2 is analogous to that of O_2. It has been suggested (as with Cl_2 p. 10) that as the vacant $3d$ orbitals are of the correct symmetry to mix with the $3p\pi$ orbitals, the antibonding orbitals may be lowered in energy increasing the bonding in S_2 relative to Si_2. It is apparent from their electronic structures that B_2, Si_2, O_2, and S_2 are diradicals and the paramagnetism of disulphur and dioxygen is well known.

The bond strength of the triple bonds declines rapidly down Group V as πp orbitals become less strongly bonding. Hence, P_2, As_2, and Sb_2 are species observed at high temperatures and they are unstable with respect to the normal forms of these elements.

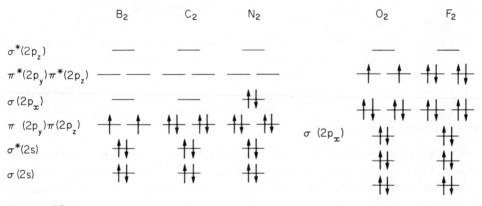

FIGURE 4.2
Orbital occupancy of first row diatomic molecules

4.3.3 Polyatomic species

The elements which yield polyatomic gaseous species are mostly those which readily form catenated compounds (Chapter 5). The main exception is boron; this forms an extensive range of catenated compounds but the stability of these increases with increasing numbers of boron atoms. There is probably such a large drop in stability between solid boron B_n and small clusters containing three to six boron atoms that the latter are not formed in vaporization.

Carbon on vaporization forms a series of polymers C_3 to at least C_7 which have no structural counterparts in the stable solid forms. The molecule C_3 is the best characterized both spectroscopically and chemically (p. 167); it is linear $:C=C=C:$. The species has been detected in space in the tail of comets. The other polymers are believed to be linear, double bonded molecules. There is no evidence yet on the structures of the poly-silicon, -germanium, and -tin species, but it is probable that they too are linear.

Phosphorus and arsenic form tetrahedral A_4 molecules. Sulphur and selenium vapour species are mainly puckered rings like S_8, although S_3 is probably a bent, open-chain molecule like ozone O_3.

4.3.4 The vaporization of condensed phases

It has been observed experimentally that there are three types of behaviour when the non-metals vaporize, which are illustrated by the following examples:

(1) Liquid nitrogen vaporizes to give just N_2 molecules, i.e. there is no dissociation or association.
(2) Liquid sulphur gives mainly S_8 molecules on vaporization at temperatures well below its boiling point, but as the temperature increases smaller molecules S_2 to S_6 are also formed.
(3) When carbon is heated under high vacuum, carbon atoms are the first species detected but as the temperature increases polymers C_2 to C_7 appear in the vapour.

The change in molecular complexity of the vapour with temperature which occurs in (2) and (3) above can be understood from the thermodynamics of the processes. Consider a solid or liquid A vaporizing to give both A(gas) and A_2(gas):

$$A(solid) \rightarrow A(gas) \quad \text{(enthalpy change } H_1) \quad \text{(i)}$$

$$2\,A(solid) \rightarrow A_2(gas) \quad \text{(enthalpy change } H_2) \quad \text{(ii)}$$

Enthalpies of vaporization are related to vapour pressures by the equation:

$$\frac{d \ln P}{dT} = \frac{\Delta H}{RT^2}$$

Thus, the greater the value of ΔH the greater the rate of increase of vapour pressure with temperature. If $H_2 > H_1$, then the proportion of dimer molecules in the vapour will increase relative to monomer atoms or molecules, but

158

if $H_2 < H_1$ the proportion of dimer in the vapour will decrease with increasing temperature.

We can relate H_2 to H_1 by considering a third process:

$$A_2(\text{gas}) \rightarrow 2\,A(\text{gas}) \quad (\text{enthalpy change } D) \qquad \text{(iii)}$$

Combining equations (i), (ii), and (iii) we find:

$$H_2 = 2H_1 - D \qquad \text{(iv)}$$

Equation (iv) shows that if $H_1 > D$, then $H_2 > H_1$, but if $H_1 < D$, then $H_1 > H_2$. The vaporization behaviour is thus determined by the relative values of H_1 and the bond dissociation energy D. Enthalpies of vaporization are roughly proportional to boiling points (Trouton's rule). High values of H_1 comparable to the bond dissociation energies represented by D are to be found among elements boiling at very high temperatures. For the Group IV elements, H_1 is greater than D and these elements give increasingly complex vapours as the temperature is raised. With elements like phosphorus or sulphur, H_1 is much less than D and the vapour species become less complicated at higher temperatures.

4.4   Special features of individual elements

4.4.1   Boron

The basic structural unit in all crystalline allotropes of boron is a B_{12} icosahedron. This structure allows the boron to participate most effectively in delocalized bonding of the type discussed fully in connection with the boron hydrides in Chapter 5.

Two of the best characterized forms of boron are based on rhombohedral structures. In α-rhombohedral boron, icosahedra are arranged at the corners of a rhombohedron [Fig. 4.3(a)]. Each icosahedron is linked to its neighbours by bonds 202 pm long in planes perpendicular to the three-fold axis [Fig. 4.3(b)], and by rhombohedrally directed bonds 175 pm long. This allotrope of boron is less stable than the β-rhombohedral allotrope for which the unit cell can be considered to contain 84 atoms as shown in Fig. 4.3(c). In this structure a B_{12} icosahedron is joined by its vertices to twelve other half-icosahedra which appear on the surface of the 84-atom unit. Each unit is

159

(a)

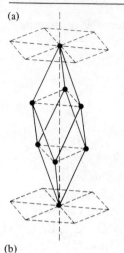

(b)

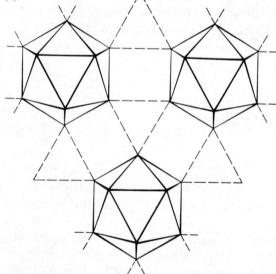

FIGURE 4.3

Structures of boron allotropes [Muetterties, E. L. (1967), *The Chemistry of Boron and its Compounds*, Ch. 2 (Hoard, J. L. and Hughes, R. E.), Wiley, New York]

(a) The general form of a rhombohedral unit cell. Note the three-fold axis and the relation to a hexagon. In the α-rhombohedral boron structure icosahedra occupy the positions of the black spots

(b) A section through the α-rhombohedral boron structure perpendicular to the three-fold axis. The broken lines indicate a possible arrangement of three-centre bonds (p. 219) linking equatorial atoms of adjacent icosahedra

(c)

(d)

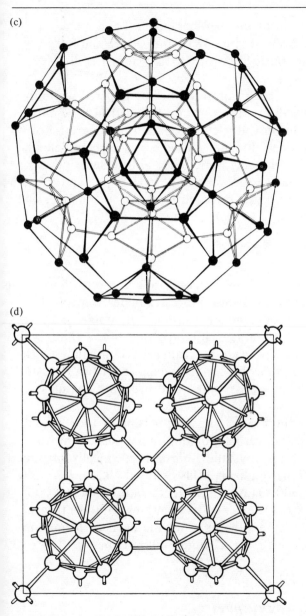

(c) The 84-atom unit of the β-rhombohedral structure viewed down the three-fold axis

(d) The bisphenoidal array of four icosahedra in the structure of tetragonal boron.

161

joined to others by juxtaposition of the half-icosahedra. Least stable of these allotropes is α-tetragonal boron [Fig. 4.3(d)], in which the links between icosahedra are in part through boron atoms external to the icosahedra.

Research into the structure of solid boron has been hampered not only by the complexity of the crystal structures but by the difficulty of obtaining pure crystalline samples. Boron is difficult to obtain pure because of its strong affinity for both metals and non-metals (see boron carbide below). Low-purity boron, obtained by reducing boric oxide with magnesium (Moissan process) can be upgraded to 99·5% purity by leaching and vacuum fusion. Boron of much higher purity is prepared from boron trihalides and hydrogen at high temperature, e.g.

$$2\,BCl_3 \; + \; 3\,H_2 \quad \xrightarrow{\text{plasma torch}} \quad 2\,B \; + \; 6\,HCl$$

or by decomposition of boranes. The α-rhombohedral and α-tetragonal forms have been made by these vapour deposition processes under controlled temperature conditions, but β-rhombohedral boron can be obtained by crystallization of molten boron. Commercially important boron fibres with remarkably high tensile strength are made by reducing boron halides with hydrogen below 1200° and allowing the boron to deposit on fine tungsten wire. The boron appears to be in a glassy phase and probably contains randomly linked icosahedra.

Next to diamond, boron is the hardest element; it is never used as a hard material in practice because boron carbide, of similar hardness, is much cheaper. At ordinary temperatures, crystalline boron is chemically very inert. It is attacked only by hot strong oxidizing acids or fused alkalis. It is only slowly oxidized in air below 500°. However, at temperatures above 1000° it will combine with all but a few elements. Its reactions with electronegative elements are predictably very exothermic, but the heats of formation of some metal borides are also high, e.g. titanium diboride has $\Delta H_f^\circ \; = \; -29$ kJ mol^{-1}.

4.4.2 *Boron carbide and related structures*

Reduction of boric oxide with carbon at high temperatures yields boron carbide of approximate empirical formula B_4C:

$$2 B_2O_3 + 7 C \xrightarrow{\quad 1800° \quad} B_4 C + 6 CO$$

As the compound is very hard it is made on a large scale for grinding, drilling, and for light-weight armour.

The structure of boron carbide is closely related to that of α-rhombohedral boron. The carbon forms a chain of three atoms down the three-fold axis of a rhombohedron of B_{12} icosahedra [Fig. 4.3(a)]. The B—C bonds are 160 pm long and the intericosahedral B—B bonds 172 pm long. Since each icosahedron can be considered to form the apex of a different rhombohedron, the 'molecular formula' of boron carbide is $B_{12}C_3$. Phases are readily obtained which have some of the carbon atoms replacing boron in the icosahedra, e.g. $(B_{11}C)(CBC)$ (see carboranes, p. 236). Other atoms can fit down the three-fold axis and may be partly incorporated in the icosahedra. The hard refractory phases of approximate compositions $B_{12}Si_3$, $B_{13}P_2$, $B_{13}O_2$, and $B_{14}S$ are all thought to be of this type. The compound $B_{12}Al$ may be related to the β-rhombohedral form with the aluminium atoms occupying 'holes' in the B_{84} units, and $B_{12}Be$ is related to α-tetragonal boron.

Although the icosahedron and larger units are dominant in boron and non-metal borides, the metal borides contain several smaller sizes of boron cages down to B_6 octahedra in the hexaborides like CaB_6.

4.4.3 Group IV

(i)   Carbon in the solid state. The best characterized crystalline modifications of carbon are diamond and graphite, although there are many other less well defined forms, some of which have great practical importance.

Graphite is the most stable allotrope; it occurs naturally but is mostly made by carbonization of hydrocarbons followed by 'graphitization' at 2000–2500°. Its crystal structure in its most common form is shown in Fig. 4.4(a). Layers of carbon rings are stacked so that alternate levels lie vertically beneath one another. Another form of graphite is known in which coincidence of the rings occurs every third layer. Each carbon atom in graphite can be regarded as forming three σ bonds with adjoining carbon atoms and one π bond; the C—C bond length of 141·5 pm is a little longer than that in benzene (139·5 pm).

163

The spacing between the layers in graphite is about 335 pm, i.e. close to twice the van der Waals radius for carbon in aromatic rings. Forces between the layers are slight and this accounts for the excellent lubricating properties of graphite. The interaction of πp electrons between the layers creates overlapping bands which permits electrical conduction. The conductivity parallel to the planes is comparable to that of some metals, but perpendicular to the planes it is a factor of a thousand less.

Graphite is chemically inert towards most aqueous reagents and resists oxidation in air to 450°. However, it is attacked by the heavier alkali metals, bromine, oxidizing acids, and fluorine, all of which increase the spacing between the carbon planes. With potassium or bromine a range of stoicheiometries for the products seems possible but C_8K and C_8Br are fairly well defined. The interlamellar separation is 776 pm in C_8K and 705 pm in C_8Br. Both materials are better electrical conductors than graphite. In these compounds the carbon rings are believed to remain planar. However, the products of oxidation and fluorination are non-conductors in which the carbon rings

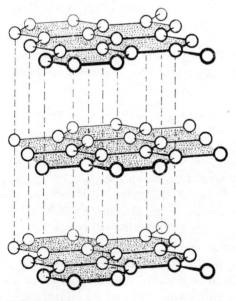

FIGURE 4.4
(a) Structure of graphite

are probably buckled, i.e. alicyclic not aromatic. When graphite is heated with a mixture of concentrated HNO_3 and H_2SO_4, a solid of rather indefinite composition is obtained with rather acidic OH groups in the enlarged interlamellar space; it has been called graphitic acid or graphite oxide. Dehydration gives a product of composition approaching C_2O. Careful treatment of graphite with fluorine at temperatures up to 500° gives a white solid $(CF)_n$. This is an excellent lubricant and is being considered for commercial use in motor oils. The interlayer separation in $(CF)_n$ of 820 pm is roughly equal to the sum of two C—F bond lengths (140 pm) plus two van der Waals radii for fluorine (260 pm). Thus, the layers can slide across each other in the same way as two pieces of polytetrafluoroethylene (Teflon).

Carbon is tetrahedrally bonded in diamond. The common form of diamond is cubic (Fig. 4.4(b)) but a hexagonal modification has been made. The C—C bond lengths of 154 pm are almost identical with those in aliphatic hydrocarbons.

Diamond is denser than graphite (3·51 g/cm³ compared with 2·22 g/cm³) and is just thermodynamically unstable with respect to graphite at room

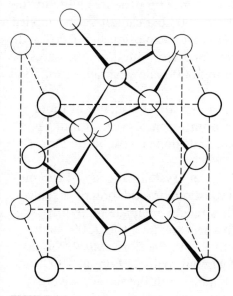

FIGURE 4.4
(b) Structure of diamond

165

temperature (ΔG° = +2·88 kJ mol^{-1}). The entropy of graphite is higher than that of diamond, so the difference in stability increases with increasing temperature. The conversion of diamond into graphite is very slow below 800° but quite rapid at 1500°.

The conversion of graphite into diamond was an aim of chemists for many years and many false claims for success were made. Genuine results had to await the development of methods for simultaneously applying high pressures (>30 kbar), to make diamonds thermodynamically the more stable allotrope, with high temperatures (>1200°) to achieve conversion at a finite rate. Practical rates of conversion are obtained at 1500° at about 45 kbar using transition metals, particularly iron–nickel alloys, as catalysts. The metal dissolves the graphite, breaking down the layer structure and allowing its conversion into the tetrahedral form. About 40% of the small diamonds used commercially in grinding are now made by this technique. Gem diamonds of up to one carat (200 mg) can be made by careful control of growth conditions, but the cost is very high at present. Direct conversion of graphite into diamond without catalysts can be achieved at higher pressures and temperatures. Figure 4.4(c) shows what is believed to be the phase dependence on pressure and temperature for carbon. Pressures greater than about 300 kbar cannot yet be applied continuously at very high temperatures. However, explosions or electrical discharges give shock waves which can create, for a short duration, pressures in excess of 1000 kbar and temperatures up to 5000°, allowing rapid formation of small diamonds.

For most practical purposes diamond is an electrical insulator at room temperature (p. 152). Doping with boron or nitrogen converts it into a *p*- or *n*-type semi-conductor; synthetic gem diamonds doped with boron have a beautiful blue colour.

Many amorphous, glassy microcrystalline, or crystalline forms of carbon can be made by controlled pyrolysis, combustion, or oxidation of organic compounds. Carbon fibres of great tensile strength are made by pyrolysis of filaments of organic polymers followed by heat treatment to 2500° under tension which orientates graphite crystallites with the fibre axis. Pyrolytic graphite, formed by thermal cracking of gaseous hydrocarbons at 1800° on surfaces, has the carbon planes oriented parallel with the surface, giving it anisotropic electrical and thermal properties characteristic of single crystals of graphite.

Polymerization of acetylene with cupric chloride followed by oxidation with ferric chloride gives highly unsaturated forms of solid carbon one of which is believed to be $(-C\equiv C-)_n$ and another $(=C=)_n$.

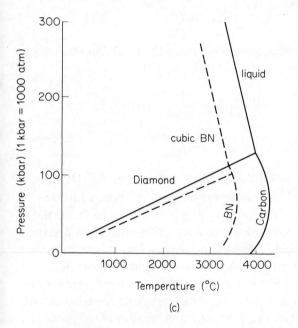

FIGURE 4.4
(c) *P-T* phase diagram for carbon (and BN)

(ii)   *Carbon vapour species.*   It has been observed by mass spectrometry that there is an alternation in the abundance and thermodynamic stability of the polymers in carbon vapour; species with an odd number of carbon atoms $(C_3, C_5, \ldots)$ are more stable than those with an even number of carbon atoms $(C_2, C_4, \ldots)$. This has been explained theoretically in terms of closed-shell electronic structures for the odd-number molecules which are not possible for the even-number molecules.

The carbon vapour species can be used in chemical synthesis. According to the method devised by P. S. Skell, carbon is vaporized from an arc struck in a vacuum. The vapour is condensed on the walls of the vacuum chamber cooled

167

in liquid nitrogen along with the vapours of inorganic or organic molecules [2]. Olefins react readily with the C_3 molecule:

$$:C=C=C: \ + \ CH_3CH=CH_2 \xrightarrow{-196°} \begin{array}{c} H_2C \\ | \\ H_3CHC \end{array} \begin{array}{c} \\ C=C=C \\ \end{array} \begin{array}{c} CHCH_3 \\ | \\ CH_2 \end{array}$$

With diboron tetrachloride, a product resulting from the insertion of carbon atoms into the B—B bond can be isolated:

$$:C: \ + \ B_2Cl_4 \xrightarrow{-196°} (:C(BCl_2)_2) \xrightarrow{B_2Cl_4} C(BCl_2)_4$$

In these reactions, carbon vapour species show behaviour typical of carbenes.

(iii)   Compounds structurally related to carbon.   Boron nitride $(BN)_n$ is isoelectronic with solid carbon. The most common form of boron nitride is the hexagonal form which is closely related to graphite. Planes of fused six-membered B—N—B—N rings are stacked above each other with B—N distances of 145 pm in the plane and 330 pm between the planes. Unlike graphite, there is superimposition of rings in alternate layers so that N and B atoms lie vertically above each other. The compound is an excellent lubricant. It is also an electrical insulator at room temperature; the difference in electronegativity between boron and nitrogen causes the 'bonding' and 'antibonding' parts of the π electron bands, which overlap in graphite, to split into two levels with a separation of about 530 kJ.

Hexagonal boron nitride is made by decomposition of boron–nitrogen compounds (Chapter 6) or by passing ammonia over a heated mixture of carbon and boric oxide:

$$2\,NH_3 \ + \ B_2O_3 \ + \ 3\,C \xrightarrow{1200°} 2\,BN \ + \ 3\,CO \ + \ 3\,H_2$$

When prepared at high temperatures the compound is fairly inert, although susceptible to hydrolysis to ammonia and boric acid. It is used to a limited extent as a high-temperature lubricant and insulator.

[2] For a review of the method and reactions, see Timms, P. L. (1972), *Adv. Inorg. Chem. Radiochem.*, **14**, 121.

Like graphite it can be converted into a cubic modification at high temperatures and pressures. At 60 kbar at 1500° in the presence of lithium or magnesium nitride catalysts, it yields the cubic form borazon which is practically as hard as diamond. The P–T phase diagram is remarkably similar to that of carbon [Fig. 4.4(c)].

None of the other Group III–Group V binary compounds (e.g. BP, AlN, GaAs, InSb) forms a layer structure analogous to graphite or boron nitride. It seems that very effective $(p–p)\pi$ overlap is required which is not found outside the first-row elements. All the compounds have diamond-like structure and some are important semi-conductors.

Silicon carbide SiC is made on a large scale industrially from quartz sand and coke in a carbon arc furnace at 2000–3000°. With a hardness intermediate between that of diamond and silicon, it is a useful grinding material. It has an enormous range of structures all based on tetrahedral silicon and carbon with alternate Si—C—Si—C bonds, i.e. no C—C or Si—Si bonds. In impure form, silicon carbide has a convenient conductivity for making electric furnace elements; it can be heated in air to 1400° with only slow oxidation on account of an adherent surface layer of SiO_2.

(iv)   Silicon, germanium, and tin.   Allotropy in silicon, germanium, and tin is much less important than in carbon. The normal forms of silicon and germanium have a diamond structure. Compression of silicon first yields a slightly more dense cubic form containing distorted tetrahedra with Si–Si bond distances of 230 pm and 239 pm (compared with 235 pm in ordinary silicon), but at 200 kbar a reversible transition to a metallic form occurs. Germanium also gives a denser tetragonal form on compression, and a metallic form at about 120 kbar.

The transition of the normal metallic form of tin to grey tin with a diamond structure is thermodynamically possible below 13°; it is a very slow process, but it is accompanied by a decrease in density from 7·3 g/cm^3 in the metallic state to 5·75 g/cm^3 in the cubic state, so that objects made out of pure metallic tin may crumble to powder after long periods below 13° – the so-called 'tin pest'.

Crude silicon is made by reduction of silica with carbon, using a slight excess of silicon to minimize silicon carbide formation. It is used as an oxygen scavenger in metallurgical processes and in the production of silicones

169

(p. 266). A chemically more challenging problem is the preparation of silicon containing less than one impurity atom per 10^6 Si atoms, which is needed for electronic work. The usual approach is to prepare a volatile silicon compound, SiH_4, $SiCl_4$, or $SiHCl_3$, from silicon or silicon compounds which are as free as possible from Group III and Group V impurities; the volatile compounds are purified by distillation, and then converted into silicon by pyrolysis or reduction by hydrogen, zinc, or magnesium. The solid silicon is finally purified and crystallized by zone melting.

Germanium is much easier to obtain pure, since GeO_2, which is fairly readily purified by wet chemical methods, can be directly reduced to germanium with hydrogen.

4.4.4 Group V

(i)   Nitrogen.   The action of an electrical discharge on gaseous nitrogen produces atomic nitrogen in its ground electronic state, ^4S, with three unpaired p electrons – so-called 'active nitrogen' [3, 4]. The recombination of the atoms to form N_2 is quite slow and it is accompanied by light emission. In the recombination process, the two nitrogen atoms might combine with each other in one of three different ways corresponding to the pairing of six, four, or two electrons.

The spectroscopic designations of the resulting states of N_2 are $^1\Sigma_g$, $^3\Sigma_u^+$, and $^5\Sigma_g^+$, and the relative probabilities of the modes of recombination are in the ratio $1:3:5$. With each of the states, combination will be followed by dissociation unless the energy of combination is removed by a third body. It has been shown spectroscopically that the most probable process, the formation of N_2 in the $^5\Sigma_g^+$ state, does occur. This is a very unstable molecule and can redissociate to atomic nitrogen. However, it can also decay to more stable states of N_2 and ultimately to the ground state.

Atomic nitrogen is very reactive. With organic compounds it commonly causes decomposition and the formation of HCN. With sulphur vapour it forms the NS radical and this polymerizes to give S_4N_4 (p. 268) among other sulphur–nitrogen polymers.

[3] Wright, A. N. and Winkler, C. A. (1968), *Active Nitrogen*, Academic Press, New York.
[4] *Advances in Chemistry Series*, No. 80 (1969), Chemical Reactions in Electrical Discharges, American Chemical Society, Washington, D.C.

The amount of atomic nitrogen in a gas stream can be estimated by a 'titration' with nitric oxide. The basic reaction is:

$$N + NO \rightarrow N_2 + O \quad (\Delta H^\circ = -312 \text{ kJ mol}^{-1})$$

In the presence of excess active nitrogen this is followed by:

$$N + O + \text{third body} \rightarrow NO^*$$

The excited NO decays with emission of a purple-blue light. In the presence of excess NO, the reaction is:

$$NO + O + \text{third body} \rightarrow NO_2^*$$

The excited NO_2 decays with emission of yellow light. Thus, NO is added at a known and adjustable rate to a gas stream containing active nitrogen until there is no light emission. This corresponds to equal concentration of N and NO.

Molecular nitrogen is obtained from air by liquefaction and fractional distillation. The liquid, b.p. -196°, is used to an increasing extent for preparing frozen foods, for preserving live biological samples, and for cooling vapour traps in high-vacuum systems.

Although N_2 is generally unreactive at room temperature, there is very great current interest in finding compounds which will react smoothly with the gas to emulate nitrogen fixation by bacteria. The ideal would be a compound which was a room temperature catalyst for the combination of nitrogen and hydrogen, currently carried out by the Haber process (p. 41).

Nitrogen is isoelectronic with CO and has been found to form complexes with some transition metals in which the bond $M-N\equiv N$ is believed to involve both σ donation from nitrogen to the metal and back-donation from filled metal d orbitals to the vacant nitrogen πp antibonding orbitals [5]. The $N-N$ stretch in the infrared spectra of compounds such as $N_2Co(PPh_3)_3H$ [compare $HCo(CO)_4$] is at a lower frequency than the $N-N$ stretching frequency in N_2, showing the influence of partially filling the πp antibonding orbitals. So far, in very few cases has it been possible to reduce the nitrogen to give ammonia or its derivatives.

[5] Allen, A. D. and Bottomley, F. (1969), *Accounts Chem. Res.*, **2**, 10. A first-hand account of the discovery of complexes of N_2.

(ii) *Phosphorus.* There are three main forms of solid phosphorus, white, red, and black. However, there are many other varieties both amorphous and crystalline as shown in Fig. 4.5(a); for the majority of these, good structural data are lacking.

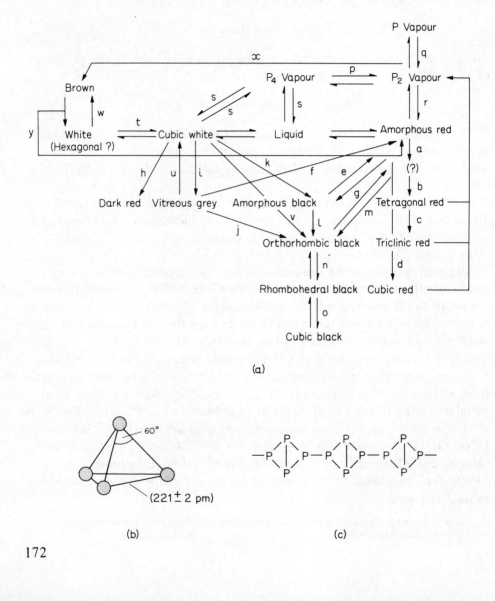

(a)

(b)   (c)

(221 ± 2 pm)

60°

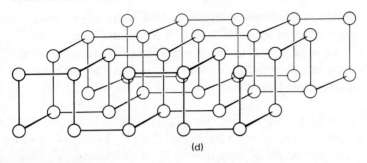

(d)

FIGURE 4.5

Allotropes of phosphorus

(a) Some relationships between the reported phase of elemental phosphorus. (a) Heat to 450°. (b) Heat to 540°. (c) Heat to 550°. (d) Heat to 600°. (e) Heat to 125°. (f) Heat to 400°. (g) Heat to 550°. (h) Heat to 300° at 8000 atm. (i) Heat to 380° with Hg or above 250° at 12 kb. (j) Heat to 400° with Hg for several days. (k) Heat at 200° under 12 000 atm. (l) Heat at 200° under 15 000 atm. (m) Heat at 200° under 12 000 atm. (n) Reversible transition in region of 50–100 kbar. (o) Reversible transition in region of 110 kbar. (p) Reversible transition at 900°. (q) Reversible transition at 1700°. (r) Reversible transition at low pressures. (s) Reversible transition at 44·1°. (t) Reversible transition at −77° or at +64·4° under 12 000 atm. (u) Sublime under vacuum. (v) Heat at 220° at 12 kbar. (w) Irradiate with ultraviolet at −190°. (x) Condense P_2 vapor at −196°. (y) Heat above −100°. (z) Heat at low pressures.

(b) P_4 molecule

(c) Red phosphorus

(d) Black phosphorus (orthorhombic form) [Corbridge, D. E. C. (1966), *Topics in Phosphorus Chemistry*, **3**, 57]

White phosphorus, consisting of tetrahedral molecules of P_4 [Fig. 4.5(b)], is the most fusible, volatile, and chemically reactive of the stable allotropes. There is confusion about bonding in the P_4 tetrahedra. The most recent calculations [6] suggest that bonding is due to overlap of $3p$ and possibly $3s$ atomic orbitals from each phosphorus atom, but that $3d$ orbitals do not contribute to the bonding. White phosphorus is readily converted into other allotropes under the influence of light or heat, suggesting that there is some strain in the tetrahedra. Molecular P_4 will complex with some transition metals [7] although the lone pairs of electrons at the corners of the tetrahedra show no other base properties.

A possible structure for red phosphorus is shown in Fig. 4.5(c). Chain linkage of tetrahedra permits a widening of the PPP bond angle for some of the phosphorus atoms from 60° to 100°.

[6] Brundle, C. R., Kuebler, N. A., Robin, N. B. and Basch, H. (1972), *Inorg. Chem.*, **11**, 20.
[7] Ginsberg, P. A. and Lindsell, W. E. (1971), *J. Amer. Chem. Soc.*, **93**, 2082.

The most stable allotrope, black phosphorus, is formed by the action of pressure on white phosphorus or by heating it with a mercury catalyst to 350° in the presence of a seed crystal of black phosphorus. Three structural forms are known but the most common, orthorhombic black phosphorus [Fig. 4.5(d)] exhibits a flakiness similar to graphite because of its layer structure.

All allotropes of phosphorus vaporize to give P_4 molecules, although the slow vaporization of red phosphorus at 300° forms some P_2 by a non-equilibrium process. Normally P_2 is formed by dissociation of P_4 at temperatures above 1000°. The partial pressures of P_2 and P_4 are equal in phosphorus vapour at 1 atm pressure at 1700°. Condensation of phosphorus vapour rich in P_2 at $-196°$ gives brown phosphorus [Fig. 4.5(a)] which may contain multiply bonded phosphorus chains, but this decomposes above $-100°$ to red and white phosphorus.

Phosphorus is made industrially by heating phosphate rock with sand and coke in an electric furnace to 1400°; the phosphorus distils out (Chapter 3). Liquid phosphorus is a bulk chemical and is the starting material for the manufacture of most phosphorus compounds including P_4O_{10} and PCl_3.

(iii)   Arsenic and antimony.   Condensation of As_4 or Sb_4 molecules does not yield a stable allotrope of arsenic or antimony. At low temperatures yellow solids are formed, but these change spontaneously at room temperature into polymeric forms which are similar in structure to black phosphorus [Fig. 4.5(d)] with a metallic lustre. In this form of arsenic, each As atom has three neighbours at 251 pm and three more at 315 pm. With antimony these values have changed to 287 pm and 337 pm respectively, i.e. the interplanar spacing is increasing less than the A—A bonding distance to give more nearly a close-packed structure. This accounts for antimony showing weak metallic conduction while arsenic is only a semi-conductor.

The elements are fairly readily oxidized by oxygen or halogens but they are not as reactive as phosphorus. They can be formed from the oxides by reduction with hydrogen or carbon.

(iv)   Compounds with related structures.   Solid phosphorus nitrides can be made by the action of ammonia on phosphazenes (p. 264) followed by heating to remove hydrogen. One of the best characterized has the formula

174

P_3N_5; it is an inert solid which on heating to 500° under vacuum yields PN and N_2. The bond length in PN is 149 pm, substantially shorter than the P—N distances in the phosphazenes (p. 258), indicating that it has a triple bond. However, it is thermodynamically unstable with respect to N_2 and P_4. The isoelectronic HC≡P, analogous to HCN, has been made by the action of phosphine on carbon in an arc. It can be condensed at low temperatures to a volatile liquid which decomposes above −100°.

In phosphorus chemistry, the P_4 tetrahedral geometry is maintained in the oxides and sulphides (p. 134) although other atoms are inserted into the P—P bonds.

4.4.5   Group VI

(i)   Oxygen.   Molecular oxygen in its triplet ground electronic state is paramagnetic as a gas, liquid, and solid, and it does not appear to associate to a diamagnetic O_4 molecule even at very low temperatures. When dry, gaseous oxygen reacts with relatively few elements or compounds at room temperature (contrast the halogens, p. 182), but it is highly reactive at elevated temperatures or in aqueous solution. Oxygen can be prepared in an excited singlet electronic state with an electron pair in the π^* orbital (ΔH_f° +92 kJ mol^{-1}) by photolysis of triplet oxygen in the presence of organic dye sensitizers or by certain chemical reactions, e.g. the interaction of hydrogen peroxide and hypochlorites. The singlet form is very reactive and will immediately oxidize many organic compounds, e.g. it adds to cyclohexa-1,3-diene:

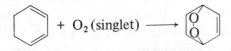

Increasing numbers of transition metal complexes of molecular oxygen are being synthesized. In those fully characterized, both oxygen atoms are coordinated to one metal atom to form a three-membered ring in which the O—O bond lengths range from about 130 pm to 165 pm depending on the metal and the other ligands attached to the metal [cf. O—O bond length in O_2 121 pm, in O_2^- ~130 pm, in O_2^{2-} (or H_2O_2) ~150 pm]. However, it is not clear that this type of coordination occurs in haemoglobin and other biological oxygen carriers containing transition metal atoms.

175

The O_2^+ cation can be stabilized by fluorine-containing anions of high electron affinity. Thus, the action of F_2 and PtF_6 on $O_2^+ PtF_6^-$, a salt which can be sublimed at 100°. The reaction of BF_3 and O_4F_2 (p. 214) gives $O_2^+ BF_4^-$ which decomposes with evolution of fluorine at 0°.

Oxygen is obtained from the air by liquefaction and distillation (O_2 b.p. $-183°$, N_2 b.p. $-196°$). The biggest use of oxygen is now in steel making.

In sharp contrast to sulphur (see below), oxygen has only one allotrope, ozone. This is formed whenever oxygen atoms are liberated and can react with molecular oxygen, e.g. in electrical discharges, by the action of ultraviolet light on O_2, or by the thermal decomposition of O_2 above 2500° followed by rapid quenching. It is endothermic ($\Delta H_f° = +142$ kJ mol^{-1}), and the liquid (b.p. $-112°$) and solid forms are dangerously explosive; the gas is more strongly blue coloured than oxygen, the liquid is deep blue, and the solid is violet-black. In all forms, ozone is diamagnetic.

Ozone has the same number of valence electrons as SO_2 (p. 77). Both are bent molecules (OOO 117°, OSO 120°) with bonds closer in length to double than to single bonds; d(O—O) 128 pm in O_3. Bonding in the two molecules is basically similar. An important reason for the great difference in stability is believed to be involvement of $3d$ orbitals in SO_2 which allows filled molecular orbitals which are antibonding in O_3 to become bonding in SO_2.

Ozone is chemically very reactive and adds readily to unsaturated organic compounds, and sometimes causes undesired cross-linking in rubber and other polymers with residual unsaturation.

(ii)   Sulphur; the solid forms [8].   The extensive allotropy of sulphur arises because there are only very small differences in energy between sulphur rings containing six to twelve atoms and 'infinite' chains of sulphur atoms. Within the series of six- to twelve-membered rings, the SSS bond angle varies from 102° to 108° and the dihedral angle [Fig. 4.6(a)] increases from 74° to 100°. Each sulphur atom is surrounded by four electron pairs, two bonding pairs and two lone pairs. It is the balance between the repulsion of the lone pairs and distortion of SSS from the tetrahedral angle which decides the relative stability of the different forms.

Cyclooctasulphur [S_8 rings; Fig. 4.6(b)] is the most stable, with a bond angle of 108° and dihedral angle of 99°. It exists in three well known crystal

[8] Schmidt, M. (1973), *Angew. Chem. Internat. Edn.*, 12, 445.

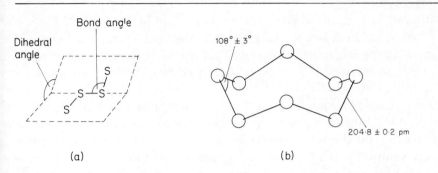

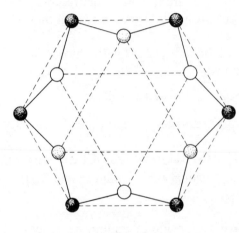

FIGURE 4.6 Sulphur structures
(a) 'Open book'
(b) S_8 ring
(c) S_{12} showing the three planes of sulphur atoms

modifications, orthorhombic (m.p. 113°), monoclinic (m.p. 118°) which is thermodynamically stable only above 95°, and nacreous monoclinic (m.p. 107°). Transitions from one form to another are slow but there is little doubt that at room temperature the orthorhombic is the most stable form. Crystals of it occur naturally, and commercial sulphur which has been made by solidification of molten sulphur is largely the orthorhombic form.

The stability of the other rings falls in the sequence $S_8 > S_6 > S_{10} > S_7 \gg S_9 \gg S_{11}$. The last three allotropes decompose slowly at room temperature.

177

The structure of S_7 is strained with four sulphur atoms in a plane [9]; S_5 has not yet been isolated. In cyclododecasulphur there are three planes of sulphur atoms in the molecule, which enables favourable bond angles of 106° and 107° to be maintained [Fig. 4.6(c)]. Larger rings S_{18} and S_{20} are known and appear to be fairly stable.

Chemical methods provide the best routes to sulphur in ring sizes other than S_8, although quenching of molten sulphur can be used (see below). The earliest chemical method was the action of concentrated hydrochloric acid on sodium thiosulphate solution at 0°. A complex reaction occurs and sulphur-containing oils are formed from which S_6 and S_8 are the main recoverable products, but small amounts of S_{10} and S_{12} are probably also formed together with high polymers not soluble in organic solvents.

The interaction of specific sulphanes (p. 205) with chlorosulphanes is more successful. The general reaction is:

$$H_2S_x + Cl_2S_y \rightarrow 2\ HCl + S_{x+y}$$

It has been most successfully applied to the formation of S_6 and S_{12}, i.e.

$H_2S_4 + Cl_2S_2 \rightarrow 2\ HCl + S_6$ (by varying the stoicheiometry this reaction can also be made to yield S_{12})

$H_2S_8 + Cl_4S_2 \rightarrow 2\ HCl + S_{12}$

The rings S_7, S_9, and S_{10} have been made by an unusual reaction between $(\pi\text{-}C_5H_5)_2Ti(SH)_2$ and chlorosulphanes or sulphuryl chloride [9]:

$$(\pi\text{-}C_5H_5)_2\ TiCl_2 \xrightarrow{H_2S,\ Et_3N} (\pi\text{-}C_5H_5)_2\ Ti(SH)_2 \xrightarrow{S_8}$$

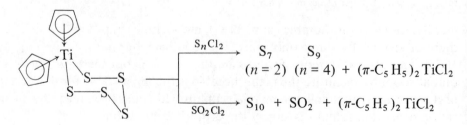

$$\xrightarrow{S_nCl_2} \quad S_7 \quad\quad S_9$$
$$(n=2)\ (n=4) + (\pi\text{-}C_5H_5)_2\ TiCl_2$$

$$\xrightarrow{SO_2Cl_2} S_{10} + SO_2 + (\pi\text{-}C_5H_5)_2\ TiCl_2$$

[9] Hellner, E. and Kawada, J. (1970), Angew. Chem. Internat. Edn., 9, 379.

Thus, with the exception of S_{11}, specific methods are available for making ring sizes from S_6 to S_{12}.

Many polymeric forms of sulphur are known although they are mostly structurally ill-defined. Unlike the discrete molecular forms they are commonly insoluble in organic solvents and CS_2. Filaments of the so-called 'plastic sulphur', made by pouring molten sulphur at 300° into cold water, can be stretched to give elastic fibres which seem to consist of helical sulphur chains with about $3\frac{1}{2}$ sulphur atoms per turn of the helix. None of the amorphous forms is very stable, and all revert slowly to cyclooctasulphur.

(iii)   Liquid sulphur.   All forms of cyclooctasulphur melt to form mobile yellow liquids which become darker in colour as the temperature is raised. At about 160° there is a marked discontinuity in the physical properties of the liquid. In particular, its viscosity increases enormously. These changes are associated with breaking of S_8 rings to give diradical species which rapidly polymerize; units containing up to 10^6 atoms may be formed. At higher temperatures depolymerization occurs with an increasing concentration of free diradicals in the liquid (about 6×10^{-3} mol l^{-1} at 300°) indicated from e.s.r. measurements.

At its boiling point liquid sulphur is a very complex mixture, containing species with two to several thousand sulphur atoms in chains and rings. The vapour composition (see below) indicates that S_8 is less abundant than S_6 or S_7 in the liquid. It is quite remarkable that, despite the complexity of the liquid and the vapour, the boiling point of 444·6° is sufficiently reproducible to have been used as a fixed point in thermometry (now replaced by the zinc point, 419·505°).

(iv)   Sulphur vapour species.   The individual ring forms of solid sulphur, S_6 to S_{12}, each give the corresponding vapour species as an important component of the vapour on non-equilibrium evaporation at very low pressures, e.g. in the inlet to a mass spectrometer.

The vapour over liquid sulphur at 200° under equilibrium conditions is mainly cyclic S_8. The variation of concentration of different species in the vapour as the temperature is raised has been determined by mass spectrometry and is shown in Fig. 4.7. Traces of S_9 and S_{10}, not shown on the figure, have also been detected. Up to the boiling point of sulphur, the small molecules S_2

179

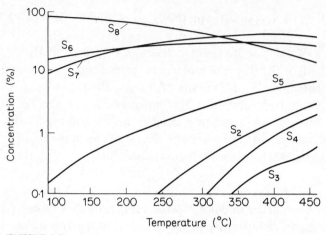

FIGURE 4.7

Composition of saturated sulphur vapour above the liquid phase [Nickless, G. (Ed.) (1968), *Inorganic Sulphur Chemistry*, Elsevier, Amsterdam; Ch. 7, Meyer, B., p. 247]

to S_5 are much less abundant in the vapour than are the larger molecules. At higher temperatures the smaller molecules become predominant, particularly S_2. No appreciable concentration of sulphur atoms can be detected until above 1600° (contrast carbon, p. 158).

(v)   Special aspects of the chemistry of sulphur.   All forms of sulphur can be burnt in air, and all react with fluorine, chlorine, and most metals. However, there are marked differences in the chemical reactivity of different forms of sulphur towards some reagents. Thus, triphenylphosphine reacts 10^4 times as fast with S_6 as with S_8 at 10° to give $(C_6H_5)_3PS$; as expected from its thermo dynamic stability, S_8 tends to be the least chemically reactive form. Stable compounds have been synthesized in which sulphur atoms in rings are partly replaced by other groups, e.g. $S_n(NH)_{8-n}$ (n = 4 to 8) (Chapter 6) and S_5CH_2. Many of the possible mixed sulphur–selenium ring species have been observed mass spectrometrically.

Sulphur can be oxidized in the presence of strong Lewis acids to give cationic species [10]. Thus, solutions of S_8 in oleum (H_2SO_4 + SO_3) contain

[10] Gillespie, R. J. and Passmore, J. (1971), *Accounts Chem. Res.*, **4**, 413. A review covering cations of Group VI elements.

the S_4^{2+} ion which has a square planar structure (see Se_4^{2+} below). Treatment of sulphur with AsF_5 at $0°$ produces blue coloured $S_8^{2+}(AsF_6^-)_2$ or red coloured $S_{16}^{2+}(AsF_6^-)_2$ depending on the ratio of reactants, i.e.

$$S_8 + 3 AsF_5 \rightarrow S_8(AsF_6)_2 + AsF_3$$
$$2 S_8 + 3 AsF_5 \rightarrow S_{16}(AsF_6)_2 + AsF_3$$

The structure of the cyclic S_8^{2+} ion is shown in Fig. 4.8. The average S—S bond length is similar to that in S_8 but the bond angles range from $91·5°$ to $104·3°$. The cross-ring distance $S(3)$—$S(7)$ is 286 pm compared with 468 pm in S_8, which suggests a weak bond. The structure of S_{16}^{2+} is not known with certainty but it may be formed from two S_8 rings joined by a single S—S bond. Solutions of sulphur in oleum have been shown by e.s.r. studies [11] to contain S_{16}^{2+} in equilibrium with paramagnetic S_8^+, and S_8^{2+} in equilibrium with S_4^+.

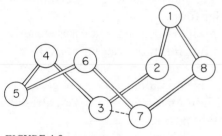

FIGURE 4.8
Structure of the S_8^{2+} ion

Although sulphur atoms are difficult to make by thermal means, they are conveniently formed by photolysis of carbonyl sulphide. Their chemistry has been studied by generating them in the presence of molecules with which they will react, e.g.

$$COS + h\nu(2290 \text{ Å}) \longrightarrow CO(^1\Sigma^+) + S(^1D_2) \text{ (excited state)}$$

$$S(^1D_2) + H_2C=CH_2 \longrightarrow |H_2C\underset{S}{\overset{\diagdown\diagup}{---}}CH_2|^* \xrightarrow{\text{third body}} H_2C\underset{S}{\overset{\diagdown\diagup}{---}}CH_2$$
$$\searrow H_2C=CH.SH$$

[11] Gillespie, R. J. and Ummat, P. K. (1972). *Inorg. Chem.*, **11**, 1674.

(vi)   *Selenium and tellurium.*   The most stable forms of selenium and tellurium are polymeric not molecular solids. The stable, trigonal, grey selenium consists of parallel infinite spiral chains of Se atoms which repeat after three atoms (dihedral angle 120°). The SeSeSe angle is 103° and each Se atom has two neighbours at 237 pm and four at 344 pm which is less than the sum of the van der Waals radii (400 pm). It is a semi-conductor and exhibits marked photoconductivity which is used in light detection and in the conversion of light into electrical energy (e.g. solar batteries). The stable form of tellurium is isomorphous with trigonal selenium; it has a smaller band gap and thus a lower electrical resistance than selenium, but it does not exhibit the photoconductivity so strongly.

Quenching of molten selenium gives a complex dark-coloured, vitreous solid from which various forms of monoclinic Se_8 can be extracted with CS_2. These molecular forms slowly revert to the trigonal form. The Se_8 molecule is similar to S_8; the Se—Se distance is 234 pm and the SeSeSe angle about 106°. Tellurium has no equivalent molecular form.

Unlike molten sulphur, the viscosity of molten selenium decreases steadily with increasing temperature. The main component in the vapour at 200° is Se_6 but smaller amounts of Se_8 and Se_2 to Se_5 are also present. Above the boiling point (685°) Se_2 becomes dominant in the vapour. The only gaseous molecule so far detected in equilibrium with molten tellurium is Te_2, although Te_5 has been reported from laser evaporation of solid tellurium.

Both selenium and tellurium can be burnt in air to give the dioxides, and they react with halogens and with most metals at elevated temperatures. Like sulphur, the elements can be oxidized to cationic forms in the presence of Lewis acids. X-Ray structure determinations on $Se_4^{2+}(HS_2O_7^-)_2$ and Te_4^{2+}-$(AlCl_4^-)_2$ have shown that the cations are both square planar with A—A bonds slightly shorter than those in solid Se or Te respectively; this is consistent with a bonding picture of the ions as 'aromatic' structures with six π electrons delocalized over four atoms. The structure of Se_8^{2+} is very similar to that of S_8^2

4.4.6   *Group VIII. The halogens*

The elemental forms of the halogens are uncomplicated compared with those of the preceding Groups. In the solid state, chlorine, bromine, and iodine have similar structures. It has been found that with iodine the I—I bond length of 271 pm in the solid is greater than the bond length in the vapour (266 pm), but the $I \cdots I$ 'non-bonding' distance (350 pm) is rather short in the solid. The effect has been ascribed to weak multicentre bonding involving the iodine $5p$ orbitals. Bromine and chlorine show only a slight shortening of the A—A bond in the solid compared with that in the vapour.

The colours of the gaseous halogen molecules are due mainly to excitation of an electron from an antibonding π orbital to an antibonding σ orbital. The energy gap between the levels decreases down the Group, giving the observed change from yellow F_2 and Cl_2 (absorbing in the blue) through brown Br_2 to violet I_2 (absorbing in the red). In solution, both iodine and bromine form weak complexes with aromatic hydrocarbons and some oxygen- and nitrogen-containing compounds, which changes their absorption spectra, e.g. iodine forms a violet solution in carbon tetrachloride but a brown solution in methanol.

Gaseous fluorine is normally made by electrolysis of a molten mixture of approximate composition $KHF_2.HF$ (m.p. $80°$) using a carbon anode and a steel cathode. As a gas at 1 atm pressure or less it can be handled fairly safely in dry Pyrex apparatus, but copper, nickel, or Monel are more commonly used. It is intensely reactive and will support combustion of many metals, oxides, and their metal salts, e.g. cement!, and practically all organic compounds. Explosive combination of elements and compounds with fluorine in a bomb calorimeter provides valuable thermodynamic data on heats of formation of compounds. Under controlled conditions, often in the presence of an inert diluent such as argon or nitrogen, direct fluorination of non-metals and their compounds can be a useful preparative procedure. All the hydrogen atoms in many aromatic hydrocarbons can be replaced by fluorine by direct reactions, and the surface of polyethylene can be converted into polytetrafluoroethylene by treatment with fluorine.

Chlorine, bromine, and iodine are far less reactive than fluorine but are still very active chemicals. Chlorine is made industrially by electrolysis of sodium chloride (either fused or in concentrated solution), bromine is liberated from bromides in sea-water by the action of chlorine, and iodine is mainly obtained from naturally occurring iodate and periodate deposits by reduction with sulphites.

4.4.7 *The noble gases*

The noble gases provide many of the best tests of theories of 'ideal' behaviour

183

in the gaseous and condensed states, since the interactions between the atoms are more strictly non-bonding than in other elements and compounds.

Long before compounds of the noble gases were prepared, many clathrates had been made. If water is crystallized slowly in the presence of argon, krypton, or xenon under pressure, solids are obtained in which noble gas atoms are trapped in cages of water molecules; clathrates containing neon or helium are not formed under such conditions. A pentagonal dodecahedron of twenty water molecules is the basic structural unit; noble gas atoms can be trapped inside the dodecahedra and in cavities which result from packing together of the dodecahedra; the limiting composition is A:5·75 H_2O. The xenon–water clathrate of close to this limiting composition has a dissociation pressure of 1 atm of xenon at $-3°$. More stable clathrates are formed by addition of a third species, e.g. the clathrates 2 $Xe.CCl_4.17\ H_2O$ and 2 $Ar.CCl_4.17\ H_2O$ have dissociation pressures of 1 atm at $14°$ and $-2°$ respectively. The radioactive isotope ^{85}Kr ($t_{1/2}$ 10·3 years) is conveniently handled in the form of its stable clathrates in hydroquinone which release negligible amounts of the gas at room temperature. The amount of ozone in air has been estimated by release of ^{85}Kr from this clathrate, i.e.

$$(C_6H_4(OH)_2)_3[^{85}Kr] + O_3 \rightarrow 3\ C_6H_4O_2 + 3\ H_2O + {}^{85}Kr\ [12]$$

Although clathrate formation is not restricted to the noble gases, it does produce particularly dramatic changes in their physical properties due to the intensity of the van der Waals interactions within the cage structures.

Helium is obtained from natural gas after condensation at low temperatures of all less volatile components. The other noble gases are obtained by fractionations of liquid air.

4.4.8 *Hydrogen*

The low mass of hydrogen causes two effects to be more important with this element than with any others. The first is that replacement of ^1H by the isotopes deuterium (^2H = D) or tritium (^3H = T) causes quite large changes in the physical properties of hydrogen and its compounds compared with isotopic replacements in other elements. The main change is in the equilibrium

[12] Tolgyessy, J. and Varga, S. (1970), *Talanta*, **17**, 659. A review of analytical uses of ^{85}Kr.

vibrational frequency of molecules containing the isotopes. For a diatomic molecule:

$$\nu_{\text{equilibrium}} \propto \left(\frac{m_1 + m_2}{m_1 m_2} \right)^{1/2}$$

where m_1 and m_2 are the atomic masses. When one of these changes by a factor of 2 or 3 for replacement of H by D or T respectively, there is a marked change in the frequency and this affects a wide range of thermodynamic and kinetic properties of the molecules.

Naturally occurring hydrogen contains about 0·016% of D but less than 10^{-15}% of the radioactive T ($t_{1/2} \approx 12$ years). Deuterium can be separated from hydrogen by making use of effects such as (i) the different volatility of D_2 and H_2 or D_2O and H_2O, (ii) the faster H_2 liberation on electrolysis of acidified water, or (iii) the position of a gas–liquid equilibrium reaction, e.g.

$$\text{HOH(l)} + \text{HSD(g)} \rightleftharpoons \text{HOD(l)} + \text{HSH(g)} \quad (K \approx 1·01)$$

Deuterium oxide is prepared on a very large scale for use as a moderator for fast neutrons in nuclear reactors. Tritium is made by neutron bombardment of lithium:

$$^{6}\text{Li} + {}^{1}\text{n} \rightarrow {}^{4}\text{He} + {}^{3}\text{H}$$

Partial replacement of hydrogen by deuterium (or by tritium in laboratories equipped to handle radioactive chemicals) can provide valuable information about mechanisms of reactions especially in biological systems.

The other effect of the low mass of hydrogen is connected with nuclear spins. The proton has spin $\frac{1}{2}$; H_2 molecules, like other homonuclear diatomic molecules between atoms with a nuclear spin, can either contain two atoms with nuclear spins aligned (orthohydrogen) or with spins opposed (para-hydrogen). At equilibrium at room temperature or above, hydrogen consists of ortho- and para-states in a 3:1 ratio. However, unlike ortho- and para-states of other diatomic molecules, ortho- and para-hydrogen have fairly different physical properties and can be separated. Below room temperature the equilibrium concentration of parahydrogen increases and essentially pure para-hydrogen can be formed by cooling hydrogen to below 20 K in the presence of metal catalysts which allow realignment of nuclei in absorbed H_2 molecules to occur.

Gaseous hydrogen is not particularly reactive at room temperature in the absence of catalysts, e.g. platinum metals; it will, however, react smoothly with some boron compounds (p. 231) and explode with fluorine. At higher temperatures, or in the presence of catalysts, it is a powerful reducing agent.

Atomic hydrogen, prepared as a short-lived gas by the action of an electric discharge on H_2, can function either as a reducing agent or as an oxidizing agent when it is bubbled through aqueous solutions, e.g.

$$Co(NH_3)_6{}^{3+} + H \rightarrow Co(NH_3)_6{}^{2+} + H^+$$
$$Fe^{2+} + H + H^+ \rightarrow Fe^{3+} + H_2$$

Catenated compounds and related systems

5

5.1 Introduction

Implicit in this chapter is the comparison between catenated compounds of carbon and those of the other non-metallic elements. The covalent compounds of carbon are so extensive and varied that their study constitutes one of the traditional branches of chemistry. Most organic compounds rely for their framework on carbon–carbon bonds. These can be single bonds only, as in alkanes or alicyclic hydrocarbons, or can include multiple bonds as well. Figure 5.1 illustrates some of the complex structures which have been found both in naturally occurring substances and in synthetic products.

Carbon is also able to bond strongly to many other elements, in particular to first-row elements such as nitrogen and oxygen, with which it forms both single and multiple bonds (e.g. $C{=}O$, $C{\equiv}N$).

An important factor in organic chemistry is the considerable stability of complex structures to reactions such as disproportionation, rearrangement, oxidation, and hydrolysis. This applies particularly to saturated or aromatic groups (alkyl, alicyclic, or aryl) which remain unchanged throughout a wide variety of chemical reactions. The persistence of the major part of a structure while a chemical change is carried out at one site enables complex organic compounds to be synthesized in a logical fashion.

Often kinetic factors are responsible for this inertness of carbon compounds. All organic compounds are, for instance, thermodynamically unstable to oxidation, e.g.

$$C_2H_6(g) + \tfrac{7}{2} O_2(g) \rightarrow 2\, CO_2(g) + 3\, H_2O(g) \quad (\Delta H = -1425 \text{ kJ mol}^{-1})$$

Disproportionation at room temperature by reactions such as:

$$CH_3(CH_2)_{n-2}CH_3 \rightarrow (n+1)/2\, CH_4(g) + (n-1)/2\, C(\text{graphite})$$

C—C single bonds only

Paraffins (alkanes) e.g.

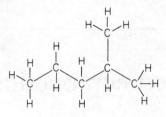

Alicyclic compounds e.g.

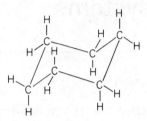

Multiple bonds

Alkenes

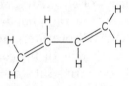

Aromatic compounds

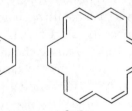

[18] Annulene

Natural products

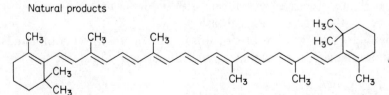

β – Carotene

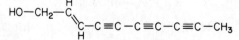

Dehydromatricarianol

FIGURE 5.1
Examples of catenated carbon compounds

is often favoured thermodynamically, and the positive entropy change increasingly favours such decomposition as the temperature is raised.

Of course, organic compounds normally do not disproportionate and are not oxidized in air under ambient conditions. This is due to high activation energy barriers to such reactions. The kinetic stability of carbon compounds is associated with the full use of carbon valence orbitals leading to an octet electronic configuration, and also with the absence of any low-lying empty orbitals. It is therefore not surprising that lower kinetic stability of the catenated derivatives is often observed where the octet is not attained (as in simple 3-coordinate boron compounds) or where 'octet expansion' can occur (as in suitable compounds of second- and third-row elements).

5.1.1 Comparison of alkanes with silanes

The chemical properties of the silanes, which contain chains of silicon atoms, contrast very markedly with those of the alkanes to which they are formally analogous. Silanes are spontaneously inflammable in air, decompose fairly readily on heating, and are hydrolysed in aqueous alkali. Clearly they are thermodynamically and also kinetically unstable to these changes. A common feature of catenated compounds of the non-metallic elements of the second and subsequent rows is their lability and reactivity in situations in which organic compounds would be inert. There are consequently considerable experimental difficulties in handling and studying many of these compounds. High-vacuum or inert-atmosphere techniques [1] are often obligatory, and reactions should be carried out under as mild conditions as possible. The ease of disproportionation and cleavage of homonuclear bonds in many of these compounds also greatly restricts the use of planned synthesis in this field. Despite these difficulties research has occasionally been rewarded by the discovery of stable and useful materials, e.g. the carboranes (p. 236).

5.2   Range of catenated compounds

The approximate range of known catenated compounds is summarized in Table 5.1. The importance of catenation decreases down Group IV, while in Groups V and VI the derivatives of phosphorus and sulphur are rather more

[1] Shriver, D. F. (1969), *The Manipulation of Air-Sensitive Compounds*, McGraw-Hill, New York.

TABLE 5.1

Catenated compounds (a summary) (excluding B)

Group IV		Group V	Group VII
(saturated compounds)	*n*		
C	C_nH_{2n+2} 1–>100	N H_2N-NH_2 stable in *gauche* configuration	O HOOH SF_5OOSF_5, CF_3OOCF_3
	C_nF_{2n+2} 1–>100	F_2N-NF_2	FOOF CF_3OOOCF_3
	C_nCl_{2n+2} 1–4 } steric	O_2N-NO_2	FOOOF
	C_nBr_{2n+2} 1–3	$FN=NF$ (*cis* and *trans*)	
		HN_3, N_3^- (p. 70)	
Si	Si_nH_{2n+2} 1–>10	P P_nH_{n+2} $n = 1–3$ or 4	S sulphanes HS_nH ⎫
	Si_nMe_{2n+2} 1–>20	F_2P-PF_2, $P(PF_2)_3$	FS_nF ⎬ $n = 1$ to 8
			ClS_nCl ⎭
	Si_nF_{2n+2}	Cl_2P-PCl_2 I_2P-PI_2	
	Si_nCl_{2n+2} 1–>20	$[P(CF_3)]_n$ $n = 4–6$ (rings)	FSSF or F–S=S–F
Ge	Ge_nH_{2n+2} 1–>10	As (As R)n where R is phenyl, alkyl,	Se thiosulphates O_3S-S^{2-}
	Ge_2Cl_6, Ge_2Br_6	etc., are stable and some are	polythionates $O_3S-S_n-SO_3^{2-}$
	no Ge_2F_6	useful drugs	catenation much less marked than
		$I_2As-AsI_2$	with S
Sn	Sn_2H_6		
	Sn_nMe_{2n+2} 1–>6		
	Sn_2Cl_6?		

Group V, P row:

$$\text{H}\quad\text{H}$$
$$\text{P—P—OH}$$
$$\text{HO}\quad\text{O}\;\;\text{O}$$

[rare example of P(V) with catenation]

extensive than those of nitrogen and oxygen respectively. Compounds containing multiple bonds, e.g. C=C, C≡C, N=N, are formed by the first-row elements carbon and nitrogen, but not by elements of later Periods, in agreement with the usual trend (p. 10).

5.2.1 Energies of homonuclear bonds

The observed range of catenated compounds can very approximately be related to the strengths of the homonuclear bonds A—A. In Table 5.2 the bond energy term values $E(A—A)$ in the dihydrides are listed. Note that the bonds get progressively weaker down Group IV, while in Groups V and VI the maximum strength comes at phosphorus and sulphur (cf. p. 150).

TABLE 5.2
$E(A—A)$ values in dihydrides (kJ mol^{-1})[a]

B_2H_4[b]	C_2H_6	N_2H_4	H_2O_2	cf. F—F
ca. 300	330	167	146	158
	Si_2H_6	P_2H_4	H_2S_2	Cl—Cl
	196	209	251	242
	Ge_2H_6	As_2H_4		Br—Br
	159	142		193
	Sn_2H_6	Sb_2H_4		I—I
	121	134		151

[a] Other values for $E(A—A)$ are often quoted. These are derived from heats of atomization of the elements, or from other compounds such as halides. We have chosen to present data derived from hydrides only, to obtain as far as possible a consistent pattern of the variation of A—A bond strength from one element to another.

[b] Estimated value. B_2H_4 is not known except in complexes, but $E(B—B)$ in several diboron compounds B_2X_4 (X = F, Cl. OH, OCH$_3$) has been shown to have approximately this value.

5.2.2 Preparation of catenated compounds

Bonds between atoms of non-metallic elements can often be formed by reactions of the general type:

$$\overset{\delta-}{A}—\overset{\delta+}{X} + \overset{\delta-}{Y}—\overset{\delta+}{A} \rightarrow A—A + X—Y$$

Commonly X is a halogen, but it can sometimes be another electronegative group such as Me$_2$N– or MeO–, and Y hydrogen, e.g.

$$A—Cl + H—A \rightarrow A—A + HCl \quad \text{(see p. 200).}$$

191

A base, such as triethylamine, is sometimes added to assist the elimination of hydrogen chloride.

Wurtz type coupling is also used, particularly for B, Si, and Ge, e.g.

$$(Me_2N)_2BCl \xrightarrow[\text{petroleum ether}]{\text{Na-K alloy}} (Me_2N)_2B\!-\!B(NMe_2)_2$$

$$Me_2SiCl_2 \xrightarrow[\text{tetrahydrofuran}]{\text{Na}} (Me_2Si)_n \text{ (rings)}$$

In these reactions an alkali metal compound may be an intermediate. Such alkali metal derivatives, where they can be prepared, can also be used to effect coupling, e.g.

$$Ph_3SiLi + Me_3SiCl \rightarrow Ph_3SiSiMe_3 + LiCl$$

An alternative approach to the synthesis of catenated compounds is to start with a structure which already contains A—A bonds. This method is often limited by the ease with which such bonds are broken. Some examples, mentioned in more detail below, include the synthesis of polysulphanes (p. 205), the oxidation of red phosphorus to various catenated oxo-acids (p. 202), and perhaps, the preparation of higher silicon chlorides by direct chlorination of calcium silicide (p. 195). Most important, however, is its application in boron hydride and carborane chemistry, where the kinetic stability of the cage structures permits considerable use of planned synthesis.

5.3 Catenated compounds of Group IV [2]

5.3.1 *Hydrides*

The range of catenated hydrides of Si, Ge, and Sn is indicated in Table 5.1. In addition, various rather ill-defined solid hydrides of silicon and germanium of approximate composition $(SiH_2)_n$ and $(GeH_2)_n$ have been described, which are no doubt mixtures of polymeric materials. The first report of a cyclic silane, Si_5H_{10}, appeared only in 1973 (p. 197). There is no evidence for the

[2] Ebsworth, E. A. V. (1963), *Volatile Silicon Compounds*, Pergamon, Oxford. General review, now somewhat out of date.

formation of 'unsaturated' compounds containing multiple Si—Si or Ge—Ge bonds.

One of the best methods for the preparation [3] of catenated silanes and germanes involves the hydrolysis of magnesium–silicon or magnesium–germanium alloys with dilute aqueous acid. This method was first used by Stock in his classical work on the silanes. In view of the extreme sensitivity of silanes to oxidation, Stock had to develop vacuum-line technique in order to handle these and similar compounds. Ammonium bromide in liquid ammonia has also been used as the acidic medium, but although the overall conversion of silicon or germanium into hydrides is higher than with aqueous acid, AH_4 and A_2H_6 are produced almost exclusively.

Although early work on silanes and germanes was done using vacuum-line techniques alone, more recently gas chromatography has been used to separate the hydrides. In this technique an oxygen-free atmosphere is maintained, and the handling of large quantities of hazardous compounds is avoided. All the possible silanes including structural isomers up to Si_7H_{16} and a few octasilanes have been observed. Plots of the logarithm of the relative retention time against the number of silicon atoms aid characterization. Points for the *n*-isomers lie on a straight line. Branched isomers elute earlier than straight chain ones of the same molecular weight. This parallels the gas chromatographic behaviour of the alkanes; the germanes behave similarly. Mixed silicon–germanium hydrides obtained from hydrolysis of mixed alloys of Si and Ge with either magnesium or calcium have also been separated and identified by this method.

Silanes and germanes tend to disproportionate on heating. These pyrolytic interconversions may involve SiH_2 or GeH_2 radicals [4], e.g.

$$Si_2H_6 \rightarrow SiH_2 + SiH_4$$
$$SiH_2 + Si_2H_6 \rightarrow Si_3H_8 \text{ etc.}$$
$$(\text{cf. } SiH_4 \rightarrow SiH_2 + H_2; SiH_4 + SiH_2 \rightarrow Si_2H_6)$$

This contrasts with the pyrolysis of alkanes, which proceeds via alkenes or alkyl radicals, and not via CH_2.

Some higher silanes and germanes are formed by controlled pyrolysis of SiH_4 (at 400°) or GeH_4 (at 280°) respectively. In addition, solid polymeric

[3] Jolly, W. L. and Norman, A. D. (1967), *Preparative Inorganic Reactions*, 4, 1, Interscience, New York. Preparation of hydrides of Groups IV and V.

[4] Bowrey, M. and Purnell, J. H. (1970), *J. Amer. Chem. Soc.*, 92, 2594.

material, AH_n, and hydrogen are produced. As the higher hydrides tend to disproportionate at lower temperatures than these, yields of them in these thermal reactions are low.

The A—M bonds in silanes and germanes are readily cleaved by chlorine and bromine to give the tetrahalides. Controlled reaction of iodine leads to mixed derivatives in which the chains remain intact, e.g.

$$Ge_2H_6 + I_2 \xrightarrow{-63°} H_3Ge.GeH_2I \text{ (decomp., room temp.)}$$

$$Si_3H_8 + I_2 \longrightarrow$$

$$\underset{\text{(A)}}{H_3Si.SiH_2.SiH_2I} + \underset{\text{(B)}}{H_3Si.SiHI.SiH_3} + H_3Si.SiHI.SiH_2I$$

These iodosilanes give approximately first-order proton magnetic resonance spectra which are useful in the characterization of isomers, e.g. (A) and (B). Thus the spectrum of (B) shows a doublet and a septet with relative intensities 6:1 [5].

Distannane Sn_2H_6 is formed in low yield, together with stannane SnH_4, by reduction of aqueous alkaline stannite solutions with sodium borohydride. It is very unstable, decomposing to the elements below 0°.

5.3.2   Alkyls and aryls

Substitution of hydrogen by alkyl and aryl groups often very greatly enhances the kinetic stability of catenated compounds to thermal decomposition, disproportion, hydrolysis, and oxidation. This is particularly true for the Group IV derivatives. Polysilanes such as $Me_{26}Si_{12}$ can be distilled in air at around 300°. The difference between these organic derivatives and the hydrides is probably associated with the much lower mobility and reactivity of alkyl or aryl groups compared with hydrogen.

Catenated alkyls and aryls are typically prepared by Wurtz coupling of organo-halides [6];

$$Me_2SiCl_2 \xrightarrow{\text{Na-K}} (Me_2Si)_n \qquad (n = 5, 6, 7)$$
$$\text{rings; cf. alicyclic compounds}$$

$$\left.\begin{array}{l} Me_3SiCl \\ Me_2SiCl_2 \end{array}\right\} \xrightarrow{\text{Na-K}} Me_3Si(SiMe_2)_nSiMe_3 \quad (n \text{ up to at least 16})$$
$$\text{chains}$$

[5] Fehér, F., Plichta, P. and Guillery, R. (1970), *Chem. Ber.*, **103**, 3028.

[6] Kumada, M. and Tameo, K. (1968), *Advances in Organometallic Chem.*, **6**, 19.

Germanium and tin compounds result by reaction of an organometallic compound with GeI_2 or $SnCl_2$ under appropriate conditions:

$$GeI_2 \xrightarrow{Me_3Al} Me_3Ge(GeMe_2)_n GeMe_3 \quad (n \text{ up to } 22)$$

$$SnCl_2 \xrightarrow{PhMgBr} \begin{array}{c} Ph_2 \quad Ph_2 \diagup SnPh_2 \\ Sn-Sn \mid \\ \mid \diagup Sn-Sn \\ \mid \diagup Ph_2 \quad Ph_2 \\ Ph_2 \, Sn \end{array}$$

'diphenyl tin'

The so-called 'diphenyl tin' has a six-membered ring of tin atoms in the chair conformation in the crystal.

5.3.3 *Halides* (Table 5.1)

Apart from the very stable fluorocarbons – the polymeric $(CF_2)_n$ is the well known Teflon plastic – catenation in saturated carbon halides is restricted. Steric interactions between bulky halogen atoms (Cl, Br, or I) may account for the instability of the higher members of the other series.

When silicon tetrafluoride is passed over silicon heated to $1100°$ at low pressure (1 torr), volatile SiF_2 is formed (see p. 50) [7]. It polymerizes rapidly to a waxy white material $(SiF_2)_n$, the silicon analogue of Teflon, which is suitable only for coating lunar frying pans since it is spontaneously in-flammable in air! Pyrolysis of this at $200–350°$ *in vacuo* yields a series of silicon fluorides, of which Si_2F_6, Si_3F_8, and Si_4F_{10} were isolated, and higher members up to $Si_{16}F_{32}$ identified by mass spectrometry (the $[\text{Parent} - F]^{+\cdot}$ ion appears in the spectrum). The polymer thus contains Si—Si bonds. It is readily hydrolysed by 20% hydrofluoric acid to a mixture of silanes (up to Si_6H_{14} at least).

Like so many fluorides, the catenated perfluorosilanes are remarkably volatile, their boiling points being comparable to those of the silanes, e.g. Si_4F_{10} $100°$, Si_4H_{10} $105°$.

Higher silicon chlorides are best produced by the chlorination of calcium silicide. Typical yields are as follows: $SiCl_4$ 65%; Si_2Cl_6 30%; Si_3Cl_8 4%;

[7] Margrave, J. L. and Wilson, P. W. (1971), *Accounts Chem. Research*, **4**, 145.

Si_4Cl_{10} + Si_5Cl_{12} + Si_6Cl_{14} 1%, so that very large scale reactions must be carried out to obtain reasonable quantities of the higher members of the series. The Si—Si bonds in chloropolysilanes are even more susceptible to cleavage by nucleophiles than those in the silanes themselves. Yields of $Me_3SiSiMe_3$ from the reaction of methylmagnesium iodide on Si_2Cl_6 are low, tetramethylsilane being a major product. Similarly, reduction of Si_2Cl_6 with lithium aluminium hydride affords silane as well as disilane, although satisfactory yields of the latter can be obtained if the products are rapidly removed from the reducing medium as they are formed. This procedure has also been applied to the preparation of trisilane from Si_3Cl_8 [8]. Such difficulties have restricted the use of perchloropolysilanes as starting materials for the synthesis of other catenated silicon compounds.

Hexachlorodisilane forms 1:1 and 1:2 complexes with trimethylamine:

$$Cl_3\underset{\underset{Me_3N}{\uparrow}}{Si}-\underset{\underset{NMe_3}{\uparrow}}{Si}Cl_3 \rightleftharpoons Cl_3\underset{\underset{Me_3N}{\uparrow}}{Si}-SiCl_3 + Me_3N \quad (\Delta H = 10\,kJ\,mol^{-1})$$

The 1:1 complex decomposes with disproportionation of the disilane to $SiCl_4$ and higher silanes. This reaction can be induced with as little as 0.1 mole % trimethylamine. If the silicon tetrachloride is removed as it is formed, the produce is the pentasilane (C), while if it is allowed to accumulate in a closed vessel, (D) is obtained quantitatively [9].

$$4\,Si_2Cl_6 \xrightarrow[\text{catalyst}]{Me_3N} 3\,SiCl_4\uparrow + Cl_3\,Si-\underset{\underset{SiCl_3}{|}}{\overset{\overset{SiCl_3}{|}}{Si}}-SiCl_3$$

$$(C)$$

$$5\,Si_2Cl_6 \xrightarrow[\text{catalyst}]{Me_3N} Si_6Cl_{14}.SiCl_4 + 3\,SiCl_4 \xrightarrow[\text{room temp.}]{\text{pump at}} Cl_3\,Si-\underset{\underset{SiCl_3}{|}}{\overset{\overset{SiCl_3}{|}}{Si}}-Si_2Cl_5$$

$$(D)$$

The different solubilities of (C) and (D) in Si_2Cl_6 or $SiCl_4$ respectively account for the different reaction paths. Four-centre intermediates may be involved:

[8] Gasper, P. P., Levy, C. A. and Adair, G. M. (1970), *Inorg. Chem.*, 9, 1272.
[9] Urry, G., (1970), Accounts Chem. Research, 3, 306.

$$\underset{Me_3N \rightarrow SiCl_3-Si}{\overset{Cl \quad Cl}{\underset{Cl \quad Si}{\diagup \diagdown}}} SiCl_3 \longrightarrow Cl_3Si-\underset{Cl}{\overset{Cl}{Si}}-SiCl_3 + SiCl_4 + Me_3N$$

Substitution of chlorine in Si_2Cl_6 by methyl very greatly reduces the rate of disproportionation, probably because this lowers the Lewis acidity and hence the ability of the disilane to complex with trimethylamine.

Decaphenylcyclopentasilane Si_5Ph_{10} is converted quantitatively by anhydrous hydrogen bromide into Si_5Br_{10}. Reduction of this with lithium aluminium hydride then yields cyclopentasilane, Si_5H_{10}, the first cyclic silicon hydride to be discovered. These reactions constitute rare specific syntheses of polysilanes.

Two catenated halides of germanium, Ge_2Cl_6 and Ge_2Br_6, are known. The latter is formed when a mixture of $GeBr_2$ and $GeBr_4$ is heated under reflux for five minutes in toluene [10]. Both compounds disproportionate on heating to about 80°:

$$GeBr_2 + GeBr_4 \underset{\text{slow heating to } 85°}{\overset{\text{rapid heating in toluene, then cooling}}{\rightleftharpoons}} \underset{\text{white crystals}}{Ge_2Br_6}$$

Hexachlorodistannane Sn_2Cl_6 has been prepared by the following route. It is extremely unstable, disproportionating to $SnCl_2$ and $SnCl_4$ at $-65°$ [11].

$$Sn_2Ph_6 \xrightarrow[(CH_3CO)_2O]{CH_3COOH-} (CH_3COO)_2Sn\underset{\overset{|}{\underset{C}{\underset{|}{\overset{O \diagdown \diagup O}{}}} CH_3}}{\overset{\overset{CH_3}{\overset{|}{C}}}{\overset{O \diagdown \diagup O}{|}}}Sn(OCOCH_3)_2 \xrightarrow[-100°]{HCl}$$

$$Sn_2Cl_6 \xrightarrow{-65°} SnCl_2 + SnCl_4$$

[10] Curtis, M. D. and Wolber, P. (1972), *Inorg. Chem.*, **11**, 431.
[11] Wiberg, E. and Behringer, H. (1964), *Z. Anorg. Chem.*, **329**, 290.

These results perhaps explain the failure to isolate other catenated halides of these elements. They are unstable with respect to AX_4 and the divalent halides AX_2 which contain no A—A bonds, unlike the solid silicon derivatives of similar formula. This trend may be associated with the increasing ionic character of the dihalides down the Group, which presumably causes them to be favoured over catenated compounds, especially for tin.

5.4 Catenated compounds of Group V (P and As) [12]

P—P bonds in a variety of compounds show remarkable constancy in length of ca. 221 pm (Table 5.3). This value applies both to 3- and to 4-coordinate phosphorus. It is difficult to say whether this is a really general phenomenon, as the range of catenated phosphorus compounds whose structures have been determined is still rather limited. Experimentally work in this area is hampered by the ready oxidation and toxicity of many of these compounds.

TABLE 5.3
Some phosphorus–phosphorus bond lengths (pm)

Black phosphorus	218	$(C_6H_5P)_5$	222
White phosphorus	221	$(C_6H_5P)_6$	223
P_2I_4	221	P sulphides	223
$(CF_3P)_4$	221	$Et_2P(S)—P(S)Et_2$	222
$(PO_2)_6^{6-}$	220		

5.4.1 *Hydrides*

Diphosphine P_2H_4 is a minor product when phosphine is prepared by the hydrolysis of calcium phosphide. Triphosphine ($H_2P.PH.PH_2$) is also formed in trace quantities. Similarly, arsine AsH_3 with small amounts of As_2H_4 and As_3H_5 result from acid hydrolysis of magnesium arsenide. The higher hydrides disproportionate readily to the monohydrides and non-volatile polymeric material. Volatile higher homologues of P_3H_5 have been detected by mass spectrometry, although none of them appears to be stable [13].

[12] Cowley, A. H. (1965), *Chem. Rev.*, **65**, 617.
[13] Baudler, M. *et al.* (1966), *Naturwissenschaften*, **53**, 106.

5.4.2 *Halides* (Table 5.1)

Diphosphorus tetrafluoride is prepared by the action of mercury on IPF_2 (p. 47). The favoured molecular conformation in the gas phase is probably *trans* and not *gauche* as in diphosphine. P_2F_4 does not dissociate into radicals as readily as N_2F_4 (p. 213). When it is passed at low pressure (2×10^{-3} torr) through a heated tube and the effluent gases are monitored by mass spectrometry, the ion PF_2^+ increases in intensity relative to $P_2F_4^+$ as the temperature is raised from 350° to 900°. On cooling the products from such pyrolysis to −196°, a yellow phosphorus–fluorine polymer is obtained, which on warming evolves PF_3, P_2F_4, and other unstable volatile fractions. From these $P(PF_3)_3$ was isolated. The ^{19}F n.m.r. spectrum showed a doublet of doublets centred at +88 p.p.m. relative to CCl_3F. The ^{31}P n.m.r. spectrum showed a triplet (J_{PF}) of doublets ($J_{PP'}$) each further split into a triplet ($J_{PP'P}$). The resonance arising from the central phosphorus atom P′ consisted of a quartet ($J_{PP'}$) of septets ($J_{P'PF}$). These spectra thus confirm the suggested structure.

When an electrical discharge is passed through the vapour over a solution of phosphorus in phosphorus trichloride, or through a mixture of hydrogen and PCl_3 vapour, diphosphorus tetrachloride is formed. The iodide P_2I_4 is obtained by direct reaction between the elements in stoicheiometric proportions. An X-ray diffraction study has shown the molecule to have a *trans* conformation in the crystal (Fig. 5.2). Diarsenic tetraiodide has been prepared similarly by heating arsenic with iodine to 220° in octahydrophenanthrene.

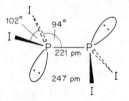

FIGURE 5.2
Structure of P_2I_4 molecules in the crystalline state

5.4.3 *Alkyls and aryls*

Catenated alkyls and aryls of phosphorus and arsenic are frequently thermally rather stable and are not susceptible to disproportionation, although they are usually oxidized in air.

The alkyls and aryls are of three main types:

(a) Diphosphines and diarsines R_2A-AR_2.
(b) Triphosphines $(R_2P)_2PR$ (R = e.g. Ph, CF_3).
(c) Cyclopolyphosphines and polyarsines $(RP)_n$ and $(RAs)_n$ where n = 4, 5, or 6.

They can be prepared by the following general methods:

(1) Elimination of hydrogen halide from a hydride and a halide, with or without the addition of base, e.g.

$$Ph_2PH + ClPPh_2 \rightarrow Ph_2P-PPh_2 + HCl$$

$$CF_3PH_2 + 2(CF_3)_2PI \rightarrow CF_3P{\overset{\displaystyle P(CF_3)_2}{\underset{\displaystyle P(CF_3)_2}{}}} + 2HI$$

(2) Wurtz type coupling reactions, e.g.

$$PhPCl_2 + Na \rightarrow (PhP)_n \quad (n = 5, 6)$$

Mercury is sometimes used to bring about such coupling, especially for the trifluoromethyl derivatives, e.g.

$$CF_3PI_2 + 2Hg \rightarrow 1/n\,(CF_3P)_n + Hg_2I_2$$

The compounds $(RP)_n$ and $(RAs)_n$ have cyclic skeletons of phosphorus or arsenic atoms. Some structures are illustrated in Fig. 5.3. The four-membered ring in $(CF_3P)_4$ is not planar, and the CF_3 groups are arranged alternately on opposite sides of the ring to minimize non-bonding interactions. The P_5 ring in $(CF_3P)_5$ is somewhat distorted, as it is not possible to alternate the substituents regularly about a five-membered ring. Arsenomethane $(CH_3As)_5$ has a very similar structure. The six-membered rings in arsenobenzene and in its phosphorus analogue are in the chair form, with the phenyl groups in equatorial positions.

Substituted arsenobenzenes were extensively studied remarkably early following the discovery in 1913 by P. Ehrlich of Salvarsan, a useful

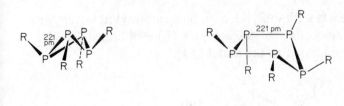

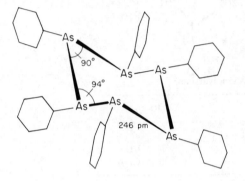

FIGURE 5.3
Structures of cyclopolyphosphines $(CF_3P)_{4,5}$ and of arsenobenzene

antitrypanosomatic drug still used in the treatment of sleeping sickness in its advanced stages. Its synthesis shows the possibility of forming As—As bonds under aqueous conditions by reduction:

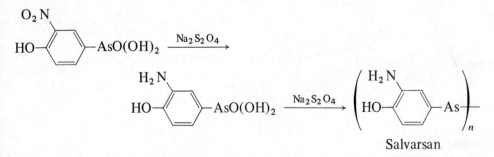

Salvarsan

It is likely that there is very little energy difference between rings of different sizes. A summary of those which have been established so far is given in Table 5.4. Other analogous compounds perhaps with larger rings could probably be made if suitable routes were chosen. When tetraethylcyclotetraphosphine $(EtP)_4$ reacts with molybdenum hexacarbonyl in tetrahydrofuran, a change in ring size occurs and the complex (E) is obtained. The five-membered ring is 1,3-coordinated to the metal [14].

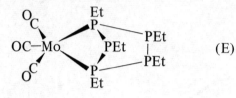

(E)

TABLE 5.4
Ring sizes in cyclopolyphosphines and cyclopolyarsines

$(RP)_n$		$(RAs)_n$
$n = 4$;	R = alkyl, CF_3, C_6H_{11}, C_6F_5	—
$n = 5$;	R = CF_3, C_6F_5, C_6H_5	R = CH_3
$n = 6$;	R = C_6H_5	R = C_6H_5

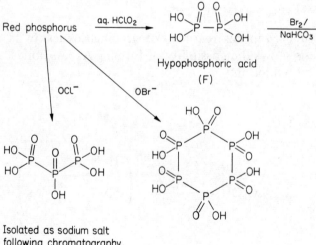

Hypophosphoric acid
(F)

Pyrophosphoric acid

Isolated as sodium salt
following chromatography

(G)   (H)

FIGURE 5.4
Products from the oxidation of red phosphorus

[14] Bush, M. A. and Woodward, P. (1968), *J. Chem. Soc.* (A), 1221.

5.4.4 *Oxo-acids*

4-Coordinate phosphorus is much less susceptible to oxidation than 3-coordinate phosphorus. Thus a few catenated oxo-acids have been prepared by the controlled oxidation of phosphorus in the presence of water. In these reactions it is likely that P—P bonds present in the element remain intact.

Hypophosphoric acid (F) (Fig. 5.4) is tetrabasic, with two fairly strong and two weakly acidic groups. Weakly alkaline bromine converts it into pyrophosphoric acid. Other catenated acids include (G) and the cyclic product (H). The structure of the latter has been established by an X-ray diffraction study of its caesium salt.

5.5   Catenated compounds of sulphur

The starting point for the preparation of catenated sulphur compounds is elemental sulphur itself, which in its stable modification at room temperature consists of S_8 cyclic molecules. S—S bonds in sulphur are rather susceptible to nucleophilic attack, for example by S^{2-} or HS^- to give polysulphide ions, by CN^- to form thiocyanate, or by SO_3^{2-} to yield thiosulphate. From solutions of sulphur in sulphides, well defined alkali metal salts $M^I_2S_n$ (n = 2 to 6) can be crystallized. Longer chains are also present in solution, and in a few cases salts containing them have been isolated with large cations.

Extensive structural data [15] show that branching does not occur in sulphur chains, although chemical evidence does not entirely exclude the participation of intermediates of the type

$$\overset{\displaystyle S}{\underset{\displaystyle R-S-R}{\uparrow}}$$

in certain reactions. The 'SSS angle in the chains is commonly between 90° and the tetrahedral angle (109·5°); 103° in the S_3^{2-} ion in BaS_3 is typical. The dihedral angles are also approximately 90° in most polysulphur compounds. This means that, for four or more sulphur atoms in a chain, the possibility of isomerism arises. For S_4^{2-} (as in $BaS_4.2H_2O$) *dl*-enantiomorphs can exist. For S_5 chains *cis* and *trans* isomers can occur. The *trans* configuration exists in two enantiomorphous forms. The *cis* form has been found in barium

[15] Rahman, R., Safe, S. and Taylor, A. (1970), *Quart. Rev.*, **24**, 208.

pentathionate, while in the potassium salt the ion is *trans* (see Fig. 5.5). The *cis* form of an S_5 chain corresponds to part of the S_8 ring, while the *trans* form is like part of the helical chain structure of metallic selenium.

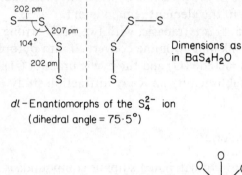

dl–Enantiomorphs of the S_4^{2-} ion
(dihedral angle = 75·5°)

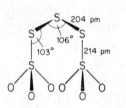

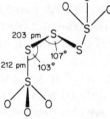

cis – $S_5O_6^{2-}$ *trans* – $S_5O_6^{2-}$

FIGURE 5.5
Isomerism in sulphur chains

In contrast to P—P bonds (p. 198). S—S bonds vary very widely in length between different types of compound (Table 5.5).

TABLE 5.5
Some S—S bond lengths (pm)

S_2	189	S_8	205
FSSF	189	S_6	207
ClSSCl	193	$BaS_4O_6.2H_2O$	212 (terminal)
BrSSBr	198	$O_3S.SO_3^{2-}$	215
$BaS_4O_6.2H_2O$	202 (internal)	$F_5S.SF_5$	221
HSSH	205	$O_2S.SO_2^{2-}$	239
CF_3SSCF_3	205?		

It appears that the 'normal' value for divalent, 2-coordinate sulphur in compounds XSSX is about 203 pm. In most compounds the dihedral angle is about 90°; with this stereochemistry, lone pair–lone pair interactions on adjacent sulphur atoms are minimized. When the dihedral angle is constrained, as in a cyclic structure, to adopt smaller or larger values (e.g. in S_6, p. 176, it is 74°), there is a slight increase in bond length attributable to the increased non-bonding pair interactions.

The very short S—S bond in FSSF is perhaps due to polarization of the molecule in the sense $F^-S=S^+-F$. The S—S bond in XSSX increases in length with decreasing electronegativity of X (X = F, Cl, Br, I).

Sulphur–sulphur bonds containing 4- or 6-valent sulphur atoms are commonly longer than bonds containing only divalent sulphur. In S_2F_{10} and $S_2O_4^{2-}$, the stability of the $SF_5\cdot$ and $SO_2^-\cdot$ radicals may contribute to the weakness and thus the length of the S—S bonds (pp. 61, 138).

5.5.1 *Sulphanes and halosulphanes*

Acidification of polysulphide solutions yields a mixture of hydrogen polysulphides or sulphanes as a heavy oil. By fractional distillation of this oil *in vacuo*, components from H_2S_2 to H_2S_6 were isolated. The crude oil does not contain H_2S_2 or H_2S_3, but it yields these by cracking. The higher sulphanes especially are very liable to such decomposition; mild heating is sufficient to cause disproportionation leading eventually to sulphur and hydrogen sulphide. Such reactions are almost thermally neutral as the number of S—S and S—H bonds is unchanged. The driving force is provided by the entropy change arising from the formation of gaseous hydrogen sulphide from liquid starting materials:

$$H_2S_n \rightarrow H_2S + (n - 1)/8\ S_8$$

The lability of catenated sulphur derivatives led Fehér and his coworkers to develop specific *in situ* syntheses which require no separation steps. They involve the reaction between a sulphane and a chlorosulphane, e.g.

$$HSSH + ClSCl + HSSH \rightarrow HS_5H + 2\ HCl$$

Secondary reactions, e.g.

$$2\ HS_5H + SCl_2 \rightarrow HS_{11}H + 2\ HCl$$

205

can occur, but are reduced by using excess H_2S_2 which can be removed *in vacuo*. Polysulphur chlorides S_nCl_2 result when SCl_2 or S_2Cl_2 is in excess:

$$ClS_2Cl + HS_4H + ClS_2Cl \rightarrow ClS_8Cl + 2\,HCl$$

Condensation between specific polysulphanes and polysulphur chlorides can yield novel sulphur rings (see p. 178).

The bromides S_nBr_2 (n = 2 to 8) are made from the chlorides by treatment with hydrogen bromide, and the iodides by using potassium iodide in cyclo-hexane. The iodides are extremely unstable and have been observed only spectrophotometrically in dilute solution.

Symmetrical S—S stretching vibrations yield strong bands in the region 440–510 cm^{-1} in the Raman spectra of catenated sulphur compounds. The spectra have been used to analyse mixtures and to assess purity. The ultra-violet absorption spectra of polysulphanes H_2S_n show a consistent red shift with increasing chain length, which has been interpreted in terms of $(p-d)\pi$ and maybe $(d-d)\pi$ delocalization of electrons along the chains (Fig. 5.6).

The reaction between AgF and sulphur gives a low yield of difluoropoly-sulphanes FS_nF (n = 2, 3, 4) which were identified by mass spectrometry, n.m.r., and chemical analysis [16].

Although branching in sulphur chains has not been found, a few compounds exist which contain the S=S grouping. S_2F_2 has two isomeric forms; the unstable one FSSF (p. 205) rearranges above $-78°$ into the more stable isomer (J).

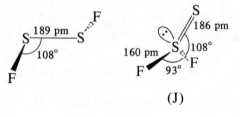

(J)

5.5.2 *Oxo-acids*

The preparations and structures of some catenated oxo-anions of sulphur are summarized in Fig. 5.7. Free thiosulphuric acid is unstable at room tempera-ture, but has been isolated as an etherate at $-78°$. Its salts, especially alkali

[16] Seel, F., Budenz, R., Gombler, W. and Seitter, H. (1971), Z. Anorg. Chem., **380**, 262.

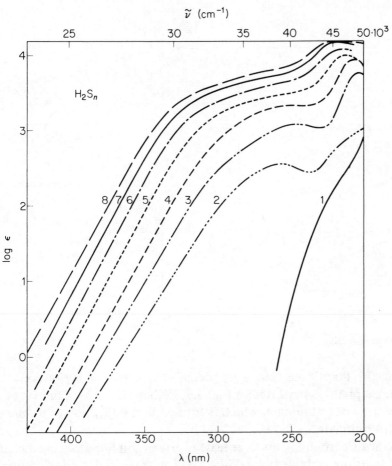

FIGURE 5.6
Ultraviolet absorption spectra of polysulphanes [Fehér, F. and Munzner, H. (1963) *Chem. Ber.*, **96**, 1131]

metal thiosulphates, are readily prepared and are used in photography to dissolve unreacted silver bromide from emulsions as thiosulphate complexes.

Dithionites are very strong reducing agents in aqueous solution: $E°(2SO_3^{2-}, 2H_2O/4OH^-, S_2O_4^{2-}) = -1·12$ V. They decompose rapidly in acid solution.

The polythionic acids $HO_3S.S_{n-2}SO_3H$ are best characterized by their salts; for the lower members of the series, especially by those of the alkali metals

207

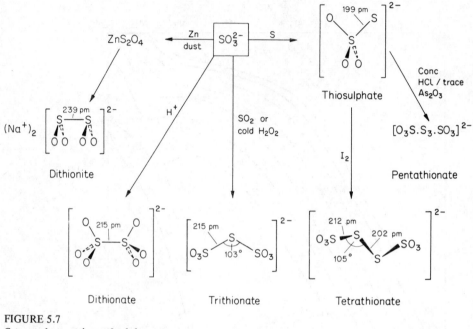

FIGURE 5.7
Catenated oxo-anions of sulphur

and alkaline earths. Polythionate ions are prepared by various reactions of sulphite or thiosulphate as indicated in Fig. 5.7. Perhaps the most familiar of these salts is sodium tetrathionate, which is formed in the titration of iodine with sodium thiosulphate.

Polythionic acids containing up to at least fourteen sulphur atoms in a chain are present in solutions obtained by adding a concentrated solution of sodium thiosulphate to cold concentrated hydrochloric acid. They also arise by reactions of the type:

$$6\,H_2S_2O_3 + (2n - 9)\,H_2S + (n - 3)\,H_2SO_3$$
$$\rightarrow 3\,H_2S_nO_6 + (3n - 9)\,H_2O$$

which, under suitable conditions, proceed stoicheiometrically without deposition of sulphur. Crystalline salts of many higher polythionic acids have been isolated from such solutions using large organic cations such as nitron. It is difficult to prove conclusively that these products consist of single species and not mixtures of homologues, but the existence of nitron polythionates with chains of up to eighteen sulphur atoms seems well established [17]. The chain lengths in polythionates can be estimated either by titration against potassium iodate, which oxidizes them quantitatively to sulphate, or by degradation by sulphite which gives trithionate and thiosulphate:

$$S_nO_6^{2-} + (n - 3) SO_3^{2-} \rightarrow S_3O_6^{2-} + (n - 3) S_2O_3^{2-}$$

The thiosulphate produced can be estimated by titration against a standard solution of iodine.

5.6   Catenated selenium and tellurium compounds

Consistent with the decrease in bond strength in the series $E(S—S) > E(Se—Se) > E(Te—Te)$, few catenated selenium or tellurium compounds are known. There are no catenated hydrides, although the molecular halides Se_2Cl_2 and Se_2Br_2, and the polymeric Te_2Cl and Te_3Cl_2, have been characterized. Selenium, and to a lesser extent tellurium, dissolve in solutions of their anions to form polyanions Se_n^{2-} and Te_n^{2-}.

Organic diselenides and ditellurides RAAR are well established, and there are a few triselenides.

It is significant that no catenated oxo-acids of Se(VI) (corresponding to the polythionates) or of As(V) (corresponding to the phosphorus derivatives) are known. Selenates and arsenates are quite strong oxidizing agents while sulphates and phosphates are not (see p. 121). Any species such as $-O_3Se—Se_n—SeO_3-$ would oxidize itself (e.g. decompose to selenite and selenium) as it contains a strongly oxidizing $-O_3Se-$ and a strongly reducing $-Se—Se-$ function.

Several selenopolythionates $[O_2S \cdot Se_n \cdot SO_3]^{2-}$ ($n = 1$ to 6), however, have been characterized. Diselenotetrathionates ($n = 2$) are obtained from the reaction of selenites with sulphur dioxide in aqueous solution:

$$2 H_2SeO_3 + 2 H_2O + 5 SO_2 \rightarrow H_2Se_2S_2O_6 + 3 H_2SO_4$$

[17] Janackis, J. (1969), *Accounts Chem. Research*, 2, 316.

The higher members of the series are formed when $K_2[O_3S.SeSO_3]$ is treated with selenous acid in concentrated hydrochloric acid; the anions are separated by fractional precipitation of their nitron salts.

5.7   Catenated compounds of nitrogen

The weakness of single N—N and O—O bonds relative to multiple bonds N≡N and O=O restricts catenation by these elements, and causes many of the compounds in which they occur to be unstable. This instability relative to the elements or to the simple hydrides is strongly emphasized by the reaction between hydrazine and hydrogen peroxide, a mixture which was once used as a rocket fuel:

$$N_2H_4(l) + 2 H_2O_2(l) \rightarrow N_2(g) + 4 H_2O(g) \quad (\Delta H^\circ = -642 \text{ kJ mol}^{-1})$$

The ease of cleavage of N—N bonds (as measured by the dissociation energy of the central bond) varies very considerably from one compound to another. There is apparently also a parallel change in bond length (see Table 5.6).

TABLE 5.6
Dissociation energies and bond lengths of some compounds containing N—N bonds

Compounds	D(N—N) (kJ mol^{-1})	N—N bond length (pm)	Structure	Symmetry point group
$(CF_3)_2N$—$N(CF_3)_2$	very stable	140		D_{2d}
H_2N—NH_2	239	145	gauche	C_2
CH_3NH—$NHCH_3$	198	145	gauche	
F_2N—NF_2	84	149	gauche & trans	C_2 C_{2h}
O_2N—NO_2	57	175	planar	D_{2h}

The stability of $(CF_3)_2NN(CF_3)_2$ relative to hydrazine is attributed to a certain amount of π character in the bonding, which arises through overlap of nitrogen p orbitals with antibonding orbitals of the CF_3 groups. There is thus some removal of non-bonding electrons from the nitrogen atoms which decreases the repulsion between them.

210

The presence of electronegative groups on nitrogen does not strengthen the N—N bond, however, in N_2F_4 or in N_2O_4. The ease of dissociation in these cases is attributed to the stability of the $\cdot NF_2$ and $\cdot NO_2$ radicals.

The structures of hydrazine and of tetrafluorohydrazine have been studied extensively by various physical techniques. In the vapour phase it is likely that hydrazine is mainly in the *gauche* form. The *trans* form, which might have been expected to minimize lone pair repulsions, is not the favoured conformer, as the molecule has a dipole moment of ca. 1.85 D. The microwave spectrum of gaseous N_2F_4 shows a *gauche* conformer to be present. Low-temperature ^{19}F n.m.r. spectra in NF_3 as solvent indicate that the *trans* form is there as well. The spectrum of *trans*-N_2F_4 consists of a single line, as all four fluorine nuclei are magnetically equivalent. The spectrum of the *gauche* form is of the AA′BB′ type and appears as four lines [see Fig. 5.8]. Subsequently electron diffraction has confirmed the presence of both conformers in the vapour phase [18]. The *trans* form does not give rise to a microwave spectrum as it has zero dipole moment.

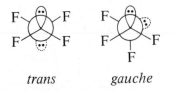

trans   gauche

The barrier to free rotation about the N—N bond in tetrafluorohydrazine is estimated at about 14 kJ mol^{-1}, similar to that in ethane. A postulated energy profile is illustrated in Fig. 5.9.

Hydrazine can be prepared by the Raschig process, which depends on the reaction of chloramine with ammonia in aqueous solution.

$$NH_3 + NaOCl \xrightarrow{\text{fast}} NaOH + ClNH_2 \qquad \text{(a)}$$

$$NH_3 + ClNH_2 + NaOH \xrightarrow{\text{slow}} N_2H_4 + NaCl + H_2O \qquad \text{(b)}$$

$$2\,ClNH_2 + N_2H_4 \longrightarrow 2\,NH_4Cl + N_2 \qquad \text{(c)}$$

[18] Cardillo, M. J. and Bauer, S. H. (1969), *Inorg. Chem.*, 8, 2086

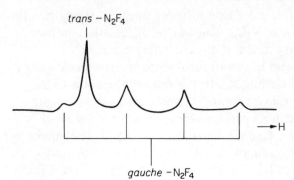

FIGURE 5.8
^{19}F n.m.r. of N_2F_4 in NF_3 at $-150°$

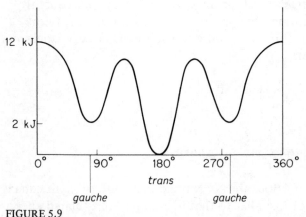

FIGURE 5.9
Postulated energy profile for rotation about N—N bond in N_2F_4 [Cardillo, M. J. and Bauer, S. H. (1969), *Inorg. Chem.*, 8, 2086]

A competing reaction (c), which is catalyzed by traces of heavy metal ions such as Cu^{2+} is suppressed by addition of gelatin which complexes with the metal ions. It seems that gelatin also catalyses reaction (b).

A good laboratory preparation of hydrazine involves the application of a Hofmann rearrangement to urea:

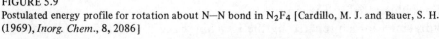

$$[O=C=N-NH_2] \xrightarrow{H_2O} H_2N-NH_2 + CO_2$$

The yields in this reaction are also sensitive to metal impurities.

Tetrafluorohydrazine [19] is obtained by reaction of nitrogen trifluoride with elements such as copper, antimony or bismuth at about 400°C.

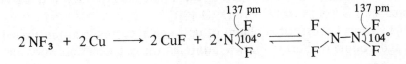

$2 NF_3 + 2 Cu \longrightarrow 2 CuF + 2 \cdot NF_2 \rightleftharpoons N_2F_4$

·NF_2 radicals are produced, which combine on cooling. The equilibrium is similar to that between NO_2 and N_2O_4 (p. 131). It has been followed spectrophotometrically, by pressure variation and by e.s.r.

The ·NF_2 radical combines with a number of other free radicals including NO, with which it forms a deeply coloured adduct:

$$2 NO + N_2F_4 \rightleftharpoons 2 F_2N.NO \rightleftharpoons 2 NO + 2 NF_2$$
$$D^{298} = 40 \text{ kJ}.$$

It can abstract a hydrogen atom from various hydrides to give the explosive and toxic compound difluoramine (see p. 45).

$$RSH + \cdot NF_2 \rightarrow RS \cdot + HNF_2 \quad (2 RS \cdot \rightarrow RSSR)$$

When molten ammonium hydrogen fluoride is electrolyzed, *cis* and *trans* isomers of difluorodiazine, together with NF_3, are formed. Electron diffraction, and for the *cis* isomer microwave spectroscopy, have shown that both molecules have planar structures.

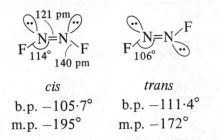

cis	*trans*
b.p. −105·7°	b.p. −111·4°
m.p. −195°	m.p. −172°

The *trans* form is converted into the *cis* form on heating. Of course, *cis*–*trans* isomerism about the N=N bond is familiar in organic chemistry, e.g. in azobenzene.

[19] Colburn, C. B., (1966), *Chem. in Britain*, **2**, 336.

213

Both the *cis* and *trans* isomers of N_2F_2 react with SbF_5 or AsF_5 to give complexes of the N_2F^+ cation, e.g. $N_2F^+ AsF_6^-$. On thermal decomposition, essentially only the *cis* isomer of N_2F_2 is formed, consistent with its higher stability. Vibrational spectroscopy indicates that the N_2F^+ ion is linear; this is expected as it is isoelectronic with N_2O [20].

Alkyl and aryl substituted chains of up to eight nitrogen atoms joined by single and double bonds are known, although the octazenes are very unstable.

5.8 Catenated oxygen compounds

Although compounds containing the –O—O– grouping, e.g. H_2O_2, F_2O_2, organic peroxides, and hydroperoxides, are common, very few are yet known in which more than two oxygen atoms are linked together. Many peroxo-compounds are liable to violent decomposition with evolution of oxygen.

As noted above for compounds containing the N—N bond, some variations in O—O bond distance occur between different peroxo-derivatives. The most striking result, however, is the very short O—O bond in F_2O_2, which is similar in length to that in the O_2 molecule. This bond is apparently much stronger than would be expected from trends in the dissociation energies of the central bonds in the series of isoelectronic compounds shown in Table 5.7.

TABLE 5.7
Some dissociation energies and bond lengths

Dissociation energies (kJ mol^{-1})			Bond lengths (pm)		
				$r_{O—O}$	$r_{O—X}$
$F_3C—CF_3$	$F_2N—NF_2$	FO—OF	OF_2	–	141
272	84	259	O_2F_2	122	158
			O_2	121	–
$H_3C—CH_3$	$H_2N—NH_2$	HO—OH	H_2O_2	148	95
351	251	201	H_2O	–	96

Dioxygen difluoride is prepared by passing a 1:1 mixture of fluorine and oxygen through an electrical discharge tube cooled in liquid air. The products condense on the walls of the reaction vessel. Radiolysis using γ-rays or photolysis has also been used. By using a higher proportion of oxygen, the prepara-

[20] Christe, K. O., Wilson, R. D. and Sawodny, W. (1971), *J. Mol. Structure*, 8, 245.

tion of higher fluorides O_nF_2 (n = 3 to 6) has been claimed. Only O_4F_2, the dimer of the $\cdot O_2F$ radical, seems established. Both O_2F_2 and O_4F_2 are very unstable thermally, decomposing below $-50°$.

The structures of peroxides such as O_2F_2 or H_2O_2 can be represented as in Fig. 4.6, by an 'open book' diagram. In H_2O_2 the angles 'HOO are less than tetrahedral as expected. In catenated oxygen and sulphur compounds the dihedral angle is usually about $90°$, so that interactions between lone pair electrons on the adjacent atoms are minimized.

A well authenticated compound containing three oxygen atoms in a chain is $F_3COOOCF_3$. Fluorine reacts with carbonyl fluoride (or carbon monoxide, which it first converts into carbonyl fluoride) best in the presence of AgF_2 catalyst to yield trifluoromethyl hypofluorite:

$$CO + F_2 \longrightarrow \begin{array}{c} F \\ \diagdown \\ F \diagup \end{array} C{=}O \xrightarrow{F_2} \begin{array}{c} F \\ \diagdown \\ F\text{-}C\text{-}OF \\ \diagup \\ F \end{array}$$

(cf. $OSF_4 + F_2 \rightarrow F_5S.OF$, p. 140)

The F–O bond of the hypofluorite can similarly add across the C=O bond of carbonyl fluoride to give bistrifluoromethyl peroxide which is stable to at least $225°$ and is not explosive, in contrast to organic peroxides. A similar stabilization of the N–N bond by CF_3 substituents was noted above (p. 210). Carbonyl fluoride reacts with alkali metal fluorides in acetonitrile to form salts $M^{+-}OCF_3$ (M = K, Rb, Cs), isoelectronic with MBF_4. These may be intermediates in the reaction between COF_2 and F_2O, which is catalysed by caesium fluoride:

$$O{=}C\begin{array}{c} \diagup F \\ \diagdown F \end{array} + CsF \rightarrow F_3CO^- \, Cs^+;$$

$$F_3CO^- + F\begin{array}{c} \diagup O \diagdown \\ \quad F \end{array} \rightarrow F_3C.OOF + F^-$$

$$F_3C.OOF + O{=}C\begin{array}{c} \diagup F \\ \diagdown F \end{array} \rightarrow F_3COOOCF_3$$

215

Groups which form fairly stable peroxides are often strongly electronegative in character, e.g. $F_5S.OOSF_5$, $FSO_2O.OSO_2F$, $CF_3C(O)O.OC(O)CF_3$, $^-O_3SO.OSO_3^-$ (p. 140). This stability may partly be associated with the inert nature of radicals such as $FSO_2O\cdot$ which can recombine, whereas radicals such as $CH_3O\cdot$ are very reactive and can initiate explosive decomposition.

5.8.1 Hydrogen peroxide and aqueous solution chemistry of peroxo-compounds [21]

Hydrogen peroxide is commonly prepared by electrolytic oxidation of sulphuric acid to peroxodisulphuric acid at low temperatures ($-20°$) and high current density. Platinum electrodes are usually used, in order to minimize oxygen evolution on account of their high overvoltages for this process. Peroxodisulphuric acid $[E°(S_2O_8^{2-}, 2\,H^+/2\,HSO_4^-) = 2\cdot18\,V]$ hydrolyses readily to give peroxomonosulphuric acid:

$$H_2S_2O_8 + H_2O \rightarrow H_2SO_5\cdot + H_2SO_4 \qquad (d)$$

This is minimized during the electrolysis by replacing some of the sulphuric acid by ammonium sulphate. The difficulty is that H_2SO_5 is destroyed by reactions such as:

$$H_2SO_5 + H_2O \rightarrow H_2SO_4 + H_2O_2 \qquad (e)$$

$$H_2SO_5 + H_2O_2 \rightarrow H_2SO_4 + O_2 + H_2O \qquad (f)$$

On completion of the electrolysis the peroxodisulphuric acid solution is hydrolysed (Equations (d) and (e)), and hydrogen peroxide isolated as an aqueous solution by rapid distillation under reduced pressure. Concentration up to 90% by low-pressure fractionation, followed by fractional crystallization, is used to prepare the pure compound.

A process involving autoxidation of 2-ethylanthraquinol is also used commercially. Air is passed through a solution of the quinol in an organic solvent, and the hydrogen peroxide extracted into water in countercurrent columns. Reduction of the quinone is effected by hydrogen in the presence of palladium

[21] Ardon, M. (1965), Oxygen: Elementary Forms and Hydrogen Peroxide, Benjamin, New York.

on an inert support, which is suspended in the liquid. The process is thus a cyclic one and requires only hydrogen and oxygen as raw materials:

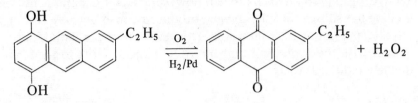

Pure hydrogen peroxide is a pale blue syrupy liquid, b.p. 152°, m.p. −0·9°. Both the free compound and its concentrated solutions are very liable to decomposition, which is catalysed by heavy metal ions. This reaction has been harnessed in torpedo propellants.

Hydrogen peroxide can act either as an oxidizing agent (e.g. with Fe^{2+} or I^-) or as a reducing agent (e.g. with MnO_4^-). Its oxidizing properties are the more important; it is used in dilute solution (ca. 3–5%) as an antiseptic and as a bleach. 30% hydrogen peroxide is a useful laboratory oxidant.

The gas phase decomposition of hydrogen peroxide in a flow system occurs homogeneously above 420°. Below this temperature the reaction takes place predominantly on the surface of the Pyrex vessel. The mechanism of the homogeneous reaction is considered to involve the steps:

$$H_2O_2 + M \rightarrow 2\ \cdot OH + M$$

$$H_2O_2 + \cdot OH \rightarrow H_2O + HO_2\cdot$$

$$HO_2\cdot + \cdot OH \rightarrow H_2O_2 + O_2$$

M is any third body; the efficiency of gas molecules lies in the order $H_2O_2 > H_2O > N_2 > O_2$. The first step in this sequence is rate-determining:

$$-d[H_2O_2]/dt = k[H_2O_2][M]$$

Radicals are also involved in aqueous reactions of hydrogen peroxide. Thus, the oxidation of ferrous ion at low hydrogen ion concentrations ([H^+] < 0·01M) proceeds according to:

$$Fe^{2+}(aq.) + H_2O_2 \longrightarrow FeOH^{2+} + \cdot OH$$

$$Fe^{2+} + OH \xrightarrow{\text{fast}} FeOH^{2+}$$

217

A mixture of H_2O_2 and Fe^{2+} in aqueous solution is a useful radical source in organic reactions (Fenton's reagent).

When hydrogen peroxide is oxidized, however, the O—O bond is not cleaved. ^{18}O labelling has shown that the oxygen produced comes entirely from hydrogen peroxide and not at all from water. This result, together with kinetic data, is consistent with the suggestion that the $HO_2\cdot$ radical is first formed, and subsequently oxidized to O_2.

5.8.2 *Peroxo-acids*

Peroxo-acids contain the grouping O—O. Many are prepared by treating the normal acid or a salt with hydrogen peroxide. Sodium peroxoborate, which is used as a bleaching and antiseptic powder, contains the ion (K) in the crystal. It comprises about 20% of many household detergents, and is also used in mouthwashes. Peroxo-carboxylic acids such as peroxoacetic acid

$$\left[\begin{array}{c} HO \\ HO \end{array} B \begin{array}{c} O\text{-}\text{-}O \\ O\text{=}O \end{array} B \begin{array}{c} OH \\ OH \end{array} \right]^{2-}$$

(K)

$CH_3CO.OOH$, trifluoroperoxoacetic acid $CF_3CO.OOH$, and peroxobenzoic acid $C_6H_5CO.OOH$ are useful reagents in organic chemistry, e.g. for the oxidation of ketones to carboxylic acids (Baeyer–Villiger oxidation), or of alkenes to epoxides. Solutions of peroxo-carboxylic acids are prepared by treating the acid anhydride with concentrated (ca. 50%) aqueous hydrogen peroxide.

Inorganic peroxo-acids are exemplified by peroxomonosulphuric acid (Caro's acid) and peroxodisulphuric acid, mentioned above. True peroxo-acids contain the grouping –O—O–. There are also some salts, e.g. $2\,Na_2CO_3.3\,H_2O_2$, $Na_4P_2O_7.nH_2O_2$, and $Na_2SiO_3.3\,H_2O_2$, which contain hydrogen peroxide of crystallization but are not true peroxo-compounds.

5.9   Catenated boron compounds and the boron hydrides

5.9.1 *Historical background*

The investigation of the boron hydrides by Alfred Stock [22] in Germany in the period 1912–1936 was of great importance in inorganic chemistry. He

[22] Stock, A. (1933), *Hydrides of Boron and Silicon,* Cornell University Press, Ithaca, N.Y. A first-hand account of early discoveries in this field.

devised elegant vacuum-line techniques to prepare, purify, and characterize the air-sensitive volatile hydrides. He described the chemistry of B_2H_6, B_4H_{10}, B_5H_9, B_5H_{11}, B_6H_{10}, and $B_{10}H_{14}$. The formulae of these compounds could not be explained by the contemporary ideas on valency which had worked so well for organic compounds and also for the silicon hydrides which Stock investigated.

In the period 1937–1953 numerous theories on bonding in the boron hydrides were proposed, but those of Longuet-Higgins and Lipscomb gained acceptance and form the basis of much of present thought on the problem. About 1954, growing military interest in missiles projected the boron hydrides into strategic importance as possible fuels for rockets. The heat of combustion per gram of boranes is higher than that of alkanes. While Stock had worked with grams and milligrams of boranes, the compounds were suddenly required in ton quantities. There was a flurry of research activity and stock-piles of the hydrides were made. Military enthusiasm waned after 1958 when it became apparent that the gain in useful energy was marginal and that this did not compensate for the difficulties of using the toxic, air-sensitive compounds.

Since 1958, research on the boranes has been to peaceful ends. The major developments have been in polyhedral anions and carboranes, compounds containing both boron and carbon in the skeleton. There is now limited commercial production of very thermally stable silicone polymers based on substituted carboranes.

5.9.2 *Boron and multi-centre bonding*

As we have commented before, the fact that boron has four atomic orbitals available for bonding but only three electrons to fill them has a strong influence on its chemistry. We have seen in Chapter 2 that BCl_3, in which there is $(p–p)\pi$ bonding from the lone pairs on the chlorine, is stable as a monomer, but that BH_3, in which the p_z orbital is vacant, is unstable with respect to the dimer, diborane B_2H_6.

Diborane has been shown by electron diffraction and Raman and infrared spectroscopy to have a hydrogen bridged structure with D_{2h} symmetry as shown in Fig. 5.10(a). A complete molecular orbital bonding scheme for this molecule is quite complicated because there are fourteen MOs arising from combinations of the $2s$ and $2p$ orbitals of boron with the $1s$ orbital of hydrogen [23]. Calculations and the photoelectron spectrum of diborane show that there are six bonding MOs filled by the twelve valence electrons in the molecule. However, the unusual part of the molecule is the $B\overset{H}{\underset{H}{<}}B$ bridge, and we can usefully discuss bonding in this in terms of localized molecular orbitals.

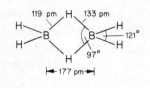
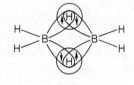

(a)

(b)

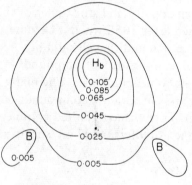
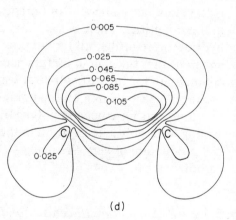

(c)

(d)

FIGURE 5.10

Bonding in diborane

(a) Diborane D_{2d} symmetry

(b) Three-centre two-electron bonds in B_2H_6

(c) Calculated electron density in B—H—B bond of B_2H_6[a]

(d) Calculated electron density in part of C=C bond of C_2H_4[a]

[a Steiner, E. (1970), *Ann. Reps. Chem. Soc. (A)*, 67, 37]

Overlap of a combination of $2s$ and $2p$ atomic orbitals on boron with the $1s$ orbital on hydrogen creates two localized MOs [Fig. 5.10(b)]. If two electrons from each boron atom in diborane are assigned to bonding to the terminal hydrogen atoms, one electron from each boron atom and one from each of

[23] Wade, K. (1971), *Electron Deficient Compounds*, Nelson, London.

the bridging hydrogen atoms is left to fill the bridging MOs. The result is two localized three-centre two-electron bonds. A calculation on the electron distribution in a bridging orbital gives the picture shown in Fig. 5.10(c).

It is interesting to compare diborane with ethylene as the two molecules are isoelectronic. The photoelectron spectra of the molecules are quite similar and a calculation of the electron distribution in the C—C bond of ethylene [Fig. 5.10(d)] is comparable to that in diborane. The main difference is the electron density along the A $\cdots$ A axis in the two molecules. In ethylene, there is appreciable electron density along the C $\cdots$ C axis corresponding to a C—C σ bond, but in diborane the density along the B $\cdots$ B axis is very low and there is no B—B bond.

Localized bonding descriptions of the higher boron hydrides require the formation of three-centre bonds by overlap of s and p orbitals of three boron atoms. In principle, any atom supplying an orbital of the correct symmetry could participate in three-centre bonding, and an increasing range of compounds are being made in which one or more of the positions in a borane structure are occupied by heteroatoms. The orbitals from carbon are most comparable in energy with those from boron, hence the large number of stable carboranes.

A delocalized MO approach is more convenient than localized bonding descriptions for borane anions, carboranes, and chloroboranes of high symmetry. However, before we consider the application of these bonding ideas to polyboron compounds, we shall survey the range of compounds which have been isolated or predicted with an emphasis on the progression in skeletal arrangements.

5.9.3 *The range of structures*

Table 5.8 shows some of the simpler boron compounds containing one to four boron atoms. Each of the compounds BX_3 can be considered as the first member of a homologous series B_nX_{n+2}. The structures of the compounds B_nX_{n+2} can be described by two-centre bonds. It can be seen from the Table that the number of members known in each series increases with the $p\pi$ donor ability of X. The dimethylamino-derivatives with particularly strong $(p-p)\pi$ bonding are known up to $n = 5$, but boron chlorides after $n = 2$ and boron hydrides after $n = 1$ are described by two- and three-centre bonding.

221

The compounds B_2H_6 and B_4H_{10} are formally the first known representatives of two different homologous series, B_nH_{n+4} and B_nH_{n+6}. However, unlike most homologous series in compounds involving only two-centre bonds, the particular requirements of three-centre bonding may cause some members of these homologous series to be very unstable and not isolable. Thus, B_3H_7 and B_4H_8 have not been isolated, although B_5H_9 (Fig. 5.11) is quite stable.

TABLE 5.8
Boron compounds containing one to four boron atoms (^{a} see p. 243)

Increasing pπ donor ability of attached atoms or groups →

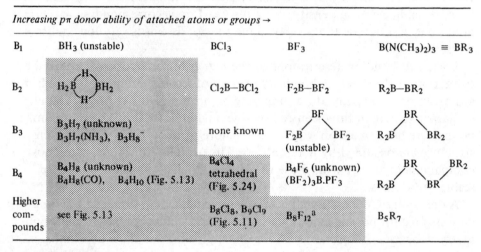

B_1	BH_3 (unstable)	BCl_3	BF_3	$B(N(CH_3)_2)_3 \equiv BR_3$
B_2	$H_2B\!\!\overset{H}{\underset{H}{\diamond}}\!\!BH_2$	$Cl_2B{-}BCl_2$	$F_2B{-}BF_2$	$R_2B{-}BR_2$
B_3	B_3H_7 (unknown) $B_3H_7(NH_3)$, $B_3H_8^-$	none known	$F_2B\diagdown^{BF}\diagup BF_2$ (unstable)	$R_2B\diagdown^{BR}\diagup BR_2$
B_4	B_4H_8 (unknown) $B_4H_8(CO)$, B_4H_{10} (Fig. 5.13)	B_4Cl_4 tetrahedral (Fig. 5.24)	B_4F_6 (unknown) $(BF_2)_3B.PF_3$	$R_2B\diagdown^{BR\quad BR_2}\diagup BR$
Higher compounds	see Fig. 5.13	B_8Cl_8, B_9Cl_9 (Fig. 5.11)	$B_8F_{12}^a$	B_5R_7

▨ multicentre bonding involved

From the few examples in Table 5.8, it can be seen that complexing with electron pair donors or conversion into anionic forms can stabilize otherwise unstable structures.

Figure 5.11 shows the boron, or boron and carbon, skeletons for some boranes, borane anions, and carboranes containing four to twelve skeletal atoms, alongside the formulae of the compounds with these skeletons. The diagrams do not show the position of bridging hydrogen atoms or terminal BH_2 groups, but full structures for some of the compounds are given in Fig. 5.1

The right-hand column in Fig. 5.11 represents the homologous series of boranes B_nH_{n+6}. They are compounds of relatively low symmetry with open structures, known as arachno- (cobweb) compounds. Each of the skeletons of arachno-compounds can be viewed in one of two ways, either as a fragment

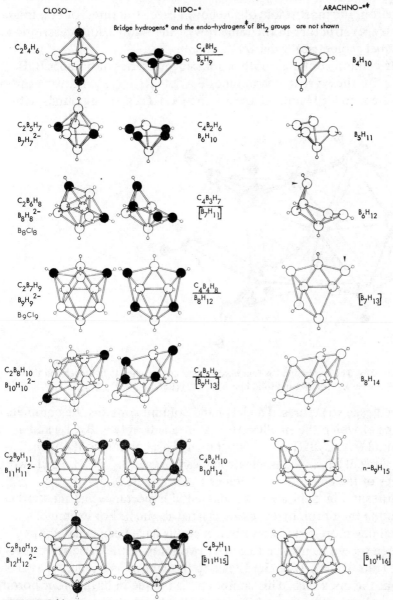

FIGURE 5.11

Boron cage structures, ● = B or C, ○ = B; additional H atoms in BHB bridges or terminal BH_2 groups are not shown. [Williams, R. E. (1971), *Inorg. Chem.* **10**, 210]

of an icosahedron, the most stable of the boron cage structures, or as a fragment of the closo- (cage) structure in the same row of the figure. Both descriptions have about equal geometrical validity.

The middle column contains another homologous series of boranes B_nH_{n+4}. Isoelectronic with these are the carboranes $B_{n-m}C_mH_{n-m+4}$, i.e. each carbon atom is equivalent to a BH unit. These are the nido- (nest) compounds with

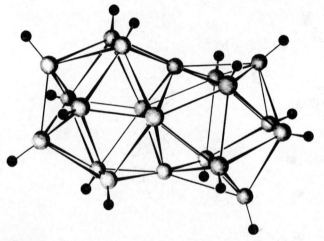

FIGURE 5.12
The structure of $B_{20}H_{16}$. The compound has four boron atoms not attached to hydrogen and thus represents a link between the boranes and solid boron (p. 159) (Ref. as in Fig. 5.13)

partially closed cage structures. The left-hand column contains the complete cage structures of which the smallest two, a tetrahedron (e.g. B_4Cl_4) and a trigonal pyramid (e.g. $C_2B_3H_5$), are not shown. This column contains the homologous series $B_nH_n^{2-}$, the isoelectronic carboranes $B_{n-2}C_2H_n$, and two representatives of the chloro-closo-boranes B_8Cl_8 and B_9Cl_9.

The structures in Fig. 5.11 are of fundamental importance and most other structures among the boron hydrides are related to them. For example, boranes containing more than twelve boron atoms have been isolated but these have been shown to involve fusion of two units of the basic structures of Fig. 5.11. Thus, $B_{20}H_{16}$ (Fig. 5.12) can be thought of as a union of two $B_{10}H_{14}$ units at the open face. This compound is unique in having four boron atoms not joined to hydrogen, and it represents a link between the boranes and the boron structures discussed in Chapter 4. Other linked polyhedral compounds include unstable B_8H_{18} (two B_4H_{10} units), fairly stable $B_{10}H_{16}$ (two B_5H_9 units), and two isomers of $B_{18}H_{22}$ (sharing of two different pairs of boron atoms between two $B_{10}H_{14}$ units).

5.9.4 *Detailed structures of some boranes*

Complete structures for many of the more stable boranes have been determined by X-ray crystallography. Electron diffraction has been used in a few cases. Preliminary evidence for structures has commonly been obtained by mass spectrometry, infrared spectroscopy, and ^{11}B and ^1H n.m.r. spectroscopy. There are two problems with the use of n.m.r. First, there may be intramolecular rearrangements which are fast on an n.m.r. time-scale, and second, boron-11 has a quadrupole moment which broadens the n.m.r. signals. The recent use of ^{11}B n.m.r. at 70·6 MHz and ^1H n.m.r. at 200 MHz, controlled spin-decoupling, and Fourier transform methods are greatly improving the usefulness of n.m.r. in this area.

Figure 5.13 shows the structures of B_4H_{10}, B_5H_9, B_5H_{11}, B_6H_{10}, B_8H_{12}, and $B_{10}H_{14}$ as examples of known structures. Normally B—B nearest neighbour distances are between 170 pm and 186 pm although there are two exceptions in the structures shown. The B(4)–B(5) distances in B_6H_{10} is only 160 pm and the B(5)–B(10) and B(7)–B(8) distances in $B_{10}H_{14}$ are relatively long at 201 pm. The B—H—B bridges in B_4H_{10} appear to be unsymmetrical. The B—H distances are 133 pm towards B(1) and B(3) and 143 pm towards B(2) and B(4). Terminal B—H distances are shorter, commonly about 119 pm. The apical BH_2 unit in B_5H_{11} is unique, and the possibility of additional hydrogen bridge bonding to B(2) and B(5) has been suggested on the basis of the n.m.r. spectrum which shows no coupling between one of the apical H atoms and B(1) to which it is directly bonded.

The B(2)B(1)B(4) angle in tetraborane is 98°. This makes it reasonable, as discussed above, to call the skeleton either an icosahedral fragment (angle 105°) or an octahedral fragment (angle 90°).

5.9.5 *Applications of localized bonding and molecular orbital theory to polyhedral boranes*

The structures in Figs. 5.11–5.13 show lines joining each pair of boron atoms which are geometrically neighbours. A relationship between this purely geometrical connectivity and localized bonding has been attempted by

225

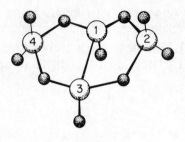

B_4H_{10}
Tetraborane(10)

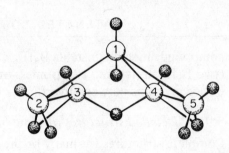

B_5H_{11}
Pentaborane(11)

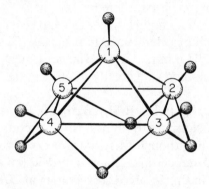

B_5H_9
Pentaborane(9)

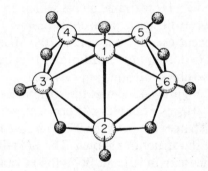

B_6H_{10}
Hexaborane(10)

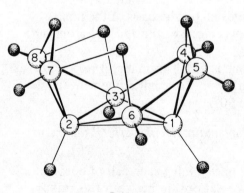

B_8H_{12}
Octaborane(12)

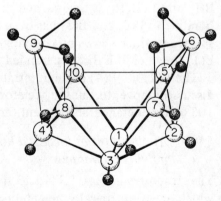

$B_{10}H_{14}$
Decaborane(14)

FIGURE 5.13
Structures of some boranes [Muetterties, E. L. (Ed.) (1967), *The Chemistry of Boron and its Compounds*, Wiley, New York]

Lipscomb [24]. Assuming that a borane of formula B_nH_{n+m} may contain BB, BH, and BH_2 two-centre bonds and BBB and BHB three-centre bonds, the following rules form a basis for assigning a localized bonding structure:

(1) Every pair of boron atoms which are geometrically neighbours must be connected by at least one BB, BHB, or BBB bond.
(2) Each boron atom, since it has four valence atomic orbitals, must participate in $(4 - x - y)$ boron framework bonds, where x is the number of terminal hydrogen atoms and y is the number of bridge hydrogen atoms bonded to a particular boron atom.
(3) No two boron atoms may be bonded together by both a two-centre and a three-centre (BBB or BHB) bond.
(4) The electron balance for boron atoms is:

$$2\,\Sigma BB + 2\,\Sigma BBB + m + n = 3n \qquad (a)$$

The hydrogen atom balance is:

$$\Sigma BHB + \Sigma BH_2 + n = n + m \qquad (b)$$

The total number of three-centre bonds will be equal to the number of boron atoms, i.e.

$$\Sigma BBB + \Sigma BHB = n \qquad (c)$$

Combining equations (a), (b), and (c), we find that the molecule B_nH_{n+m} must have $(\Sigma BHB - \tfrac{1}{2}m)$ BB bonds and $(n - \Sigma BHB)$ BBB bonds.

For example, B_5H_9 is known experimentally to contain four hydrogen bridge bonds. From rule (4) it follows that it must contain two BB bonds and one BBB bond. A representation of this bonding is shown as a topological diagram in Fig. 5.14(a). There are four such representations all of which are of equivalent symmetry. With the larger boranes the number of possibilities for arrangements of bonds increases. Decaborane(14) is known to contain four hydrogen bridges, and thus must contain two BB and six BBB bonds. The representation of this bonding shown in Fig. 5.14(b) is one of twenty-four possibilities. A computer programme is used to apply rules (1)–(4) to find allowable representations.

[24] Epstein, I. R. and Lipscomb, W. N. (1971), *Inorg. Chem.*, **10**, 1921. Lipscomb, E. N. (1963), *Boron Hydrides*, Benjamin, New York.

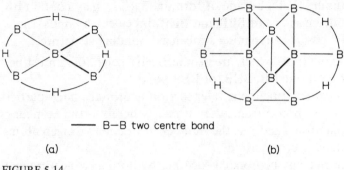

——— B—B two centre bond

(a)   (b)

FIGURE 5.14
(a) Topological representation of $B_5H_9^a$ (one of four structures)
(b) Topological representation of $B_{10}H_{14}^a$ (one of 24 structures)
(^{a} Terminal hydrogen atoms excluded)

   For the closo-borane anions of high symmetry, a satisfactory picture of the bonding can be obtained by a simple molecular orbital model. In the $B_6H_6^{2-}$ ion, for example, with O_h symmetry the structure can be arbitrarily considered in two parts, an equatorial plane $B_4H_4^{2-}$, and two apical BH units (Fig. 5.15). Only the ψ_1 and the degenerate ψ_1 and ψ_2 π molecular orbitals of $B_4H_4^{2-}$ are of appropriate symmetry to combine with orbitals of corresponding symmetry from the two BH groups. Four electron pairs are involved in equatorial B—B bonds, and an additional three electron pairs are required to fill the bonding molecular orbitals to the BH groups, making a total of seven electron pairs for B—B bonding in the $B_6H_6^{2-}$ ion.

   Similar molecular orbital treatment of any of the other closo-borane anion structures shows that the n skeletal bonding electron pairs are associated with an $(n - 1)$-cornered polyhedron. This principle gives a rationale for the geometrical relationships across the rows in Fig. 5.11. The compounds $B_6H_6^{2-}$, B_5H_9, and B_4H_{10}, for example, can be considered to have the same number of skeletal bonding electron pairs [25]. The compounds are formally related by removal of BH^{2+} and additions of H^+, ions which do not contribute electrons to skeletal bonding, i.e.

$$B_6H_6^{2-} \text{ (7 electron pairs)} \xrightarrow{-BH^{2+}, +4H^+} B_5H_9 \xrightarrow{-BH^{2+}, +2H^+}$$

$$B_4H_{10} \text{ (7 electron pairs)}$$

[25] Wade, K. (1971), Chem. Comm., 792.

In this formal replacement of BH^{2+} units by two or four H^+ ions, the number and symmetry of the skeletal bonding molecular orbitals will be unaffected if the H^+ ions are located in sites which reflect the skeletal symmetry. Thus, the boron atoms in B_5H_9 and B_4H_{10} are found in positions which are part of an octahedron, and the bridging hydrogen atoms and the hydrogen atoms in BH_2 groups are in positions as close as possible to vacant positions in the octahedron.

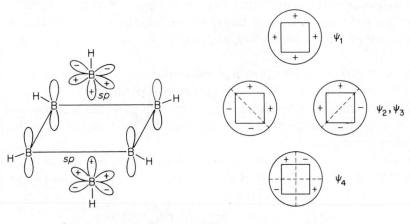

$B_6H_6^{2-}$ represented as
$B_4H_4^{2-} + 2BH$

symmetry of π molecular
orbitals of $B_4H_4^{2-}$

FIGURE 5.15
Molecular orbital model of the bonding in the $B_6H_6^{2-}$ ion

This 'hole-in-polyhedron' approach to nido- and arachno-compounds is most fully justified with boron cage compounds containing a heteroatom as discussed on p. 240.

5.9.6 Arachno- and nido-boranes; some physical and chemical properties

The boranes are generally slightly less volatile than alkanes of equivalent molecular weight. Thus, while B_2H_6 and B_4H_{10} are gases at $25°$, $B_{10}H_{14}$ is a slightly volatile solid. Although some boranes, e.g. B_8H_{12}, are unstable below $0°$, decomposition of most of the arachno- and nido-compounds commences in the temperature range $50-200°$. Total decomposition to the elements is usually complete only above $500°$ because of the stability of higher boranes

229

formed by pyrolysis of lower boranes. The boranes are all endothermic compounds, e.g. ΔH_f° values for B_2H_6, B_5H_9, and $B_{10}H_{14}$ are respectively 36, 73, and 31 kJ mol^{-1}.

The lower boranes may inflame on exposure to air, and they are normally handled in the laboratory on a vacuum line. Decaborane(14) is less reactive and is slowly oxidized by air at room temperature; solutions of $B_{10}H_{14}$ in chlorinated hydrocarbons, particularly CCl_4, are dangerously explosive. All the arachno- and nido-compounds instantly reduce solutions of silver salts to silver metal (contrast closo-compounds, p. 235).

(i)   Reactions with bases and chemical reduction.   Acid–base reactions and the addition of electrons in chemical reduction are distinct processes. Nevertheless, they are closely intertwined in the reactions of the arachno- and nido-boranes, and a high proportion of the known chemistry of the compounds involves these effects.

Diborane is cleaved by bases in two ways. With CO, phosphorus, and sulphur bases it is split symmetrically to give $H_3B.L$ (p. 35). With ammonia and other strong bases it is split asymmetrically, i.e.

$$B_2H_6 + 2L \rightarrow (BH_2L_2)^+ BH_4^-$$

There is evidence that water reacts in this way with diborane below -70° [26], but at room temperature B_2H_6 is oxidized by water to boric acid and hydrogen. Solutions of diborane in some ethers have n.m.r. spectra which indicate that all the protons are magnetically equivalent on the n.m.r. time-scale. Reversible complexing to give a species with a single BHB bridge has been suggested as a way in which the hydrogen atoms are rapidly scrambled.

The action of sodium or preferably sodium borohydride on B_2H_6 in ether solution produces the $B_3H_8^-$ ion:

$$NaBH_4 + B_2H_6 \xrightarrow[\text{diglyme}]{100^\circ} NaB_3H_8 + 2H_2$$

At higher temperatures this reaction provides a route to a number of the closo-borane anions, particularly $B_{10}H_{10}^{2-}$ and $B_{12}H_{12}^{2-}$ (see below). The $B_3H_8^-$ ion has the structure shown in Fig. 5.16. Rapid intramolecular exchange

[26] Finn, P. and Jolly, W. L. (1970), *Chem. Comm.*, 1090.

230

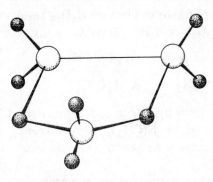

FIGURE 5.16
Structure of $B_3H_8^-$

between BH_2 and BHB groups makes all the protons appear equivalent in the ^1H n.m.r. spectrum. Closely related to $B_3H_8^-$ are complexes of formula B_3H_7L; the structure of the ammonia complex which is formed from NaB_3H_8 and ammonium chloride is shown in topographical form in Fig. 5.17. The dimethyl ether complex of triborane(7) reacts rapidly with PF_3 to give a diborane(4) complex:

$$B_3H_7O(CH_3)_2 + 3\,PF_3 \rightarrow B_2H_4(PF_3)_2 + BH_3PF_3 + (CH_3)_2O$$

The structure of the complex is believed to be ethane-like, i.e.

$$\underset{H}{\overset{H}{F_3P \rightarrow B}} - \underset{H}{\overset{H}{B \leftarrow PF_3}}$$

It reacts quantitatively with hydrogen at room temperature to give two molecules of BH_3PF_3, and with diborane to form B_4H_{10}:

$$B_2H_4(PF_3)_2 + B_2H_6 \rightarrow B_4H_{10} + 2\,PF_3$$

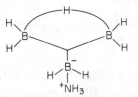

FIGURE 5.17
Representation of structure of $B_3H_7.NH_3$

The action of bases donating through nitrogen or oxygen on B_4H_{10} results in the elimination of BH_2 or BH_3 to give $B_3H_8^-$ or B_3H_7L derivatives, e.g.

$$B_4H_{10} + 2N(CH_3)_3 \longrightarrow B_3H_7N(CH_3)_3 + H_3BN(CH_3)_3$$

$$2B_4H_{10} + 3CN^- \xrightarrow{\text{ether}} H_3BCNBH_3^- + 2B_3H_7CN^-$$

When heated with carbon monoxide, B_4H_{10} loses hydrogen and forms $B_4H_8.CO$ A single-crystal X-ray study on the related $B_4H_8PF_2N(CH_3)_2$, formed from B_4H_8CO and $F_2PN(CH_3)_2$, shows the B_4H_8 moiety to have a structure like B_4H_{10}.

Deprotonation of B_5H_9 or B_6H_{10} with lithium alkyls or alkali metal hydrides produces salts of the highly reactive $B_5H_8^-$ or $B_6H_9^-$ ions. When LiB_5H_8 is treated with RCl where R is, for example, deuterium, $(CH_3)_3Si-$, $(CH_3)_2B-$, or $(CH_3)_2P-$, the product contains R in a basal bridging position [27]

$$LiB_5H_8 + RCl \longrightarrow$$

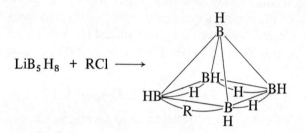

The bridged compounds are readily isomerized to $2\text{-}RB_5H_8$, although when R is $(CH_3)_2B-$ the isomerization leads to cage expansion and the product is a derivative of hexaborane(10).

The acid–base chemistry of $B_{10}H_{14}$ has been studied in greater detail than that of the other boranes. In aqueous media, $B_{10}H_{14}$ can be titrated as a mono-basic acid with hydroxides:

$$B_{10}H_{14} + OH^- \rightleftharpoons B_{10}H_{13}^- + H_2O$$

The $B_{10}H_{13}^-$ ion is not stable in the presence of excess OH^-, and degrades to $B_9H_{14}^-$. This and related changes are summarized in Fig. 5.18.

(ii)   *Other reactions.*   Unless controlled, the reaction of the boranes with halogens in very vigorous, but at low temperatures it is possible to replace one

[27] Gaines, D. F. and Iorns, T. V. (1970), *J. Amer. Chem. Soc.,* **92,** 4571.

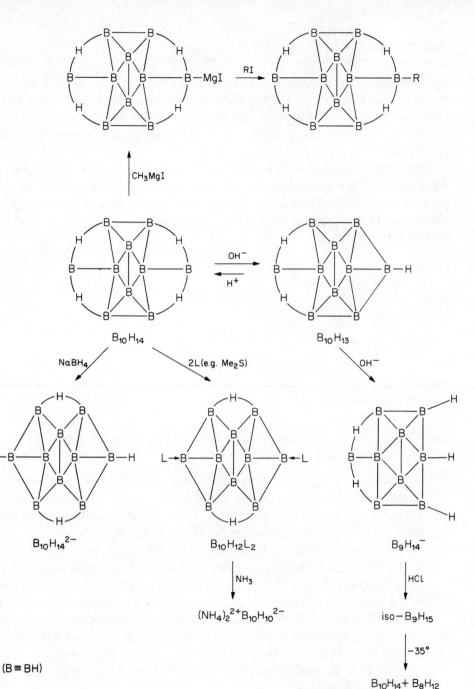

(B ≡ BH)

FIGURE 5.18
Some reactions of decaborane(14). (Note that the bonding representations are not necessarily unique; other bonding arrangements may also satisfy the equations of balance)

hydrogen atom by a halogen atom in many of the arachno- and nido-compounds. With pentaborane(9) the difference in energy between 1- and 2-chloro-substituted compounds is slight and the constant for the equilibrium, $1\text{-ClB}_5\text{H}_8 \rightleftharpoons 2\text{-ClB}_5\text{H}_8$ is about 4 at $25°$. Halogens attack decaborane(14) mainly in the 1-, 2-, 3-, and 4-positions.

Many of the boranes react readily with unsaturated organic compounds. With alkynes the reactions commonly lead to the formation of nido- or closo-carboranes (p. 236). The reaction of tetraborane(10) with ethylene produces the carbon-bridged species $C_2H_4B_4H_8$, the probable structure of which is shown in Fig. 5.19.

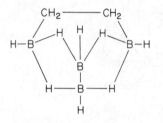

FIGURE 5.19
Structure of $B_4H_8C_2H_4$

(iii)   Synthesis.   A variety of methods are used to make the arachno- and nido-boranes of which the more general are:

(1) Hydrolysis of magnesium boride; as Stock showed, when magnesium boride of stoicheiometry Mg_3B_2 is dissolved in aqueous acids, mainly B_4H_{10}, B_5H_9, and B_6H_{10} are formed. The method is useful for preparing B_6H_{10} (about 6% yield based on the boron in Mg_3B_2).

(2) By pyrolysis of diborane; this provides the best route to B_4H_{10}, B_5H_9, B_5H_{11}, and $B_{10}H_{14}$. The mechanism of pyrolysis is complex although BH_3 is certainly involved, and by varying the temperature, the rate of cooling of the gases, and the concentration of additional components such as H_2 or dimethyl ether, the formation of particular hydrides can be enhanced. Thus, B_5H_{11} is formed in maximum yield at about $100°$ but B_5H_9 is formed more efficiently at $240°$ in the presence of H_2. Pyrolysis of a mixture of B_2H_6 and B_6H_{10} gives a small yield of B_6H_{12}, one of the less easily made hydrides.

The diborane required for these preparations is conveniently made from phosphoric acid and $NaBH_4$ (p. 49).

(3) By the action of an electric discharge on lower boranes; the method is most used for the preparation of linked cage compounds, e.g.

$$2\, B_5 H_9 \xrightarrow{\text{discharge}} H_8 B_5 - B_5 H_8 + H_2$$

$$2\, B_{10} H_{14} \xrightarrow[\text{amine catalyst}]{\text{discharge}} B_{20} H_{16} \qquad \text{(Fig. 5.12)}$$

(4) By acid–base reactions; acidification of salts of $B_3 H_8^-$ with phosphoric acid gives small yields of several uncommon boranes including $B_8 H_{18}$ and $B_6 H_{12}$. Pentaborane(11) is readily disproportionated by bases; ethers give $B_6 H_{10}$, and hexamethylenetetramine gives $n\text{-}B_9 H_{15}$. The formation of $B_8 H_{12}$ from $B_{10} H_{14}$ is shown in Fig. 5.18.

5.9.7 *The closo-borane anions*

The chemistry of the closo-borane anions stands apart from that of the arachno- and nido-compounds because of the high stability of the closo-borane skeletons. Alkali metal salts of $B_6 H_6^{2-}$, $B_8 H_8^{2-}$, and $B_{10} H_{10}^{2-}$ can be heated to 600° under vacuum without hydrogen loss, while $B_{12} H_{12}^{2-}$ salts are stable to 800°. Apart from $B_7 H_7^{2-}$ and $B_8 H_8^{2-}$, silver salts of the anions can be isolated although some are sensitive to light. The greatest chemical stability is achieved in $B_{10} H_{10}^{2-}$ and $B_{12} H_{12}^{2-}$, particularly the latter. Neither anion is destroyed by aqueous alkali although $B_{10} H_{10}^{2-}$ is decomposed by strong acids. All the hydrogen atoms in the anions can be replaced by chlorine, bromine, or iodine with no degradation of the cage. The B—Cl bonds in $B_{10} Cl_{10}^{2-}$ and $B_{12} Cl_{12}^{2-}$ are resistant to hydrolysis unlike those in the uncharged chloro-closoboranes (p. 242). The stability of the B_{10} and B_{12} cages in $B_{10} H_{10}^{2-}$ and $B_{12} H_{12}^{2-}$ and their derivatives can be compared with the stability of the C_6 aromatic ring system in benzene and its derivatives. In one sense $B_{12} H_{12}^{2-}$ can be regarded as a three-dimensional benzene; the volume of the ion is comparable to the volume that would be swept out by a benzene nucleus spinning on a two-fold axis [28].

Oxidation of $B_{10} H_{10}^{2-}$ with Fe^{3+} gives the dimer $B_{20} H_{18}^{2-}$ with three-centre linkages between two boron atoms on each $B_{10} H_9^-$ unit; on photolysis this

[28] Longuet-Higgins, H. C. and Roberts, M. (1955), *Proc. Roy. Soc.*, A, **230**, 110.

isomerizes as shown in Fig. 5.20. Reduction of $B_{20}H_{18}^=$ gives $B_{20}H_{18}^{4-}$ with an apical B—B bond between two $B_{10}H_9^{2-}$ units. Similar linked B_{12} units have been made by electrolytic oxidation of $B_{12}H_{12}^{2-}$.

The stability of the closo-borane anions is only kinetic. Even $B_{12}H_{12}^{2-}$ is thermodynamically unstable with respect to boric acid and hydrogen in contact with water.

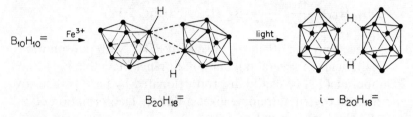

$$B_{10}H_{10}^= \xrightarrow{Fe^{3+}} \quad \xrightarrow{light}$$

$$B_{20}H_{18}^= \qquad\qquad i - B_{20}H_{18}^=$$

FIGURE 5.20
The formation and isomerization of $B_{20}H_{18}^{2-}$

There are three main methods for synthesizing the anions;

(1) By the action of BH_4^- ion on a borane, e.g.

$$2\,NaBH_4 \;+\; 5\,B_2H_6 \xrightarrow[180°]{(C_2H_5)_3N} Na_2\,B_{12}\,H_{12} \;+\; 13\,H_2$$

(2) By pyrolysis of a salt of a simple borane anion, e.g.

$$CsB_3H_8 \xrightarrow{180-250°} Cs_2\,B_9\,H_9 \;+\; Cs_2\,B_{10}\,H_{10} \;+\; Cs_2\,B_{12}\,H_{12} \;+\; H_2$$

(3) Degradative oxidation of $B_9H_9^{2-}$ with air in the presence of methanol gives $B_8H_8^{2-}$, $B_7H_7^{2-}$, and $B_6H_6^{2-}$.

None of these three processes is mechanistically well understood.

5.9.8 *Carboranes* [29, 30]

closo-Carboranes of formula $C_2B_{n-2}H_n$, isoelectronic with $B_nH_n^{2-}$, have the same high thermal and chemical stability as the closo-borane anions. The

[29] Grimes, R. (1970), *Carboranes*, Academic Press, New York.
[30] Haworth, D. T. (1972), *Endeavour*, **31**, 16.

majority of carboranes in this class are made by the reaction of a borane and an alkyne as the following two examples show:

$$B_2H_6 + C_2H_2 \xrightarrow[\text{flow system}]{\text{exothermic reaction}}$$

$$1,5\text{-}C_2B_3H_5 + 1,6\text{-}C_2B_4H_6 + 3,4\text{-}C_2B_5H_7 + \text{other minor products}$$

$$B_{10}H_{14} + 2\,CH_3CN \longrightarrow B_{10}H_{12}(CH_3CN)_2 \xrightarrow{C_2H_2}$$

$$1,2\text{-}C_2B_{10}H_{12} + 2\,CH_3CN + H_2 \ (80\% \text{ yield})$$

Figure 5.11 shows the distribution of carbon atoms in the most stable form of the compounds. It will be seen that in closo structures the carbon atoms are located as far apart as possible, the configuration that minimizes $C^+\!-\!C^+$ repulsion.

If a preparative method produces a carborane with adjacent carbon atoms, it can sometimes be isomerized by heating to give the more stable form. This isomerization is most important for converting $1,2\text{-}C_2B_{10}H_{12}$ (*ortho*carborane) into 1,7- (*meta*) or 1,12- (*para*) isomers. Figure 5.21 shows one suggested mechanism for isomerization involving the intermediacy of a cubo-octahedral structure, but another suggestion is that there is an internal rotation of a triangular B_2C face of the icosahedron.

FIGURE 5.21
Isomerization of $1,2\text{-}C_2B_{10}H_{12}$ to $1,7\text{-}C_2B_{10}H_{12}$ via a possible cube octahedron intermediate

In $1,2\text{-}C_2B_{10}H_{12}$, and to a lesser extent in $1,7\text{-}C_2B_{10}H_{12}$, the H atoms on C are slightly acidic and can be replaced by metals to give, for example, *C*-lithiocarboranes. Halogenation of all three isomers of $C_2B_{10}H_{12}$ results in substitution of all the H atoms on B but not those on C. A range of both *C*- and

B-substituted carborane derivatives is known. Silicone polymers containing *meta*-carborane units have been synthesized thus:

$$\underset{(1,2\text{-}C_2B_{10}H_{12})}{\underset{B_{10}H_{10}}{HC\!\!-\!\!CH}} \xrightarrow{\;C_4H_9Li\;} \underset{B_{10}H_{10}}{LiC\!\!-\!\!CLi} \xrightarrow{\;(CH_3)_2SiCl_2\;} \underset{B_{10}H_{10}}{Cl(CH_3)_2SiC\!\!-\!\!CSi(CH_3)_2Cl}$$

$$\Big\downarrow 320°$$

$$1,2 \rightarrow 1,7 \text{ isomerization}$$

$$\Big\downarrow$$

$$CH_3O(CH_3)_2SiCB_{10}H_{10}CSi(CH_3)_2OCH_3 \xleftarrow{\;CH_3OH\;} Cl(CH_3)_2SiCB_{10}H_{10}CSi(CH_3)_2Cl$$

$$\Big\downarrow (CH_3)_2SiCl_2$$

$$\left[\begin{array}{ccc} CH_3 & CH_3 & CH_3 \\ | & | & | \\ -SiCB_{10}H_{10}CSi\!-\!O\!-\!Si\!-\!O\!- \\ | & | & | \\ CH_3 & CH_3 & CH_3 \end{array} \right]_n + 2n\,CH_3Cl$$

The polymer shown is an elastomer. The presence of the $1,7\text{-}C_2B_{10}H_{10}$ group in the backbone imparts exceptional heat and oxidation resistance, superior to that of any other silicone rubber. Various polymers of this type are now being produced commercially for special applications.

One boron atom can be removed from icosahedral 1,2- or $1,7\text{-}C_2B_{10}H_{12}$ to give the corresponding isomers of the nido-anion $C_2B_9H_{11}^{2-}$, the so-called 'dicarbollide' ions [31]:

$$C_2B_{10}H_{12} \xrightarrow{\;MeOH,\ KOH\;} C_2B_9H_{11}^{-} \xrightarrow{\;NaH\;} C_2B_9H_{11}^{2-}$$

This corresponds to the loss of BH^{2+} from $C_2B_{10}H_{12}$, i.e. the number of skeletal bonding electron pairs is unchanged and $C_2B_9H_{11}^{2-}$ will have a pseudo-icosahedral structure with one vacant apical position above a pentagonal face. A simple molecular orbital model assigns six electrons to five orbitals pointing

[31] Hawthorne, M. F. (1968), *Accounts Chem. Research*, **1**, 281.

towards the missing position as shown in Fig. 5.22(a). The symmetry of the orbitals and the number of electrons are virtually identical to those found in the cyclopentadienide ion $C_5H_5^-$. Transition metal complexes can be made with the dicarbollide ions which have a 'sandwich' structure analogous to complexes such as ferrocene. The structure of the red, paramagnetic iron(III) complex $(\pi\text{-}1,2\text{-}C_2B_9H_{11})Fe(\pi\text{-}C_5H_5)$ is shown in Fig. 5.22(b). It is one of the products when salts of $C_5H_5^-$ and $C_2B_9H_{11}^{2-}$ are refluxed with $FeCl_2$ in tetrahydrofuran, and it can be easily reduced to the diamagnetic anion $(\pi\text{-}1,2\text{-}C_2B_9H_{11})Fe\text{-}(\pi\text{-}C_5H_5)^-$.

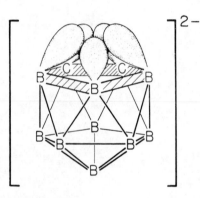

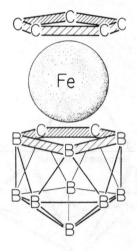

FIGURE 5.22
(a) Schematic structure of the $C_2B_9H_{11}^{2-}$ ion
(b) Structure of $(\pi\text{-}C_2B_9H_{11})Fe(\pi\text{-}C_5H_5)$

Since the discovery of the dicarbollide ion complexes in 1965, many related compounds have been synthesized. Treatment of $(C_2B_9H_{11})_2Co^-$ with $CoCl_2$ and NaOH gives small yields of the bridged species shown in Fig. 5.23. The bridging unit, a $C_2B_8H_{10}^{4-}$ ion, is two BH^{2+} ions short of an icosahedron and thus has two unfilled icosahedral positions. The ion has been called the 1,2-dicarbcanastride(4−) ion from the Spanish word for a basket.

Other nido-anions such as $C_2B_7H_9^{2-}$, $C_2B_6H_8^{2-}$, and $C_3B_3H_6^{2-}$, which are derived from non-icosahedral closo structures by effective loss of BH^{2+} ions, have also been shown to form complexes with transition metals.

239

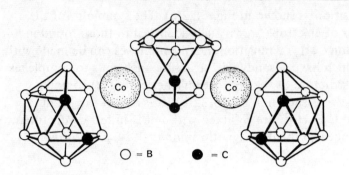

$\bigcirc$ = B $\quad$ $\bullet$ = C

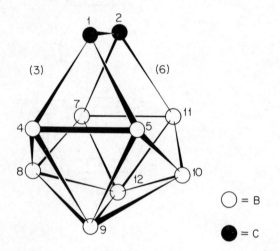

$\bigcirc$ = B

$\bullet$ = C

FIGURE 5.23
(a) Structure of the complex ion $(\pi\text{-}C_2B_9H_{11})Co(\pi\text{-}C_2B_8H_{10})Co(\pi\text{-}C_2B_9H_{11})^{2-}$
(b) Structure of the $1,2\text{-}C_2B_8H_{10}{}^{4-}$ ion

5.9.9 *Other heteroatom borane derivatives*

Just as there are many compounds analogous to boron carbide (p. 163), so the possibilities for replacing one boron atom in nido- or closo-borane structures or in carboranes seem endless. Structures are known containing, for example, Be, Ga, Ge, Sn, N, P. As, Sb, and S. There are also structures containing transition metal atoms in the cage rather than external to it as in the sandwich compounds, e.g. $L_2PtB_8H_{12}$. The number of electrons available for bonding in the cage is generally the same in these compounds as in known borane or carborane structures; thus $CPB_{10}H_{11}$ is 'isoelectronic' with $C_2B_{10}H_{12}$. The phosphorus compounds in particular show a marked similarity in properties to the carboranes and undergo thermal isomerization.

The formation of these heteroatom boron cage compounds involves no new structural principle. However, their existence shows that the bonding orbitals supplied by the cage to the heteroatoms can tolerate perturbations in size, charge density, and orbital energy remarkably well. Structures with electronegative oxygen in the cage have not yet been reported but even this may be possible as solid phases such as 'B_7O' are known (p. 163).

5.9.10 *Catenated and closo-boron halides and related compounds*

The simplest catenated boron compound is the gaseous high-temperature species $O=B-B=O$, isoelectronic with cyanogen $N\equiv C-C\equiv N$. It is formed from B_2O_3 and boron above $1200°$ but at ordinary temperatures it condenses to a solid $(BO)_n$ containing $B-B$ bonds.

Part of the range of known compounds of type Y_2B-BY_2 was shown in Table 5.8, but other compounds such as $B_2(OH)_4$ and $B_2(O\text{-alkyl})_4$ are known; in all cases the substituents are capable of donating $p\pi$ electrons to boron. The thermal stability decreases in the order of decreasing $(p-p)\pi$ bonding, i.e.

$$B_2[N(CH_3)_2]_4 > B_2(OCH_3)_4 > B_2(OH)_4 > B_2F_4 > B_2Cl_4 > B_2Br_4$$

The volatile compounds B_2F_4 (b.p. $-34°$) and B_2Cl_4 (b.p. $60°$) are spontaneously inflammable in air. They react with hydrogen, B_2Cl_4 at $0°$, and B_2F_4 at $150°$ to give HBX_2 as the initial product in each case. This is analogous to the addition of H_2 to $B_2H_4(PF_3)_2$ (p. 231). They add across carbon–carbon multiple bonds, e.g.

$$C_2H_2 + B_2Cl_4 \xrightarrow{25°} \underset{Cl_2B}{\overset{H}{}}C=C\underset{BCl_2}{\overset{H}{}} \xrightarrow{50°} \underset{Cl_2B}{\overset{Cl_2B}{}}H-C-C\underset{BCl_2}{\overset{BCl_2}{}}H$$

They will react with two molecules of a Lewis base to give complexes $B_2X_4L_2$; B_2Cl_4 is a stronger acid than B_2F_4 and forms a crystalline complex with PCl_3

which dissociates in the gas phase to B_2Cl_4 and PCl_3. Some of the ways of making these diboron tetrahalides are shown below:

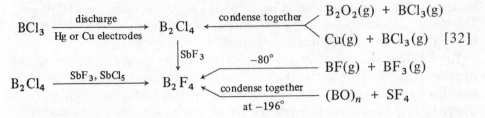

The discharge synthesis of B_2Cl_4 involves BCl as an intermediate. Polymers of BCl are isolated from the discharge reaction or from the slow decomposition of B_2Cl_4 at room temperature. The best characterized of these BCl polymers are B_4Cl_4, B_8Cl_8, and B_9Cl_9. These are chloro-closo-boranes which, although very sensitive to air and water, are much more thermally stable than B_2Cl_4, and their stability increases with skeletal size as in the other closo-borane systems. The structure of the pale green solid B_4Cl_4 is shown in Fig. 5.24 (the skeletal structures of B_8Cl_8 and B_9Cl_9 are shown in Fig. 5.11).

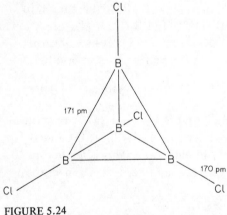

FIGURE 5.24
Structure of B_4Cl_4

In a molecular orbital description of the bonding in B_4Cl_4, the eight electrons available for skeletal bonding from four BCl groups fill four bonding molecular orbitals of class A_1 and T_2 in T_d symmetry, but two additional

[32] Timms, P. L. (1972), *J.C.S. Dalton*, 830.

bonding molecular orbitals of class E are of correct symmetry to mix with chlorine $p\pi$ orbitals. In a localized bond model there is one three-centre two-electron bond in each face of the tetrahedron with additional $(p-p)\pi$ bonding from chlorine to boron.

Boron monofluoride (p. 47) provides the route to the higher boron fluorides. When it reacts with B_2F_4 at low temperatures $F_2B.BF.BF_2$ is formed as an unstable solid which quickly disproportionates to a yellow liquid B_8F_{12} and B_2F_4. Evidence from its ^{19}F n.m.r. spectrum suggests that B_8F_{12} is $B_2(BF_2)_6$ and it behaves chemically like diborane, reacting with many Lewis bases to give stable complexes $(BF_2)_3BL$, analogous to H_3BL. The affinity of $B_2(BF_2)_6$ for bases is very great, and it is certainly the strongest boron-containing Lewis acid [33]. No polyhedral boron fluorides have yet been characterized.

Aqueous solutions containing 'sub-boric' acid $B_2(OH)_4$ can be made by dissolving $(BO)_n$ in water, by hydrolysis of B_2Cl_4 at $0°$, or by acid hydrolysis of $B_2[N(CH_3)_2]_4$. The acid is very weak; it is a strong reducing agent and its solutions decomposes slowly with evolution of hydrogen and traces of boranes.

The relatively very stable and oxidation resistant tetrakisdimethylaminodiborane(4) is made by a sodium coupling reaction:

$$2\,R_2BCl + 2\,Na \rightarrow B_2R_4 + 2\,NaCl \quad [R = (CH_3)_2N]$$

This reaction can be adapted to give the higher homologues, e.g.

$$2\,R_2BCl + RBCl_2 + 4\,K \rightarrow R_2B.BR.BR_2 + 4\,KCl$$

Although detailed structures of these boron chain compounds are not yet known, n.m.r. evidence suggests that they are akin to the carbon and silicon chain compounds and are not multicentre bonded.

[33] Kirk, R. W., Smith, D. L., Airey, W. and Timms, P. L. (1972), *J.C.S. Dalton*, 1392.

Borazines, phosphazenes, silicones, and related systems

6

6.1 Introduction

In this chapter some ring and chain compounds which are based on alternating, heteroatomic skeletons are discussed. First we consider some systems, in particular those with boron–nitrogen frameworks, which are isoelectronic with organic compounds such as alkenes, alkynes, and benzenes. The second part is concerned with other isoelectronic series, including silicones, phosphazenes, and thiazyl halides, which involve second-row elements as heteroatoms. These series of compounds possess many common structural and bonding features.

6.2 Boron–nitrogen compounds [1]

Perhaps the most extensive group of inorganic compounds which are formally analogous to organic systems are those based on the grouping B—N, which is isoelectronic with C—C. Some examples are listed in Fig. 6.1. In the sections which follow, structural and chemical features of several of these systems are compared with those of the corresponding carbon derivatives, and with some other formally isoelectronic species.

6.2.1 *Aminoboranes (Borazenes)*

The aminoboranes R_2N—BR_2 are isoelectronic with alkenes R_2C=CR_2. The B—N bond, however, apparently has considerably less double bond character

[1] Niedenzu, K. and Dawson, J. W. (1965), *Boron-nitrogen Compounds*, Springer Verlag, Berlin. Good, comprehensive coverage.

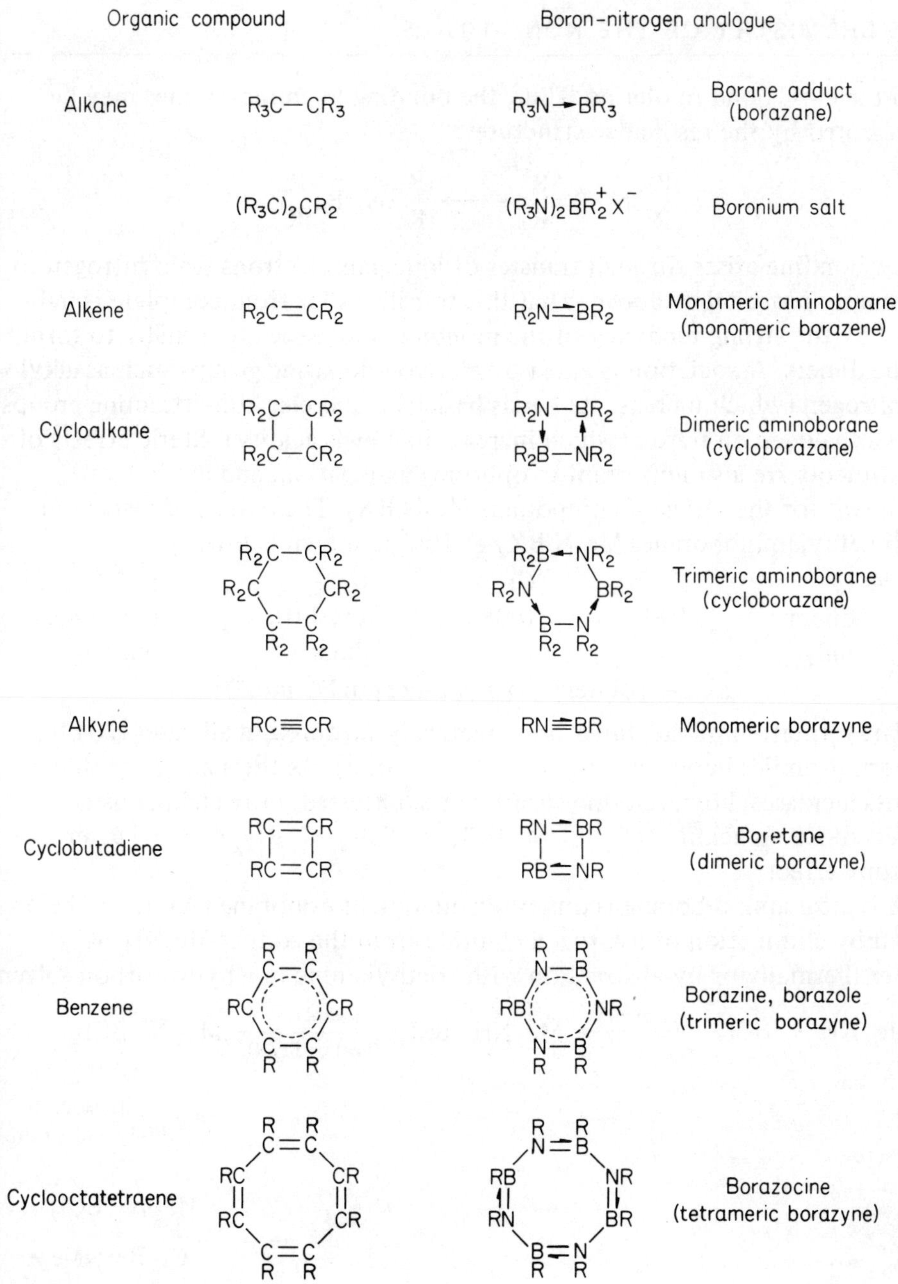

Organic compound		Boron-nitrogen analogue	
Alkane	R_3C-CR_3	$R_3N \rightarrow BR_3$	Borane adduct (borazane)
	$(R_3C)_2CR_2$	$(R_3N)_2BR_2^+ X^-$	Boronium salt
Alkene	$R_2C=CR_2$	$R_2N \overset{\rightharpoonup}{=} BR_2$	Monomeric aminoborane (monomeric borazene)
Cycloalkane	$\begin{array}{c} R_2C-CR_2 \\ \mid \quad\ \mid \\ R_2C-CR_2 \end{array}$	$\begin{array}{c} R_2N-BR_2 \\ \uparrow \quad\ \downarrow \\ R_2B-NR_2 \end{array}$	Dimeric aminoborane (cycloborazane)
	$\begin{array}{c} R_2C-CR_2 \\ R_2C \quad\quad CR_2 \\ C-C \\ R_2 \ R_2 \end{array}$	$\begin{array}{c} R_2B \leftarrow NR_2 \\ R_2N \quad\quad BR_2 \\ B-N \\ R_2 \ R_2 \end{array}$	Trimeric aminoborane (cycloborazane)
Alkyne	$RC \equiv CR$	$RN \equiv BR$	Monomeric borazyne
Cyclobutadiene	$\begin{array}{c} RC=CR \\ \mid \quad\ \mid \\ RC=CR \end{array}$	$\begin{array}{c} RN=BR \\ \mid \quad\ \mid \\ RB=NR \end{array}$	Boretane (dimeric borazyne)
Benzene	$\begin{array}{c} R \quad R \\ C-C \\ RC \quad CR \\ C-C \\ R \quad R \end{array}$	$\begin{array}{c} R \quad R \\ N-B \\ RB \quad NR \\ N-B \\ R \quad R \end{array}$	Borazine, borazole (trimeric borazyne)
Cyclooctatetraene	$\begin{array}{c} R \quad R \\ C=C \\ RC \quad\quad CR \\ \| \quad\quad\quad \| \\ RC \quad\quad CR \\ C=C \\ R \quad R \end{array}$	$\begin{array}{c} R \quad R \\ N=B \\ RB \quad\quad NR \\ \| \quad\quad\quad \| \\ RN \quad\quad BR \\ B=N \\ R \quad R \end{array}$	Borazocine (tetrameric borazyne)

FIGURE 6.1
Boron–nitrogen analogues of organic systems

than the C=C bond in olefins. Thus, the bonding in aminoboranes may be represented by the resonance structures:

$$\underset{R}{\overset{R}{>}}N-B\underset{R'}{\overset{R'}{<}} \longleftrightarrow \underset{R}{\overset{R}{>}}\overset{+}{N}=\overset{-}{B}\underset{R'}{\overset{R'}{<}}$$

The π bonding arises through transfer of lone pair electrons from nitrogen to the empty p orbital of boron. That this transfer is far from complete is indicated by the strong tendency of the monomers to associate, usually to form cyclic dimers. Association is aided by electron-donating groups such as alkyl on nitrogen (which increase its Lewis basicity), and electron-attracting groups such as halogen on boron (which increase its Lewis acidity). Steric effects of substituents are also important in opposing association, and are in fact dominant for the series of compounds $Me_2N.BX_2$. The extent of association of dimethylaminoboranes $Me_2N.BX_2$ at 100° is shown below.

X =	H	F	Cl	Br	I
K_x	dimer only	100	0·085	very little dimer	monomer only

$$K_x = [\text{dimer}]^{1/2}/[\text{monomer}] \text{ in } l^{1/2} \text{ mol}^{-1/2}$$

The formation of the dimer is energetically favoured in all cases (ΔH for dimerization lies between −40 and −80 kJ mol^{-1}). As the size of the substituents increases, however, dimerization is suppressed, outweighing usual orders of Lewis acidity (cf. $BF_3 < BCl_3 < BBr_3 < BI_3$, p. 35), i.e. an entropy effect.

A typical amino-borane is dimethylaminodichloroborane (A). It can be prepared by elimination of hydrogen chloride from the adduct $Me_2NH.BCl_3$ either thermally or by abstraction with triethylamine in a hydrocarbon solvent

$$Me_2NH + BCl_3 \xrightarrow{\text{petroleum}} Me_2NH.BCl_3 \xrightarrow[\text{(heat or Et}_3\text{N)}]{\text{ether}} Me_2N-BCl_2$$
$$(A)$$

$$\text{heat} \updownarrow \updownarrow \text{stand, room temp.}$$

$$\underset{Cl_2 \overset{-}{B}-\underset{+}{N}Me_2}{\overset{+}{Me_2}\overset{}{N}-\overset{-}{B}Cl_2}$$
$$(B)$$

246

Such elimination reactions are frequently used for the formation of bonds between atoms of the non-metallic elements (cf. P—P and S—S, Chapter 5; P—N, p. 263; Si—O, p. 266).

The monomer (A) is a colourless mobile liquid which is rapidly hydrolysed in moist air. Electron diffraction studies have shown that, within experimental error, the molecule is planar in the gas phase. On standing, it dimerizes gradually to a white crystalline solid which is much more resistant to hydrolysis. The structure (B) of the dimer has been determined by X-ray diffraction. The B—N bond length is characteristic of a single bond, and the B_2N_2 ring is planar. Note that *cis–trans* isomerism may occur in cyclic dimeric aminoboranes, as in substituted cyclobutanes. This has been observed by proton magnetic resonance for the compounds $(RBCl.NMe_2)_2$ (Fig. 6.2).

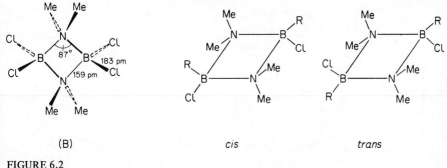

FIGURE 6.2
cis–trans Isomerism in cyclic dimeric aminoboranes

cis–trans Isomerism in alkenes is well known, and arises because the barrier to rotation about the C=C bond is high (ca. 220 kJ mol^{-1}). If the B—N bond in aminoboranes has double bond character, significant restricted rotation about it is expected, and the size of the barrier will indicate the extent of B=N bonding. Proton magnetic resonance spectra have shown the existence of such *cis–trans* isomers in several cases. For example, at 296 K the ^{1}H n.m.r. spectrum of (C) shows two single resonances of equal intensity, which are due to the N—CH$_3$ groups in different environments, frozen in the planar form. As the temperature is raised, these bands broaden and finally merge into a sharp singlet as the environment of the two N—CH$_3$ groups becomes averaged. This indicates increasingly rapid rotation about the B—N bond (Fig. 6.3). The

247

activation enthalpy for this process is about 84 kJ mol^{-1}. A barrier of at least 100 kJ mol^{-1} is required to enable stable *cis–trans* isomers to be isolated at room temperature.

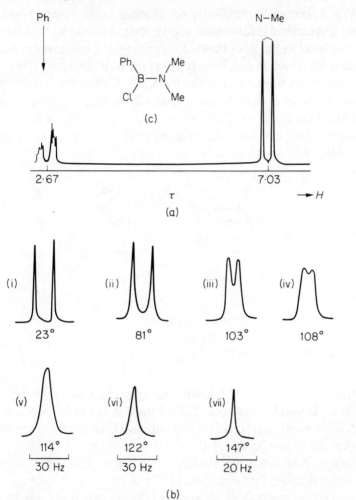

FIGURE 6.3

Proton magnetic resonance spectrum of chlorodimethylaminophenylborane

(a) Spectrum at 23°C

(b) Temperature variation of the –NMe$_2$ band. [After Barfield, P. A., Lappert, M. F. and Lee, J. (1968), *J. Chem. Soc.* (A), 554; (1968), *Trans. Faraday Soc.*, 2571]

248

6.2.2 Borazines

(i) *Synthesis.* Of particular interest are the cyclic compounds $(RBNR')_3$, which are called borazines or borazoles. They are isoelectronic with benzenoid hydrocarbons, and therefore might be expected to show some aromatic character.

The parent compound (D) was first prepared by Stock and Pohland [2] in 1926 by pyrolysis of the adduct of diborane and ammonia, which subsequently was shown to have the structure $(H_3N.BH_2.NH_3)^+BH_4^-$.

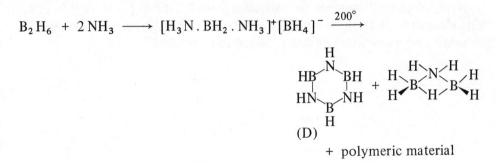

(D)

+ polymeric material

To avoid handling diborane it is convenient to use an alkali metal borohydride and ammonium chloride as reagents. Tri-*N*-alkylborazines can be prepared by this method in high yield.

$$RNH_3Cl + LiBH_4 \xrightarrow{\text{ether}} RNH_2, BH_3 + LiCl$$

$$\downarrow {-H_2}\Big|{150-200°}$$

$$(RNBH)_3$$

The mechanism of the decomposition of the adducts $RNH_2.BH_3$ is not entirely clear. Controlled heating can yield 'saturated' cyclic species. Isomers of these compounds have been characterized in several cases as *cis* and *trans* forms, analogous to trisubstituted cyclohexanes with which they are isoelectronic. It is thought that the rings have chair conformations with as many alkyl groups in equatorial positions as possible.

[2] Stock, A. and Pohland, E. (1926), *Ber.*, **59**, 2215.

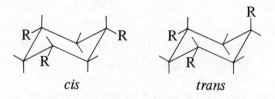

cis *trans*

Dimers $(RNHBH_2)_2$ rather than trimers are formed when bulky alkyl groups R such as t-butyl are present, but their pyrolysis still leads to borazines.

The tri-*B*-chloroborazines are particularly useful starting materials in borazine chemistry. *B*-Trichloroborazine itself can be made by passing boron trichloride over ammonium chloride heated to about 200°:

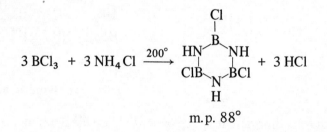

m.p. 88°

N-Substituted chloroborazines are prepared similarly from the amine and boron trichloride. Hydrogen chloride can be eliminated from the adduct $RNH_2.BCl_3$ either thermally by heating in chlorobenzene under reflux, or by treatment with triethylamine in toluene at room temperature. When boron trichloride is mixed with primary aliphatic amines in solution, a mixture of the adduct $RNH_2.BCl_3$, the salt $RNH_3^+ BCl_4^-$, and the borazene $RNH.BCl_2$ is usually formed. There is evidence that elimination of hydrogen halide takes place via the following steps. Linear boronamines are probable intermediates in the polymerizations.

$$RNH_3^+BCl_4^- \xrightarrow{-HCl} RNH_2.BCl_3 \xrightarrow{-HCl} RNH.BCl_2 \xrightarrow{-HCl}$$

$$H(NR.BCl)_n NHR \longrightarrow (RN.BCl)_3$$
boronamine
intermediates

250

With highly hindered amines such as t-butylamine, the thermal reaction stops at the borazene $Bu^tNH.BCl_2$. In reactions assisted by triethylamine a tetrameric borazyne is formed. Unlike chloroborazines (p. 254), this tetramer is remarkably stable to hydrolysis since nucleophilic attack on the B—Cl groups is hindered by the bulky alkyl substituents. The linear anions NCO^-, NCS^-, and N_3^-, which have low steric requirements, however, can displace Cl^-. The properties of these tetramers contrast very strongly with those of cyclooctatetraenes, with which they are isoelectronic. The structure of $(Bu^tN.B.NCS)_4$, determined by X-ray diffraction, shows an eight-membered ring in the boat form, in which the bonds alternate in length.

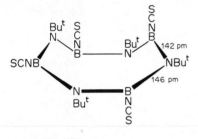

FIGURE 6.4
Structure of $(Bu^tN.B.NCS)_4$

Possible large-scale applications of boron–nitrogen compounds have been hampered by the lack of convenient syntheses from boron–oxygen compounds, which are cheap and readily available, rather than from boron halides or hydrides. It has now been shown that triphenyl borate can be converted in high yield into borazines or aminoboranes by reaction with primary or secondary amines respectively, in the presence of aluminium, under moderate pressures of hydrogen [3]:

$$RNH_2 + B(OPh)_3 + Al \xrightarrow[150°]{H_2/200\ atm} \tfrac{1}{3}(RNBH)_3 + Al(OPh)_3 + \tfrac{1}{2}H_2$$

$$2\,R_2NH + B(OPh)_3 + Al \xrightarrow[150°]{H_2/200\ atm} HB(NR_2)_2 + Al(OPh)_3 + \tfrac{1}{2}H_2$$

[3] Ashby, E. C. and Covar, R. A. (1971), *Inorg. Chem.*, 10, 1524.

(ii)   Structures of borazines; physical properties.   The physical properties of borazine and of its alkyl and aryl derivatives are rather similar to those of the corresponding benzenes. Borazine itself (b.p. 53°) and tri-*N*-alkylborazines are liquids at room temperature, somewhat more volatile than their benzene analogues. Structural studies of borazine, including electron diffraction and thorough normal-coordinate analyses of the vibrational spectra, are consistent with a planar ring with equal B—N bond lengths and equal angles (D_{3h} symmetry) [4]. The isoelectronic molecule boroxine (p. 255) is similar (Fig. 6.5).

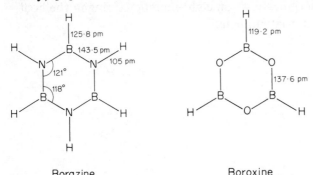

Borazine   Boroxine

FIGURE 6.5
Structures of borazine and boroxine

X-Ray diffraction studies of $B_3X_3N_3H_3$ (X = F, Cl) also indicate planar regular rings. A variety of studies, including electronic spectra supported by molecular orbital calculations, give an estimate of 40–50% aromatic character for borazine and its simple derivatives (compared with benzene 100%).

The photoelectron spectra of borazine and benzene resemble each other closely and can be correlated by assuming a similar sequence of molecular orbitals consistent with the lowering of symmetry from D_{6h} in benzene to D_{3h} in borazine [5]. These conclusions are supported by *ab initio* molecular orbital calculations. In both compounds the highest occupied MO is of π type. Ionization potential measurements show that, as expected, introduction of electron-donating substitutents (N—CH$_3$ or B—CH$_3$) raises the energy of this orbital relative to that in the parent compound, facilitating ionization; B—F or B—Cl substituents, however, lower its energy, but only slightly since their inductive effects ($-I$) are opposed by their mesomeric effects ($+M$).

[4] Blick, K. E., Dawson, J. W. and Niedenzu, K. (1970), *Inorg. Chem.*, 9, 1416.
[5] Bock, H. and Fuss, W. (1971), *Angew. Chem. Internat. Edn.*, 10, 182.

(iii)   Heats of formation; bond energies.   From the heats of hydrolysis of several borazines, and ancillary data, the B—N bond energies have been found to lie in the range 518–439 kJ mol^{-1} depending on the substituents. This represents a fairly strong bond (cf. C=C in benzene ca. 500 kJ mol^{-1}), but is of the same order of magnitude as that in $(Me_2N)_3B$ (439 kJ mol^{-1}). There has been little work on directive effects of substituents across the borazine ring, which might indicate the extent of electron delocalization within it.

(iv)   Chemical properties.   Borazines show very different chemical properties from those of benzenoid compounds. This is not surprising, as there is an alternation of electron density round the $(BN)_3$ ring owing to the presence of alternate B and N atoms. It is worth emphasizing, however, that the ring itself has fairly high innate stability and remains intact in many reactions. Consistent with the high B—N bond strength, the thermal stability of substituted borazines, particularly those with methyl and phenyl groups, is high. Hexamethylborazine may be heated to 460° for 3 hours without significant decomposition. This thermal stability suggested that useful polymers might be derived from borazines. Although such polymers are often fairly resistant to heat, their brittle nature and their susceptibility to hydrolysis and other chemical attack are unsatisfactory for commercial use.

Borazine itself and *B*-trihaloborazines are less stable than the alkyls on account of their tendency to polymerize by elimination of hydrogen or hydrogen halide. Borazine, on heating to 380° for 5 days or on standing at room temperature for several months, loses hydrogen to yield the naphthalene and biphenyl analogues, together with more highly polymeric material.

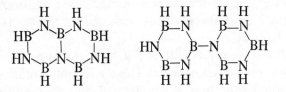

Nucleophilic attack at boron is a typical mode of reaction. Borazines are usually rather easily hydrolysed, although the rate of hydrolysis is reduced by the presence of bulky alkyl or aryl substituents. Where good leaving groups

253

such as halogen are present, nucleophilic substitution can occur with a wide variety of reagents in suitable solvents:

$$(R'S)_3 B_3 N_3 R_3 \xleftarrow{Pb(SR')_2} \quad \xrightarrow{R'Li \text{ or } R'MgX} R'_3 B_3 N_3 R_3$$

$$(SCN)_3 B_3 N_3 R_3 \xleftarrow{KNCS} Cl_3 B_3 N_3 R_3 \xrightarrow{K^+FSO_2^-} F_3 B_3 N_3 R_3$$

$$H_3 B_3 N_3 R_3 \xleftarrow{LiBH_4} \quad \xrightarrow{R'_2 NH} (R'_2 N)_3 B_3 N_3 R$$

Very strong nucleophiles such as Grignard reagents can displace hydride from B—H groups, e.g.

$$B_3 H_3 N_3 R'_3 \xrightarrow[\text{or } 3 RLi]{3 RMgX} B_3 R_3 N_3 R'_3$$

Borazine itself undergoes a number of addition reactions with, for example, hydrogen halides, methanol, and water. In the last two instances very mild conditions must be used or disruption of the ring occurs. Bromine reacts to give (E), probably via formation of *B*-tribromoborazine followed by addition of hydrogen bromide:

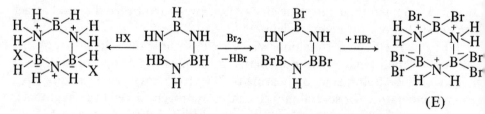

(E)

In contrast to benzenoid hydrocarbons, there is no evidence that electrophilic substitution of the borazine ring occurs. The conditions required for electrophilic attack in aromatic compounds disrupt the borazine ring by oxidation or solvolysis.

Hexamethylborazine reacts with $(CH_3CN)_3Cr(CO)_3$ to form a stable complex, the physical properties of which closely resemble those of hexamethylbenzene-tricarbonylchromium. It is suggested that the bonding in both complexes is similar, and involves interaction of the π electron system of the ligand with metal orbitals of suitable symmetry [6].

[6] Werner, H., Prinz, R. and Deckelmann, E. (1969), *Chem. Ber.*, **102**, 95.

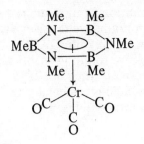

6.2.3 *Other related systems*

Isoelectronic with the borazines are the boroxines $(RBO)_3$; they are cyclic anhydrides of boronic acids $RB(OH)_2$:

$$B(OR)_3 \xrightarrow[\text{(ii) } H_2O]{\text{(i) } RMgX} RB(OH)_2 \xrightarrow[\substack{\text{azeotropic} \\ \text{distillation} \\ \text{in toluene}}]{-H_2O} \tfrac{1}{3}(RBO)_3$$

The B—O bond energy and bond length in boroxines are similar to those in alkyl borates (Fig. 6.5). Although there is probably significant π bonding in both classes of compounds, aromatic character in boroxines is thought to be low. As the electronegativity difference between adjacent ring atoms increases across the series $(HCCH)_3$, $(HBNH)_3$, $(HBO)_3$, electrons become more localized at the more electronegative centres, so that aromatic character decreases.

The parent compound $(HBO)_3$ can be made by passing hydrogen over a mixture of boron and B_2O_3 at about $1100°$. It is thermodynamically stable with respect to these reactants at high temperatures but disproportionates at room temperature to diborane and boric oxide:

$$2(HBO)_3 \rightarrow B_2H_6 + 2B_2O_3$$

Its structure, as determined by electron diffraction of the vapour, is in Fig. 6.5.

Analogous derivatives $(FBO)_3$ and $(ClBO)_3$ are formed when BF_3 or BCl_3 is passed over heated boric oxide. The stability of boroxines to disproportionation at ordinary temperatures lies in the order $(HBO)_3 < (FBO)_3 < (RBO)_3$.

Monomeric thioborine HBS has been detected from the low-pressure reaction of hydrogen sulphide with boron at high temperatures:

$$H_2S + B \rightarrow HBS + \tfrac{1}{2}H_2$$

Its half-lifetime at room temperature in the gas phase at $0\cdot2$ torr is only about 1 minute. It forms solid polymers on condensation. A number of dimeric, e.g. $(FBS)_2$, and trimeric, e.g. $(XBS)_3$ ($X = Cl$, SH, alkyl), species have also been described.

The balance between formation of monomer, dimer, trimer, or higher polymers in the series of compounds is thus very varied. The resistance of the monomers to association lies in the order XCCX' > XCN > XBNX' > XBS > XBO. While alkynes are thermodynamically unstable with respect to their trimers (benzene derivatives), they are kinetically stable in the absence o suitable catalysts. Cyanogen halides, especially FCN, polymerize much more readily to form trimeric cyanuric halides, e.g.

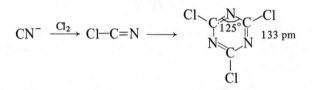

which are derivatives of *s*-triazine. The six-membered ring in cyanuric chloride is planar but is not a regular hexagon.

The kinetic stability of the monomers may well be associated with the polarity of the central bond. The more polar this bond, the greater will be the tendency to polymerize. This is supported by the recent isolation of stable monomeric borazynes, in which electron transfer from nitrogen is aided by the presence of strongly electron-attracting C_6F_5 groups on boron [7].

$$C_6F_5BCl_2 + ArNH_2 \longrightarrow C_6F_5B\equiv NAr + 2 HCl$$

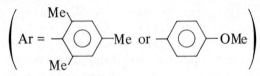

The high B—N bond order is indicated by its stretching frequency (ν_{BN} 1710 cm^{-1} in Raman; cf. ν_{BN} ca. 1450 cm^{-1} in borazines). As the vibration is strongly Raman active, but is infrared-inactive, the B—N bond is essentially non-polar.

6.3   Boron–phosphorus and boron–arsenic compounds

It is likely that $(p-p)\pi$ bonding boron (a first-row element) and phosphorus or arsenic will be weak. No boron–phosphorus analogues of the borazines have

[7] Paetzold, P. I. and Simson, W. M. (1966), *Angew. Chem. Internat. Edn.*, 5, 842.

been prepared. Compounds of formula $(R_2BPX_2)_n$ are known with varying degrees of polymerization. Bulky substituents such as aryl are often present in the monomers, which can be prepared by elimination reactions, e.g.

$$Ph_2Ph + Ph_2BCl \xrightarrow[-Et_3NHCl]{Et_3N} Ph_2PBPh_2 \quad (\gamma_{BP}\ 1445\ cm^{-1})$$

Cyclic trimers, however, are the major products when borane adducts of secondary phosphines decompose thermally:

$$3\ R_2PH,BH_3 \rightarrow (R_2P.BH_2)_3 + 3\ H_2 \quad (R\ =\ alkyl, CF_3)$$

Some tetramers and higher polymeric material are also produced. The cyclic trimers are generally stable up to about 250°. They are rather resistant to hydrolysis; P-hexamethylcyclotriboraphane $(Me_2PBH_2)_3$ for instance is unchanged after heating at 100° with water, 4N-hydrochloric acid, or concentrated sodium hydroxide.

Similar boron–arsenic compounds $(Me_2AsBH_2)_{3\ and\ 4}$ are prepared by elimination of hydrogen from $Me_2AsH.BH_3$ at 75–100°.

There are no aluminium–nitrogen compounds corresponding to the monomeric aminoboranes or to the borazines. Products from elimination reactions of adducts such as $RNH_2.AlH_3$ are often highly polymeric, and 4-coordination about aluminium is always retained. These are further illustrations of the reluctance of second-row elements, especially Al, Si, and P, to take part in $(p-p)\pi$ multiple bonding rather than forming four formal single bonds.

6.4 Some cyclic and linear heteroatomic compounds of silicon, phosphorus, and sulphur

Multiple bonding among first-row elements is due to strong $(2p-2p)\pi$ overlap. Multiple bonding between first- and second-row elements can be due either to weaker $(2p-3p)\pi$ overlap or to $(2p-3d)\pi$ overlap. In this section we describe compounds, both cyclic and acyclic, in which significant electron delocalization via $(2p-3d)\pi$ overlap is believed to occur [8].

[8] Mitchell, K. A. R. (1969), *Chem. Rev.*, **69**, 167. π-Bonding in cyclic systems, including phosphazenes.

There are several series of closely related compounds, many of which are formally isoelectronic, which are based on either rings or chains of alternate atoms $(X—Y)_n$ (where X = Si, P, or S, and Y = N or O), and which possess common features of structure and bonding. Some typical cyclic derivatives are illustrated in Fig. 6.6. We have seen that boron–nitrogen and boron–oxygen

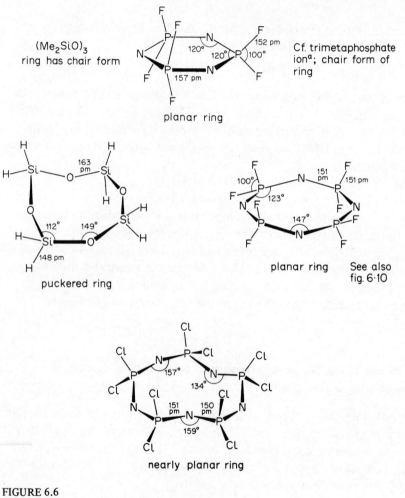

FIGURE 6.6
Structures of some cyclic Si—O and P—N compounds
([a] See p. 110)

systems are dominated by the cyclic trimers. In the silicon–oxygen, phosphorus–nitrogen, and related systems cyclic species of varying ring size as well as linear polymers all exist and are of comparable stability one with another.

First, consider some structural features of silicon–nitrogen and silicon–oxygen compounds and related species. The structure of trisilylamine $(H_3Si)_3N$, which has a planar Si_3N skeleton, contrasts sharply with that of trimethylamine which is pyramidal. The bonding in trisilylamine can be described in terms of sp^2 hybridization of nitrogen orbitals to form the σ bonds to silicon. The lone pair electrons in the remaining p orbital on nitrogen can be delocalized over the molecule by donation into $3d$ silicon orbitals. Maximum overlap occurs for the planar structure (Fig. 6.7). In agreement with this, trisilylamine is a very much weaker Lewis base than trimethylamine. Thus it does not react with trimethylboron, whereas trimethylamine forms a strong 1:1 complex. Trigermylamine $(H_3Ge)_3N$ also has a planar skeleton; it is, however, much less stable thermally than trisilylamine.

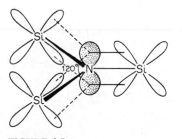

FIGURE 6.7
Multiple bonding in trisilylamine

Similarly, disilyl ether $(H_3Si)_2O$ and digermyl ether $(H_3Ge)_2O$ have wide bond angles at oxygen, consistent with significant $(p–d)\pi$ bonding [9]. A linear structure in which it might be expected that maximum delocalization of oxygen p electrons would occur is not attained.

When silicon or germanium is bonded to a second-row (P, S) or to a third-row (As) element, the bond angle is narrow. This indicates less $(p–d)\pi$ bonding than in the nitrogen or oxygen compounds, but does not necessarily mean that it is absent (see Table 6.1).

[9] Drake, J. E. and Riddle, C. (1970), *Quart. Rev.*, **24**, 263. Structures, preparation, and reactions of compounds of hydrides of Si and Ge with elements of Groups V and VI.

Trisilylamine is prepared by allowing silyl chloride or silyl iodide to mix with ammonia in the gas phase under vacuum. Like the free hydrides, these silyl and germyl compounds are very easily oxidized and must be handled under vacuum-line or oxygen-free conditions.

TABLE 6.1
Structural data[a] for trimethyl, trisilyl, and trigermyl compounds

Compound	M—A (pm)	Angle MAM	Structure
$(H_3C)_3N$	147	108°	pyramidal
$(H_3Si)_3N$	174	119	planar
$(H_3Ge)_3N$	184	120	planar
$(H_3Si)_3P$	225	95	pyramidal
$(H_3Ge)_3P$	231	95	pyramidal
$(H_3C)_2O$	142	111	tetrahedral angle
$(H_3Si)_2O$	163	144	wide angle
$(H_3Si)_2S$	214	97	narrow angle

[a] The structures of most of these volatile molecules were determined by electron diffraction.

6.4.1 Bonding in phosphazenes

Phosphorus–nitrogen polymers have been known for many years [10]. The trimeric chloride $(NPCl_2)_3$ was discovered by Liebig in 1834, although its molecular formula was not established until later. Stokes (1897) obtained a series of compounds $(NPCl_2)_n$ (n = 3 to 7) and suggested cyclic formulae for them. More recently cyclic fluorides $(NPF_2)_n$ have been isolated up to n = 17, and rubbery linear polymers of high thermal stability obtained.

A common feature of the cyclic species is that the bonds within any symmetrically substituted ring are usually equal in length. The cyclic trimers are planar or very nearly so, while the tetramers and higher oligomers generally have puckered ring systems. The P—N bonds in cyclophosphazenes are considerably shorter than the value assessed for a P—N single bond, viz. 178 pm in $(H_3N.PO_3)^-$. Ring angles at phosphorus are always approximately 120°, whereas those at nitrogen are larger, except in the trimers where an angle of approximately 120° is determined by the geometry. Exocyclic bond angles at phosphorus are about 100° (Fig. 6.6).

To describe the bonding in phosphazenes we have chosen to use a model which involves hybridization of s and p orbitals (after Craig, Paddock, and

[10] Paddock, N. L. (1964), *Quart Rev.*, **18**, 168. Excellent article, containing references to more detailed reviews.

others), as it provides a more readily understood approach than a delocalized molecular orbital treatment.

The σ bond skeleton can be considered as derived from approximately sp^3 hybrid orbitals of phosphorus, two of which are used in forming exocyclic bonds to the substituents and the other two in forming ring bonds to nitrogen, which uses sp^2 type hybrid orbitals. The remaining two nitrogen orbitals – an sp^2 type hybrid in the plane of the ring and a p_z orbital perpendicular to this plane – are available for π bonding to phosphorus $3d$ orbitals. Two mutually perpendicular π systems are therefore present, the first in the plane of the ring, and the second perpendicular to this plane. (We have assumed planar ring systems in this discussion for simplicity, but the same general argument can be applied with modification to puckered ring systems.)

Carbocylic and related compounds in which the bonding involves $(2p-2p)\pi$ overlap obey Hückel's rule, that is, there is an alternation in delocalization energy with the number of π electrons. Those systems which possess $(4n + 2)\pi$ electrons are stabilized (have 'aromatic character') relative to those with $4n\pi$ electrons (aromatic character absent). Hückel's rule is obeyed by what are known as homomorphic systems, that is, those in which the sign of the orbital wave function on alternate atoms is the same throughout in the π molecular orbital of lowest energy (see Fig. 6.8).

Delocalized systems derived from $(p-p)\pi$ overlap are homomorphic. Those derived from $(p-d)\pi$ overlap can be of this type, or of a second type, termed heteromorphic, in which the signs of the orbital wave functions on alternate atoms in the most delocalized MO alternate. Unlike homomorphic systems, heteromorphic systems do not show the alternation in stability with ring size.

Figure 6.8 shows that the π system in the plane of a phosphazene ring is homomorphic, and is derived chiefly from the nitrogen sp^2 hybrid orbitals and the $d_{x^2-y^2}$ orbitals of phosphorus. (The d_{xy} orbital also contributes to some extent.) The π system perpendicular to the ring, however, is heteromorphic. It is derived chiefly from the nitrogen p_z orbitals and the d_{zx} orbitals of phosphorus. (The d_{yz} orbitals also contribute to some extent.)

In the phosphazenes the heteromorphic π system is the more important one [11]. Unlike carbocyclic systems, therefore, there is no alternation in properties with ring size in phosphazenes. For example, the bond lengths

[11] Branton, G. R., Brion, G. E., Frost, D. C., Mitchell, K. A. R. and Paddock, N. L. (1970), *J. Chem. Soc.* (A), 151. Photoelectron spectra and MO description of phosphazenes.

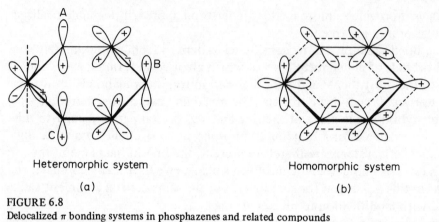

Heteromorphic system

(a)

Homomorphic system

(b)

FIGURE 6.8

Delocalized π bonding systems in phosphazenes and related compounds

(a) Heteromorphic system perpendicular to plane of ring. Signs of orbital wave functions on alternate atoms, viz. A, B, C, alternate

(b) Homomorphic system in plane of ring. Signs of orbital wave functions of alternate atoms the same

P—N in symmetrically substituted phosphazenes $(NPX_2)_n$ are equal within any ring and essentially independent of ring size. While all the C—C bonds in benzene are equal in length, this is not so in cyclooctatetraene in which alternate double and single bonds occur. The P=N stretching frequency in the infrared spectrum shows a smooth variation with ring size, and no alternation (Fig. 6.9). The same seems to apply to the P—N bond strength which is

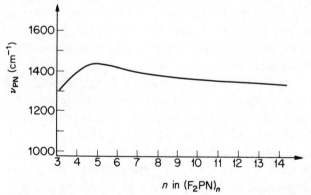

FIGURE 6.9

The effect of ring size on the P—N stretching frequency in the fluorophosphazenes $(F_2PN)_n$.

[Paddock, N. L., in Lappert, M. F. and Leigh, G. J. (1962), *Developments in Inorganic Polymer Chemistry*, Elsevier, Amsterdam]

262

approximately 300 kJ mol^{-1} in cyclic compounds, compared with 275 kJ in P(NMe$_2$)$_3$.

The two mutually perpendicular π bonds in phosphazenes together have approximately cylindrical symmetry as in acetylene. This means that there is very little resistance to torsional motion. Phosphazenes, both rings and chains, and especially the fluorides, are very flexible, and like silicone polymers have low temperature coefficients of viscosity.

6.4.2 *Preparation of chlorophosphazenes*

The chlorides are the starting materials for most work on phosphazenes. They can be prepared once again by an elimination reaction:

$$PCl_5 + NH_4Cl \xrightarrow[\text{reflux, 138°}]{\text{CHCl}_2\text{CHCl}_2} (Cl_2PN)_n + 4HCl$$

According to the conditions used, either cyclic or linear products can predominate. Early on in the reaction the ionic species P_3NCl_{12} precipitates from the solution:

$$3PCl_5 + NH_4Cl \xrightarrow[\text{1 h}]{\text{reflux}} [Cl_3P.N.PCl_3]^+[PCl_6]^- + 4HCl$$

Chain growth then occurs, perhaps as follows:

$$[Cl_3P.N.PCl_3]^+[PCl_6]^- + NH_4Cl \longrightarrow$$

$$[Cl_3P.N.PCl_2.N.PCl_3]^+Cl^- + 4HCl$$

$$\xrightarrow{\text{HN=PCl}_3} [Cl_3P.N.PCl_2.N.PCl_2.N.PCl_3]^+Cl^- + HCl$$

The ionic, linear derivatives $Cl_3P(NPCl_2)_nN.PCl_3^+$ are thought to be the precursors of the cyclic compounds, by elimination of PCl_4^+ ion. Thus the tetrameric chain leads to the cyclic trimer:

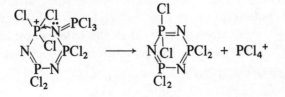

Evidence for this mechanism was obtained, in part, by following the reactions using ^{31}P n.m.r. spectroscopy [12].

6.4.3   *Some structural features in phosphazenes*

As noted above, geometry tends to impose an approximately regular hexagonal, planar structure on the rings of phosphazene trimers. Geometrical isomerism arises when the phosphorus atoms are unsymmetrically substituted. For example, *cis* and *trans* isomers of $(PhClPN)_3$ are known.

The tetramers exhibit a considerable range of conformations, of which four extreme forms are illustrated in Fig. 6.10. The chloride $(Cl_2PN)_4$ exists in two

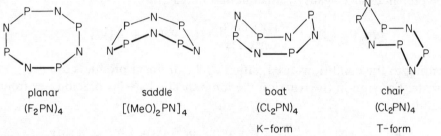

planar	saddle	boat	chair
$(F_2PN)_4$	$[(MeO)_2PN]_4$	$(Cl_2PN)_4$	$(Cl_2PN)_4$
		K–form	T–form

FIGURE 6.10

Ring shapes in some tetrameric phosphazenes. $(Me_2PN)_4$ has a structure intermediate between the saddle and boat forms

crystalline forms, named K and T, which have boat and chair conformations respectively. The two forms are readily interconvertible:

$$K\text{-form} \underset{\substack{\text{recrystallize} \\ \text{at room temp.}}}{\overset{\text{heat at } 70°}{\rightleftharpoons}} T\text{-form}$$

6.4.4   *Chemical properties of phosphazenes* [13]

Consistent with the idea of delocalization of the lone pairs of electrons into the ring, the chlorophosphazenes are very weak bases. Protonation takes place at ring nitrogen atoms; this is also true of *P*-amino-derivatives $[(R_2N)_2PN]_3$ where there are potentially both exo- and endo-cyclic basic sites. The ethyl-phosphazenes are more strongly basic than the chlorophosphazenes on account of the inductive effects of the ethyl groups feeding electrons into the ring.

[12] Emsley, J. and Udy, P. B. (1970), *J. Chem. Soc.* (A), 3025.
[13] Allcock, H. R. (1972), *Chem. Rev.*, **72**, 315.

The chlorophosphazenes polymerize on heating at about 300°, to form long-chain rubbery polymers having molecular weights of the order of 100 000. The chains have a helical structure which is almost flat. Unfortunately the polymers are less resistant to hydrolysis than the cyclic compounds. Related derivatives containing bulky substituents seem to be on the verge of commercial use as high-temperature elastomers. Very pure cyclic starting materials must be used, otherwise the polymers tend to unzip to give rings.

Typical reactions of chlorophosphazenes include nucleophilic displacements of chloride (cf. chloroborazines). Two patterns of substitution occur. If the entering group decreases the electron density at phosphorus, attack of a second nucleophilic group at the same phosphorus site (i.e. geminal substitution) is favoured. This applies to the fluorination by potassium fluorosulphite of $(Cl_2PN)_3$:

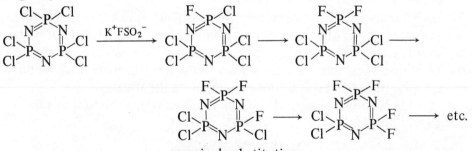

geminal substitution

When the entering group increases electron density at phosphorus, however, attack of the second nucleophile is likely to occur at another phosphorus site (i.e. non-geminal substitution):

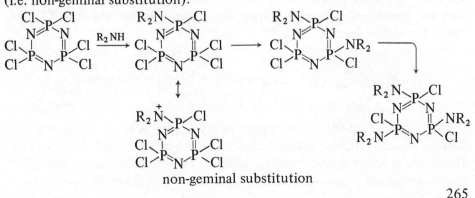

non-geminal substitution

Reaction of aryl-lithium or aryl-magnesium reagents with the trimeric chloride does not proceed cleanly. The fluoride, however, with phenyl-lithium gives mainly non-geminal substitution as expected. A mixture of 1,3-*cis* and 1,3-*trans* diphenyl compounds is obtained. Other nucleophilic substitutions are brought about by water (initially to form metaphosphimic acids),

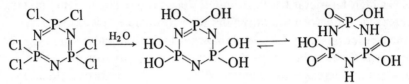

and by alkoxides which yield the alkoxy-derivatives $[P(OR)_2N]_n$.

6.4.5   *Silicones and related compounds*

When a bifunctional silicon compound such as R_2SiCl_2 reacts with ammonia or with water, cyclic oligomers or linear polymers may be formed. Of particular importance are the products which result from the hydrolysis of alkyl and aryl dichlorosilanes. These are the silicone polymers which are manufactured in large quantities (ca. 50 000 tons per annum in the West).

In the 'direct process' methyl chloride is passed over a mixture of silicon and copper powder heated to 280–300°:

$$2\ MeCl + Si \rightarrow Me_2SiCl_2$$

The major product is dimethyldichlorosilane (80%), together with smaller quantities of $MeSiCl_3$, Me_3SiCl, Me_2HSiCl, and various disilanes. The reaction occurs on the surface of a reactive copper–silicon alloy (approx. Cu_2Si). Methyl and chloride transfer occurs as shown, leading to chemisorbed Me_2SiCl_2 and hence to the free product:

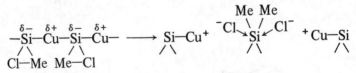

The formation of silicone polymers by hydrolysis is illustrated in Fig. 6.11. Initially dimethyldichlorosilane forms a mixture of cyclic and linear species. This crude product is heated with a catalyst, commonly sulphuric acid. This causes the silanol oligomers to condense further, and the cyclic species to

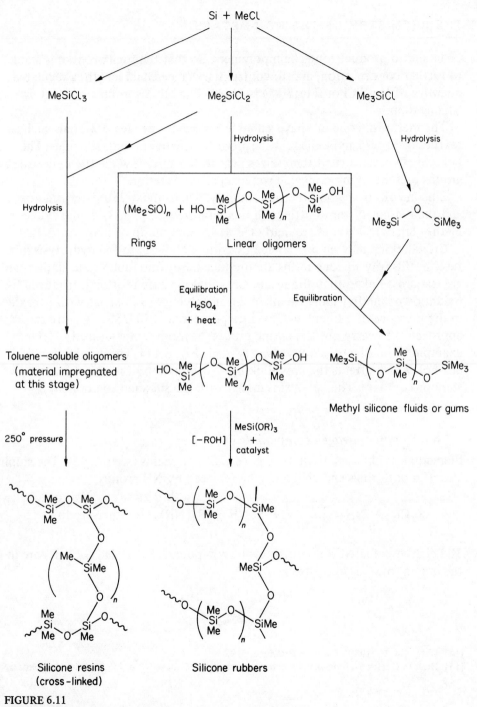

FIGURE 6.11
The formation of silicone polymers

open and to produce long-chain polymers. So that the final product is stable to further condensation, and to control its average chain length, a regulated quantity of Me_3SiCl or $(Me_3Si)_2O$ is added. The Me_3Si- groups thus act as 'chain stoppers'.

The methylsilicone oils have valuable surface properties. Materials such as textiles or paper can be made waterproof by treatment with silicones. The polar $Si-O$ bonds orient themselves near to the surface while the hydrocarbon groups present an impermeable water-repellant exterior.

Silicone oils have good thermal stability. Their life at $250°$ is satisfactory and their viscosity varies little with temperature (see p. 263). Some cyclic methyl phenyl siloxanes are marketed as vacuum pump oils.

Cross-linking may be introduced by adding $MeSiCl_3$ to the hydrolysis mixture. In this way silicone resins are produced. Silicone rubbers are similar, but are less cross-linked than the resins. Cross-linking here is often introduced by oxidation of methyl substituents in linear polymethylsiloxanes with peroxides in the presence of a filler, such as silica powder, at $150-250°$. A more recent approach is to carry out the curing process at room temperature [14]. One example is the silanol–alkoxysilane system (Fig. 6.11). The elimination of alcohol, which effects the cross-linking, is catalysed by tin salts such as stannous octoate. The catalyst is mixed with the siloxane component as required.

6.4.6 *Sulphur–nitrogen compounds* [15]

Elemental sulphur can exist as rings (e.g. S_8) or chains (see p. 176). The sulphur atoms in both rings and chains can be replaced by NH groups:

$$S_2Cl_2 + NH_3 \xrightarrow[\text{formamide}]{\text{dimethyl-}} S_7NH + S_6(NH)_2 + \text{other products}$$

The eight-membered rings in the cyclic compounds S_7NH and $S_6(NH)_2$ are in the crown form, as in S_8 itself:

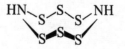

[14] Watt, J. A. C. (1970), *Chem. in Britain*, **6**, 519.
[15] Heal, H. G. (1968), *Inorganic Sulphur Chemistry* (Ed. Nickless, G.) p. 459, Elsevier, Amsterdam.

Tetrasulphur tetranitride, which also results from the reaction of ammonia with sulphur chlorides, best SCl_2, is an orange crystalline substance which is detonated by shock, especially when pure. It has a cage structure (Fig. 6.12) with the four nitrogen atoms in one plane. The S—N distances (163 pm) are equal and correspond to a bond order between 1 and 2. The S—S distance (258 pm) (dotted in the figure) is less than the sum of the van der Waals radii (370 pm). This indicates that some interaction between the sulphur atoms occurs. The structure can be interpreted in terms of significant $(p–d)\pi$ bonding within the ring.

Syntheses and structures of some other sulphur–nitrogen compounds are illustrated in Fig. 6.12. Surprisingly, perhaps, the S—N bonds in $S_4F_4N_4$ alternate in length round the ring, which may indicate that delocalization occurs only to a small extent in this molecule. Note that the monomer NSF can be isolated at room temperature, unlike the phosphazene or siloxane monomers. The polarity of the S—N bond is presumably rather lower than that of P—N or Si—O bonds, and sulphur is also better able to form multiple bonds than P or Si (cf. oxides). NSF slowly trimerizes to $N_3S_3F_3$.

In contrast to NSF, NSF_3 is extremely stable, both thermally and to chemical attack. Sodium, for example, does not attack it at room temperature [16, 17].

α-Sulphanuric chloride is similar to trithiazyl trichloride, with oxygen atoms replacing lone pairs. The rings in both of these molecules are in a shallow chair form, with all three chlorine atoms axial. An isomer, β-sulphanuric chloride, is probably *trans*. *cis* and *trans* Isomers of sulphanuric fluoride separated by preparative gas chromatography from the mixture obtained by reaction of sodium fluoride with $(NS(O)Cl)_3$ in acetonitrile, have in fact been characterized by ^{19}F n.m.r. spectroscopy. The *cis* isomer, in which all three fluorine atoms are equivalent, gives a single resonance, whereas the spectrum of the *trans* form shows an AB_2 pattern.

Treatment of S_4N_4 with thionyl chloride in the presence of aluminium chloride [18] yields a mixture of the tetrachloroaluminate salts of three cyclic

[16] Glemser, O. (1963), *Angew. Chem. Internat. Edn.*, **2**, 530. A short, clearly presented account of sulphur–nitrogen–fluorine compounds.
[17] Glemser, O. and Mews, R. (1972), *Adv. Inorg. Chem. Radiochem.*, **14**, 333. Recent, comprehensive review of sulphur–nitrogen–fluorine compounds.
[18] Banister, A. J. and Dainty, P. J. (1972), *J.C.S. Dalton*, 2658.

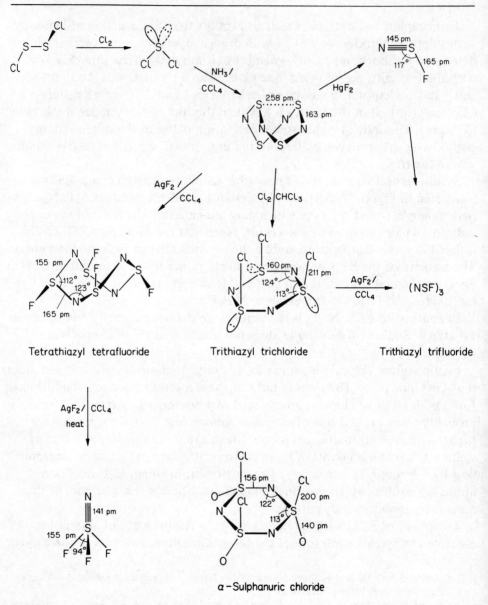

FIGURE 6.12
Some sulphur–nitrogen compounds

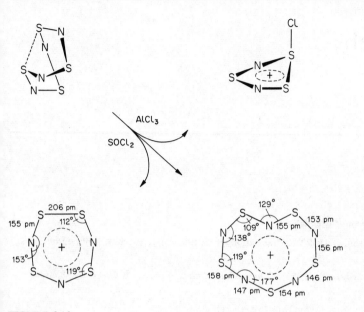

FIGURE 6.13
Three sulphur–nitrogen cations, $[S_3N_2Cl]^+$, $[S_4N_3]^+$, and $[S_5N_5]^+$

cations, $S_3N_2Cl^+$, $S_4N_3^+$, and $S_5N_5^+$. The rings in these species are essentially planar; that in $S_5N_5^+$ is heart-shaped (Fig. 6.13). The close structural relationship between S_4N_4 and $S_3N_2Cl^+$ is apparent from the figure. $S_5N_5^+$ is thought to result from the attack of NS^+ on S_4N_4 via the reaction sequence:

$$S_4N_4 \xrightarrow{SOCl_2} [NSCl] \xrightarrow{AlCl_3} [NS^+][AlCl_4^-] \xrightarrow{S_4N_4} S_5N_5^+ AlCl_4^-$$
(intermediates, not isolated)

It has been suggested, on the basis of MO calculations and the electronic spectrum of $S_4N_3^+$, that these cations represent members of a new series of aromatic compounds, obeying Hückel's rule, with six, ten, and fourteen π electrons respectively. Each S atom is presumed to provide two electrons, and each N atom one electron to the delocalized π system.

These ideas open up intriguing possibilities for the future of inorganic aromatic chemistry.

271

Bibliography

General textbooks of inorganic chemistry

Cotton, F. A. and Wilkinson, G. (1972), *Advanced Inorganic Chemistry*, 3rd Edn., Wiley-Interscience, New York.

Douglas, B. E. and McDaniel, D. H. (1965), *Concepts and Models of Inorganic Chemistry*, Blaisdell, Waltham, Mass.

Massey, A. G. (1972), *The Typical Elements,* Penguin, London.

Phillips, C. S. G. and Williams, R. J. P. (1966), *Inorganic Chemistry*, Vols. I and II, Clarendon Press, Oxford.

Wells, A. F. (1962), *Structural Inorganic Chemistry*, 3rd Edn., Clarendon Press, Oxford.

Theoretical inorganic chemistry

Huheey, J. E. (1972), *Inorganic Chemistry: Principles of Structure and Reactivity*, Harper and Row, New York.

Pimentel, G. C. and Spratley, R. D. (1969), *Chemical Bonding Clarified through Quantum Mechanics*, Holden-Day, San Francisco. Very readable, non-mathematical approach; strongly recommended.

Symmetry and related topics

Cotton, F. A. (1971), *Chemical Applications of Group Theory*, 2nd Edn., Wiley-Interscience, New York.

Hollas, J. M. (1972), *Symmetry in Molecules*, Chapman and Hall, London.

Synthesis and characterization

Brauer, G. (1963), *Handbook of Preparative Inorganic Chemistry*, Academic Press, New York. Contains descriptions of recommended preparative methods of several hundred common inorganic compounds.

Hill, H. O. A. and Day, P. (1968), *Physical Methods in Advanced Inorganic Chemistry*, Wiley-Interscience, New York.

272

Jolly, W. L. (1970), *The Synthesis and Characterisation of Inorganic Compounds*, Prentice-Hall, Englewood Cliffs, N.J.

Acids and bases; non-aqueous solvents

Bell, R. P. (1969), *Acids and Bases; Their Quantitative Behaviour*, 2nd Edn., Chapman and Hall, London. Clear and concise student text.

Waddington, T. C. (1969), *Non-aqueous solvents*, Nelson, London. General account at undergraduate level.

Thermochemistry

Dasent, W. E. (1970), *Inorganic Energetics*, Penguin, London.

Johnson, D. A. (1968), *Some Thermodynamic Aspects of Inorganic Chemistry*, Cambridge University Press, London. Good, but not in SI units.

Non-existent compounds

Dasent, W. E. (1965), *Non-Existent Compounds; Compounds of Low Stability*, Dekker, New York. It is interesting to note how many of these have been made since 1965.

Texts on the chemistry of some particular elements

Bartlett, N. (1971), *The Chemistry of the Noble Gases*, Elsevier, Amsterdam.

Eméleus, H. J. (1969), *The Chemistry of Fluorine and its Compounds*, Academic Press, New York. Brief, readable account of some recent fluorine chemistry, especially of the non-metallic elements.

Eméleus, H. J. (Ed.) (1972), *MTP International Review of Science, Inorganic Chemistry, Series One*, Vols. I–X, Butterworths, London. Series containing up-to-date review articles on important aspects of the whole field of inorganic chemistry. The following three volumes cover the chemistry of the non-metallic elements.

Lappert, M. F. (Ed.), *Hydrogen and Groups I–IV*, Vol. I.

Addison, C. C. and Sowerby, D. B. (Eds.), *Groups V and VI*, Vol. II.

Gutmann, V. (Ed.), *Group VII and the Noble Gases*, Vol. III.

Holloway, J. H. (1968), *Noble-Gas Chemistry*, Methuen, London.

Jolly, W. L. (1964), *The Inorganic Chemistry of Nitrogen*, Benjamin, New York.

Muetterties, E. L. (1967), *The Chemistry of Boron and its Compounds*, Wiley, New York. Detailed coverage of most aspects.

Nickless, G. (Ed.) (1968), *Inorganic Sulphur Chemistry*, Elsevier, Amsterdam. Extensive treatise.

van Waser, J. R., (1958), *Phosphorus and its Compounds*, Vol. I, Wiley-Interscience, New York. A comprehensive account of phosphorus chemistry, (1961), Vol. II, *Technology, Biological Functions and Applications*.

273

Index